The rules
of integration

MANCHESTER
UNIVERSITY PRESS

European Policy Research Unit Series

Series Editors: *Simon Bulmer* and *Mick Moran*

The European Policy Research Unit Series aims to provide advanced text-books and thematic studies of key public policy issues in Europe. They concentrate, in particular, on comparing patterns of national policy content, but pay due attention to the European Union dimension. The thematic studies are guided by the character of the policy issue under examination.

The European Policy Research Unit (EPRU) was set up in 1989 within the University of Manchester's Department of Government to promote research on European politics and public policy. The series is part of EPRU's effort to facilitate intellectual exchange and substantive debate on the key policy issues confronting the European states and the European Union.

Titles in the series also include:

The governance of the Single European Market   Kenneth Armstrong and Simon Bulmer

The politics of health in Europe   Richard Freeman

Immigration and European integration   Andrew Geddes

Mass media and media policy in Western Europe   Peter Humphreys

The regions and the new Europe   ed. Martin Rhodes

Political economy of financial integration in Europe   Jonathan Story and Ingo Walter

Regulatory politics in the enlarging European Union   Alasdair Young and Helen Wallace

The rules
of integration

Institutionalist approaches
to the study of Europe

Edited by

Gerald Schneider and Mark Aspinwall

Manchester University Press
Manchester and New York

distributed exclusively in the USA by Palgrave

Published by Manchester University Press
Oxford Road, Manchester M13 9NR, UK
and Room 400, 175 Fifth Avenue, New York, NY 10010, USA
http://www.manchesteruniversitypress.co.uk

Distributed exclusively in the USA by
Palgrave, 175 Fifth Avenue, New York,
NY 10010, USA

Distributed exclusively in Canada by
UBC Press, University of British Columbia, 2029 West Mall,
Vancouver, BC, Canada V6T 1Z2

British Library Cataloguing-in-Publication Data
A catalogue record for this book is available from the British Library

Library of Congress Cataloging-in-Publication Data applied for

ISBN 0 7190 5798 1 *hardback*
       0 7190 5799 X *paperback*

First published 2001

06 05 04 03 02 01   10 9 8 7 6 5 4 3 2 1

Typeset in Sabon
by Action Publishing Technology Ltd, Gloucester
Printed in Great Britain
by Biddles Ltd, Guildford and King's Lynn

Contents

Figures and tables

Figures

Tables

Contributors

Mark Aspinwall is a Lecturer in Politics at the University of Durham.

Thomas Bräuninger is a Lecturer and Research Collaborator at the Faculty of Public Policy and Management of the University of Konstanz.

Simon Bulmer is Jean Monnet Professor of European Politics at the University of Manchester.

Martin Burch is Director of the Graduate Centre and Senior Lecturer in Government at the University of Manchester.

Jeffrey T. Checkel is Senior Researcher and Co-ordinator, Research on European Identity Change, ARENA/Universitetet i Oslo.

Tanja Cornelius is a Research Assistant at the Faculty of Public Policy and Management of the University of Konstanz.

Christophe Crombez is Associate Professor of Political Economy, University of Leuven.

Philipp Genschel is a Research Fellow at the Max Planck Institute for the Study of Societies, Cologne.

Adrienne Héritier is Co-Director of the Max-Planck Project Group 'Common Goods: Law, Politics and Economics' and part-time Professor at the European University Institute, Florence.

Liesbet Hooghe is Associate Professor at the Department of Political Science, University of Toronto.

Simon Hug is Lecturer at the Department of Political Science, University of Geneva.

Thomas König is Professor of Political Science at the Faculty of Public Policy and Management of the University of Konstanz.

Susanne K. Schmidt is a Research Fellow at the Max Planck Institute for the Study of Societies, Cologne.

Gerald Schneider is Professor of Political Science at the Faculty of Public Policy and Management of the University of Konstanz, and Executive Editor of *European Union Politics*.

Thomas Schuster is a PhD candidate at the Mannheim Department of Economics.

Bernard Steunenberg is Professor of Public Administration at the University of Leiden.

Preface

The genesis of this book was a meeting of the Standing Group on the European Union at the joint sessions of the European Consortium for Political Research in Oslo in 1996. At that meeting, we decided collectively to assemble an international group of academics to draw together the fields of European studies and institutionalism, broadly conceived. The purposes were two-fold. One was to bring the conceptual lens of institutionalist research to bear on the issue of European integration in a comprehensive way. The second was to connect scholars in the diverse traditions of institutionalist research in such a way that new understandings about the influence of institutions might be gained, which would be of use to those beyond the relatively narrow confines of European studies.

If Fulvio Attinà, the Chairman of the Standing Group, was the matchmaker, we were the (tentative) parents. Tentative because the task before us seemed a daunting one. The European Union represents an amazingly complex set of rules, procedures, practices and norms at a variety of levels. There is both a vertical and a horizontal proliferation of institutions, some formal, others informal. These institutions are historically rooted but are also undergoing frequent change. In addition, the approaches scholars take to studying these institutions differ widely. Their assumptions, world views, scientific approaches and many other aspects of their research can be so far apart as to produce entirely divergent results about virtually the same puzzle. In an initial working paper, we used the metaphor 'Same menu, different tables' to describe this dismal incoherence (Aspinwall and Schneider, forthcoming). The menu is the influence that institutions have on the political behaviour of European actors; the tables represent different approaches, which we subsume under the (increasingly accepted) names rational choice, historical, and sociological institutionalism.

Ironically, the results produced by these competing schools (or sects) may be incompatible. To explore the potential for convergence, we convened an international research group. The tables carried on civilised discussions among themselves, which may be rare among academic works on this subject. This volume shows that the overlap between the different schools is considerable and not restricted to the common substantive interest. We have structured the volume in a way that hopefully facilitates communication. We particularly invited responses to the findings by representatives of one of the three approaches from scholars from a competing camp. We believe that the comment sections following each chapter highlight theoretical considerations and illuminate conceptual and methodological disputes to a degree not normally found in edited collections. The result of our effort may not be a synthesised institutionalism, but we are convinced that a better understanding of European institutions and of the limitations of the different approaches is the result. If we were the parents of this project, we had numerous midwives to assist us. From its conception in Oslo the gestation period included a panel at the 5th biennial conference of the European Community Studies Association in 1997 in Seattle, an ECPR research workshop in Bergen in 1997, a workshop at the joint sessions of the ECPR in Warwick in 1998 and finally a meeting of all contributors at the University of Konstanz in 1998. For financial and logistical support for these meetings we are indebted to the universities of Durham, Konstanz and Bergen. The Thyssen Foundation provided generous support for the Konstanz meeting, the European Consortium for Political Research for the session in Bergen. We also gratefully acknowledge the assistance of Bettina Lassen and Simona Scheele in the preparation of the Konstanz meeting and the final manuscript. Tobias Bachteler, Christian Martin and Sabine Zanger also helped in the production of the final manuscript. Without the tireless efforts of our collaborators this project would have been much later in appearing.

Abbreviations

AA	Federal Foreign Office (FRG)
BKA	Federal Chancellor's Office (FRG)
BMF	Federal Finance Ministry (FRG)
BML	Federal Ministry for Food, Agriculture and Forestry (FRG)
BMWi	Federal Ministry for Economics (FRG)
CE	Council of Europe
CFSP	Common Foreign and Security Policy
COES	Cabinet Office European Secretariat
COREPER	Committee of Permanent Representatives
DG	Directorate General
DTI	Department of Trade and Industry
EC	European Community
ECJ	European Court of Justice
ECSC	European Coal and Steel Community
EdF	Électricité de France
(E)DOP	(European) Defence and Overseas Policy
EMU	Economic and Monetary Union
EP	European Parliament
EPP	European People's Party
ESRC	Economic and Social Research Council
EU	European Union
FCO	Foreign and Commonwealth Office
FRG	Federal Republic of Germany
IGC	intergovernmental conference
IR	international relations
JHA	Justice and Home Affairs
MAFF	Ministry of Agriculture, Fisheries and Food
MEP	Member of European Parliament
NATO	North Atlantic Treaty Organisation
NGO	non-governmental organisation
PES	Party of European Socialists

QMV   Qualified Majority Voting
SEA   Single European Act
TEU   Treaty on European Union

Institutional research on the European Union: mapping the field[1]

The study of institutions has come a long way, especially in European studies. In an earlier era, institutions were studied as formal, static organisations, such as the legal system or the courts. Interest in the subject waned during the long behaviouralist interlude, but for political scientists, institutions were resuscitated when March and Olsen breathed new life into the field with groundbreaking work in the 1980s (1984; 1989). By the mid-1990s, Europeanists had imported 'new' institutionalist research into the field of European integration (Bulmer, 1994; Pierson, 1996). The longevity of the two main theoretical 'institutions', neofunctionalism and intergovernmentalism, prevented scholars from jumping earlier on to the bandwagon of the new paradigm.

What are institutions? At a basic level, they have been defined as 'a relatively stable collection of practices and rules defining appropriate behaviour for specific groups of actors in specific situations' (March and Olsen, 1998: 948). More specific is Peter Hall's often-cited definition – 'the formal rules, compliance procedures, and standard operating practices that structure the relationship between individuals in various units of the polity and economy' (1986: 19).

Even more crucial than definitional distinctions is that different scholars perceive the influence of institutions on social action in seemingly incompatible ways. New institutionalists in political science have been promiscuous in importing concepts from the cognate disciplines of economics and sociology, and the source of their importation makes a difference in how they interpret the influence of institutions.[2] Those borrowing from the economics tradition tend to see them as a set of rules which actors create or use in a strategic fashion to achieve desired but unrelated goals. Those borrowing from the sociological tradition tend to see institutions as constitutive of identities and preferences – helping actors to interpret and give meaning to appropriate behaviour.

The basic premise of neoinstitutionalist analysis, agreed by virtually all scholars, is that institutions affect outcomes. Institutions contain the bias individual agents have built into their society over time, which in turn leads to important distributional consequences. They structure political actions and outcomes, rather than simply mirroring social activity and rational competition among disaggregated units (March and Olsen, 1984; 1989; Thelen and Steinmo, 1992; Lindberg and Campbell, 1991). This leaves a great many questions in its wake, however. This book seeks to engage this debate in the context of the European Union (EU). It brings together some of the foremost scholars working in the fields of institutionalism and European integration. Our objectives are to explore the differences between the institutionalist theoretical traditions as they are applied to European integration studies and, to the extent possible, search for common ground. Where common ground does not exist, we hope to build bridges between the traditions so that a better understanding of their fundamental differences may be realised. We follow up on our earlier observation that institutionalism in European studies is characterised by both substantive convergence and theoretical divergence (Aspinwall and Schneider, forthcoming).

In order to make some sense of the vast output in this field we place institutional variants along a spectrum from the economist end to the sociological end. We adopt the distinction by Hall and Taylor (1996) of three institutionalisms – sociological, historical and rationalist.[3] At the economist end of the spectrum, rationalists see institutions mainly as 'long-lived equilibrium patterns of rational behaviour' and thus realised outcomes in a strategic game 'that society plays' (Calvert, 1995: 218). At the sociological end, institutions are inseparable from human identity and behavioural choice. From this perspective, 'all problems are common; all solutions socially constructed and reified; all expectations common and publicly hegemonic' (Berger and Luckmann, cited in Jepperson, 1991: 151). A polarisation between these two approaches, labelled rationalist and constructivist, has emerged in the international relations literature (see for example the special issue of *International Organization*, Autumn, 1998). This polarisation is spilling into European studies as well; the September 1999 special issue of *Journal of European Public Policy* features for instance an all-constructivist line-up.

These are two ends of the same spectrum, which varies according to the extent to which institutions are internalised by agents and therefore the extent to which agents are capable of acting independently of them. In the centre of this spectrum is historical institutionalism, which shares some characteristics with each of the other two variants. Historical institutionalist theorists generally believe that actor intentionality exists, at least in the short term, but that strategic choice is limited by long-term iterated interaction.

This book is based on the understanding that each of these ways of viewing institutions is valid. It also assumes the relevance and importance of both formal and informal structures in human behaviour. In the EU, formal institutions include administrative rules, legislative procedures and the voting rights attributed to diverse collective actors. Informal institutions include the Council's efforts to promote consensus solutions even when qualified majority decisions are possible. Cultural practices and cognitive patterns also fall into this category. One instance where both academics and practitioners believe that culture matters is the organisation of the European Commission, where the various directorates are seemingly characterised by divergent administrative habits and conventions. However, Liesbet Hooghe's contribution (Chapter 7) casts doubt upon that widely-held belief showing that the world views of civil servants are primarily structured by ideology rather than bureaucratic interests.

The effects of institutions on human action can be either constraining or empowering. On the one hand, rules prevent actions that might otherwise be pursued. National constitutions or deeply entrenched social traditions might for instance hinder the development of certain types of integration in the European arena. On the other hand, newly created institutions also open up avenues which could not have been pursued earlier. Pierson (1996) observes that the European Court of Justice referred to Article 119 of the Treaty of Rome which obliges the introduction of measures guaranteeing 'equal pay for equal work' to promote gender equality in reluctant member states. Equally, shared cultural and cognitive-based understandings may promote common action, whereas different understandings may act as a constraint. Governments with an integration-sceptic population typically prove to be the most difficult negotiation partners in interstate negotiations (Schneider and Cederman, 1994).

Contributors to this volume use institutions as independent, intervening and outcome variables. Institutions as independent variables include norms, ideas and values, such as the notion of the EU representing democratic ideals, or the state representing a variant of capitalism. Institutions as independent variables are mainly examined through the sociological and historical variants of institutionalism. As intervening variables, institutions influence movement towards or away from integration. They may comprise codified, clearly-visible rules or they may be routines and standard practices which are less visible but equally important determinants of social behaviour. To rational choice institutionalists, actors navigate these institutions as ships navigate a reef, with a clearly marked channel as the route to a well-known port. A rational navigator is assumed to strive for the best route. Pirates (other actors) or an unforeseen storm (uncertainty) might, however, prevent the helmsman from choosing the optimal way. To historical institutionalists, intervening institutions permanently transform the actor's preferences – dangerous reef systems mean that some ports are avoided, others more frequently visited. To continue the metaphor, the consequence of repeated and consistent visits to certain ports may be the establishment of particular and not necessarily ideal patterns of trade. The longevity of traditions is illustrated by Bulmer and Burch in Chapter 4. In a careful examination of the British and the German central government structures they show how long-lived certain institutions are despite tremendous changes in the outside world.

As dependent variables, institutions include equilibria and patterns of behaviour that characterise the process of European collaboration. Rational choice theorists have traditionally examined the design of institutions with the help of game-theoretic concepts. A typical example of how these instruments can be used successfully in an applied setup is Chapter 3 by Bräuninger et al. They persuasively demonstrate how actors are concerned about a future power distribution when they negotiate over treaty reforms. The chapter draws on the rich tradition in social and public choice reasoning pioneered by Arrow, Black, Buchanan, Downs, Olson, Tullock and others. These classic authors were the first who systematically examined the role of institutions after World War II. The tradition has made us alert to the ambiguous role that rules can play. Although unanimity might be socially optimal, it entails the danger that nothing can be changed in the future and that individual actors might be able to dictate the development of an organisation like the EU. It is exactly this reasoning which has led to the increased use of qualified majority voting since the mid-1980s.

Although public choice theorists have been the first to examine constitutional choices, sociological variants within the neoinstitutionalist tradition are beginning to do the same. Finnemore and Sikkink (1998), for example, suggest that norm entrepreneurs, motivated by noble ideals, help to persuade governments to adopt certain norms that subsequently become deeply embedded in international society (see also Checkel, Chapter 2). Hooghe´s contribution illustrates how powerful the impact of norms is in the European Commission. This notion of norm entrepreneurs is implicit in the analysis of the agency role of EU actors (among others, see Cram, 1997a; Armstrong and Bulmer, 1997; Pierson, 1996; Burley and Mattli, 1993). The European Commission and the European Court of Justice (ECJ) have actively constructed a European competence in important ways, through rulings, proposals and alliances with actors at various levels across the EU. This activism may be an unwelcome (from the point of view of member states) by-product of principal-agent delegation, because as we stated earlier, agents sometimes have their own agendas. In the case of the Commission, this activity is ongoing through an identification of new issues, proposed solutions and establishment of alliances. Throughout its work, the Commission strives both to legitimise itself and to create a demand for European level public goods that might not be created by principals acting jointly. Again, the effect of this is to shift (often very slowly) or create preferences, strategies, interests and identities which would not have occurred without supranational agency activism. Susanne K. Schmidt shows in Chapter 6 how the Commission uses informal power resources to integrationist ends. Her chapter highlights that political entrepreneurs not only depend on their legal competence, but rather that they actively try to change the rules or at least try to profit from the disagreement among other actors.

Since rules affect behaviour at all levels of societal interaction, the new institutionalism has no theoretical bias toward either 'high' or 'low' politics or toward either vertical or horizontal forms of co-operation. It is important, for example, not to conflate rational choice approaches with intergovernmental approaches. Many intergovernmental theorists have taken a broadly rational angle in their theorising, but neither is necessary to the other. In the reform of the structural funds, institutions such as federal-regional powersharing or the dominant bargaining principles have for instance proved to be important in the administration of funds (Payne, Mokken, and Stokman, 1997). Such vertical checks and balances are accompanied by rules that structure the interactions within the European Union and in particular between the Commission, the Parliament and the Council (Moser and Schneider, 1997b).

As we suggested earlier, there may be considerable convergence between the 'new institutionalisms' in certain respects. For example, some historical institutionalists share with rational choice institutionalists an emphasis on actor intentionality in the short term (Pierson, 1996). Other historical institutionalists tend to emphasise the long-term consequences of institutions – particularly their tendency to influence preferences (Bulmer, 1994) – and thus share with sociological institutionalists a preoccupation with endogenous sources of behaviour.

Nonetheless, no synthesising approach is in sight. One of the most important underlying differences between theorists is the temporal dimension. Rational choice theorists tend to concentrate on short-term decision-making. Sociological institutionalists concentrate on long-term institutional effects. Likewise, historical institutionalists concentrate on the long term effects of specific (possibly rational) decisions (Wiener, 1998). Closely related to this (and possibly co-varying with temporal differences) is the extent to which institutions are 'internalised' by agents. From the rational choice perspective, institutions are most often external to the agent – including voting procedures and conflict resolution mechanisms – unless actors are engaged in the conscious creation of rules.[4] From the sociological perspective institutions are internalised – including identitive institutions such as nationality or religion. It follows that these different emphases will cause observers to stress alternative explanations for the logic of action, the interpretation of rules and the formation of preferences and strategies. Yet these are not mutually exclusive – to put it another way, against 'the background of habitualised activity opens up a foreground for deliberation and innovation' (Berger and Luckmann, 1967: 71).

However, these approaches to institutions are not without their critics. Koelble (1995: 239), for example, criticises the feedback conceptualisation of institutions and states: 'Individuals are not helpless when it comes to institutional choice, but historical institutionalists insist that institutions guide their choices. In the end, it is unclear whether the intentions of individuals or the constraints imposed by institutions shape outcomes.' Moreover, it is very difficult to measure the effect of culturally-derived institutions, because it is virtually impossible to surmise, except by counterfactuals, what a given outcome would have been in the absence of these institutions. Control groups do not exist in the EU laboratory. According to the very paradigm, it is impossible to imagine individuals acting without reference to cultural roots; to ascertain the effects of these roots becomes exceedingly difficult.

New institutionalism and European integration

Like in the new institutionalism as a whole, there is no consensus on how to think about the role of institutions in European integration. Yet the examination of institutions in integration studies is not completely new. One early contribution was Scharpf 's (1985, 1988) seminal articles on the joint-decision trap. His complaint that traditional approaches such as neofunctionalism have largely overseen the impact of decision-making rules on the integration process coincided with the publication of March and Olsen's (1984) pioneering piece which heralded the new institutionalist turn in political science. In the meantime, institutionalist analysis has been turned into the mainstream approach not just in political science, but also in European studies. Studies on the relative power of institutional actors, examinations of the complexities of bargaining between actors from different levels and evaluations of the role that norms and socialisation play in the process of European integration proliferate at an ever-increasing speed.

Although these achievements are impressive, they are not based on a common understanding of European institutions. On the contrary, a considerable promiscuity characterises the way in which researchers deal with different facets of rule-based behaviour. This partly reflects the state of the art in the general discussion where no consensus definition of institutions and their salient attributes has been reached. The conceptual indeterminacy matters more, however, in the relatively volatile field of European studies where only a gradual turn towards theoretically innovative and empirically systematic research designs can be observed. Instead of offering insights to other sub-disciplines, integration research is still heavily dependent upon imports from other disciplines. We argue that epistemological disagreements between the contending approaches are at least as important as theoretical divisions. Yet, important ontological differences separate the institutionalist traditions as well, and these are perhaps less reconcilable. These different ontologies can, however, co-exist in the same field if scholars are careful to observe a scientific approach. We explore these differences in more detail below.

Rational choice

The starting point of all rationalist reasoning on the EU is the assumption that actors in all relevant decision-making arenas behave strategically to reach their preferred outcome.[5] Since the EU has gradually evolved from an intergovernmental form into a complex power sharing system, most interactions are affected by the way in which principals delegate power to agents. These agents include the Commission, but also the member states in the event that they have to implement a supranational decision. As we know from numerous principal-agent-models, delegating power is not trivial since agents often exploit their superior knowledge and experience to reach their goals. This might be particularly the case in the EU where information is largely controlled by the supranational Commission. Rational choice theorists have only recently started to analyse how agents exploit the uncertainty which results from the imperfect division of power between competing European actors (e.g., Franchino, 2000).

Signalling games and the spatial theory of voting have been the major source of inspiration. It should, however, be noted that rationalist research on European integration has its predecessor in voting power studies where the ex ante power of individual actors is assessed (e.g., Brams and Affuso, 1976). As Garrett and Tsebelis (1996) correctly point out, this kind of study largely focuses on individual institutional actors, thereby missing the increasing tendency towards power sharing and ignoring institutional complexities of decision-making in the European Union.[6] Substantial contributions within the rationalist branch of neoinstitutionalist research has mainly come from those scholars who build their own models, although game-theoretic concepts have also been a major source for the metaphorical analysis of the EU. Yet, these 'soft' applications of the rationalist paradigm often have major difficulties in detecting a convincing causal mechanism to explain a social phenomenon. It has to be expected that these informal models will increasingly disappear the more the field matures.

Theoretical progress first occurred in the analysis of the ways in which institutional reforms such as the introduction of the Single European Act (SEA) or the Maastricht Treaty have redistributed decision-making power among the competing actors. The major legislative rules that have been studied are the co-operation and the co-decision procedures. This latter procedure exists in a Maastricht and an Amsterdam version and will subsequently be called 'co-decision I' and 'co-decision II'. The main question of research in this area has been whether the European Parliament (EP) evolves into a major institutional player through the three main treaty reforms. Technically, the dispute is over the so-called agenda-setting power of the legislature and thus the possibility that it may independently put forward legislative proposals.

According to Steunenberg (1994, similarly: Crombez, 1996), the introduction of the co-operation procedure and the co-decision I procedure did not, by and large, diminish the influence of the European Commission in comparison with the EP. This view is partly challenged by Moser (1997a, 1997b) who contends that co-decision can force the Commission to accept proposals by the EP which deviate from its own preference. In his evaluation of Tsebelis' study (1994/5) of the Parliament's alleged conditional agenda setting power, Moser shows that the legislature can only exert an independent effect under the co-operation procedure if the decision-making context changes over time. Under co-decision I, by contrast, the EP has obtained for the first time unconditional veto power (Schneider, 1995a). This gradual strengthening will continue under the co-decision II since the Council has now definitively lost the possibility to return to its initial proposal after a failed compromise (Steunenberg, 1998). Whether the Commission, however, lost as much influence as predicted by some modellers (e.g., Tsebelis and Garrett, 2000) remains disputed. In Chapter 5 Crombez proposes that the danger of indecision has grown with the last treaty reform.

The introduction of rules on the implementation of EU measures (the so-called 'comitology' procedures) has led, by contrast, to a strengthening of the intergovernmentalist rather than the supranationalist actors. As Steunenberg, Koboldt and Schmidtchen (1996, 1997) demonstrate, the Council has obtained considerable 'gatekeeping' power on some supranational proposals. This means that the member states can control, at least to some extent, the policy proposals of the Commission. Franchino (2000) shows in a macroquantitative study that strategic considerations are highly important in this context and that the levels of uncertainty especially affect the comitology outcomes. Another institution within the EU that has been studied by rationalists is the European Court of Justice (ECJ). Garrett (1992) offered a first strategic interpretation of ECJ decision-making. He conjectured that 'the actions of all courts are fundamentally political in that they anticipate the possible reactions of other political actors in order to avoid their interpretation.' Although he qualified this interpretation, Garrett (1995) used an exchange with Mattli and Slaughter (1995) to reiterate that the ECJ behaves in a strategic fashion and systematically takes member states' possible reactions into account. Alter (1998) as well as Mattli and Slaughter (1998) seem to agree with this.

The first generation of game-theoretic models on decision-making in the EU has been largely devoted to the actors' objective influence, without systematically analysing the very individual ways in which actors make use of different institutional settings. In our view, this narrow and some-times overly constitutionalist focus is problematic since it might nurture generalisations that are not well founded in the reality of EU decision-making. Models within the booming branch of spatial games often do not capture the most important features of the empirical situation under scrutiny. Schmidt (Chapter 6) shows in a set of convincing case studies that actors might also rely on other power resources in the inter-institutional competition. However, the lack of empirical foundation of these models is largely a consequence of the absence of meaningful data.

The conflicting interpretations of co-decision I might serve as an illustration why the empiricism typical of most non-rational choice institutionalists should play a more prominent role in the process of EU theorising. Moser (1997b), for instance, demonstrates in contrast to Tsebelis (1997) that this now renovated procedure empowered the legislature in comparison with the Council of Ministers. As Kaiser's (1996) empirical study shows, this power shift is, however, not due to limitations on the Council's power to propose, as Moser's interpretation of the Treaty on European Union (TEU) suggests. It seems largely to have been a consequence of the costs that are involved with the use of vetos and inflexible bargaining positions.[7] This finding shows that the strategic use of institutions rather than the power potential arising from a legalist interpretation of the constitutional rules should be one of the key topics in rationalist reasoning on EU institutions.

One exception to the formalistic trend is the two-level game literature on European integration. Schneider and Cederman (1994) show how member states use domestic institutions to strengthen their bargaining stance in the negotiating rounds of the European Council. A possible threat involving a formal rule is modelled in the referendum game where a laggard state can hint at popular resistance towards further integration in order to obtain a different treaty.[8] Hug's (1997) discussion of the feasibility of direct democracy at the level of the EU reiterates this point and demonstrates that the future development of the organisation depends heavily on how future procedures are designed. Constituents at the domestic level are more likely to go along with the opinion of their preferred party if referendums are binding than in a situation of a non-committing vote (Hug and Sciarini, 2000).

However, rational choice research has not yet devoted sufficient attention to the impact of informal institutions. One example is the possibility of employing a potential government crisis to bolster a threat in the realm of the EU (Schneider and Cederman, 1994). Another example of the considerable influence of informal rather than formal rules is seniority, which influences not least the way in which the European Commission is formed or how members of the EP are selected (Schneider, 1997). Finally, and probably most importantly, no rationalist work on the impact of cultural factors on the integration process exists.

Historical institutionalism
It would be a mistake for Europeanists to permit a degeneration of the theoretical debate into the polarised rationalist-constructivist arguments that characterise many recent international relations studies. Such a polarisation, essentially between economic and sociological ontologies, would overlook the important link provided by what is normally termed historical institutionalism. The historical institutionalist approach takes a different cut on institutional dynamics and decision-making in the EU. In historical institutionalism the focus is on the ways prior institutional commitments condition further action, limit the scope of what is possible and cause agents to redefine their interests (Bulmer, 1994; Pierson, 1996). Institutional and policy change become 'path dependent' as actors define their preferences endogenously, based upon what has occurred in the past. The image is one of a ratchet, in which institutional arrangements are winched into placed slowly over time, thus constraining human behaviour. History creates context, which shapes choice.

Causality flows both ways – while agents choose institutions, institutions then constrain agents. It bears some similarities to structuration on these grounds (Giddens, 1976; 1984). EU institutional and policy development may ultimately follow one of any number of 'paths,' and historical institutionalism does not show favouritism for one path over another. There is no reason why agents may not subsequently alter institutional arrangements to better suit their needs, but extant research points to the 'stickiness' and longevity of prior structural arrangements. Thus, institutions may prove inefficient over time, as social changes are not met by a corresponding evolution of the institutional framework.

Pierson raises our awareness of the evolution of co-operation over time and the importance of past decisions on interstate negotiations. Gaps emerge in member state control over institutional evolution, and these gaps are extremely difficult to close. Using the development towards a European social policy as an illustration, he shows the path-dependency of collaboration within the EU: 'In a number of instances, the short-term preoccupations of institutional designers have led them to make decisions that undermined long-term member-state control' (Pierson, 1996: 156).[9] The ubiquity of unintended consequences, the autonomy of supranational institutions and the instability of policy preferences in member states are further factors that have contributed to the inadvertent loss of control.

Pierson's essay is a response to the intergovernmentalist notion of state choice, and he uses the language of choice in delineating initial institutional arrangements. The implication is that member state preferences continue to be defined externally to the integration process – in other words they are less influenced by the development of EU institutions and policies than purely non-rational choice theorists would have us believe. Although he does suggest that 'altered circumstances' (1996: 140) might force a change of governmental policy preferences, he also places emphasis on the partisan sources of preference. The inference is that exogenous preference formation – member state governments seeking to maximise national benefits rather than achieve a common solution in the 'European interest' – is still an important source of motivation.[10] Thus, as he acknowledges, his research straddles the rationalist/nonrationalist divide.

Historical institutionalists differ over the role of culture in institutional influence, however. Where Pierson or Immergut (1992) see constrained rational actors, Armstrong and Bulmer (1997) give emphasis to the different aspects of culture within European organisations, such as the Commission. Historical institutionalists also differ over the issue of power. Pierson's discussion of historical institutionalism at the EU level omits the profound importance of structural bias, which is an important aspect of the historical agenda (Hall and Taylor, 1996: 940–1; Skocpol, 1985; Armstrong and Bulmer, 1997: 52). The structure of supranational institutions and policy competence privileges certain *types* of policy over others, and by extension, certain actors over others.

The normative aspect of historical institutionalism is evident here: institutions are not necessarily the product of neutral bargaining or efficient historical evolution. They have ideas built into them, which then influence the chances of agents. For example, the market orientation of European policy, and the existence of producer and consumer directorates with shared competence over policy marginalises non-market interests. The dominant mode of policy-making has been negative, reflecting both the ascendant normative bias of liberalism and the structure of EU institutions, which privileged negative over positive integration.[11]

Therefore, along these two dimensions at least – structural bias and culture – it is possible to distinguish among historical institutionalists working on European-level politics. In general, those closest to the rationalist camp discount culture and see institutions as power-neutral; those closest to the sociological camp take culture into account and see the institutions as having important implications for the power of social groups.

Although Europeanists working from a historical institutionalist perspective tend to focus on the EU level, there is a much larger comparativist literature using the historical approach at the level of the nation state. Numerous scholars have examined the unique economic and political traditions which colour state responses to social demands or external change (see the contributors to Evans et al., 1985; Hall, 1986; Schmidt,

1995; Crouch, 1993; Katzenstein, 1985; Putnam, 1993). For example, the similarities in corporatist arrangements among small European states distinguished their responses to economic change from those of the large industrial states (Katzenstein, 1985).

One of the shortcomings of historical institutionalism is its failure to integrate the effects of institutions over time at these two levels. As the mutual influences of the member states and the EU are increasingly felt, historical institutionalist research should endeavour to examine the interaction of institutions between the supranational and national polities. The challenge for research in this theoretical tradition is breaking the cycle to determine causality. The notion of feedback mechanisms, where institutions influence choice and behaviour but are also subject to alteration, leaves analysts without a theoretical purchase if they wish to test causality.

In sum, historical institutionalism, while not a coherent body of thought, stresses the role of prior commitments and institutional and policy stickiness in the process of European integration. Unlike neofunctionalism, with which it shares some traits, historical institutionalism does not predict movement toward or away from integration; rather it predicts that agency rationality, strategic bargaining and preference formation are conditioned by institutional context. European integration is a cumulative process, where prior decisions form a basis upon which new decisions are made. In the view of some theorists, historical institutionalism also infers a relationship between organisational culture and political outcomes (Armstrong and Bulmer, 1997) and sees an important structural bias on the part of institutional design (Hall and Taylor, 1996; Armstrong and Bulmer, 1997), which privileges some actors over others.

Sociological institutionalism
Sociological institutionalism has also contributed important insights to European integration studies and there seems to have been a veritable explosion in recent years in the number of scholars taking a broadly sociological or constructivist approach to this subject (see: Joergensen, 1997; Wiener, 1998; Christiansen et al., 1999). This trend builds upon scholarship in international relations which has sought to identify normative and cultural mechanisms by which both state behaviour and state identity are constrained or constructed, and additionally how identity itself influences state interests and practices, as well as international normative structures. The work in this area has sought to counter the rationalist thread linking both neoliberal institutionalism and neorealism (for an excellent overview see: Katzenstein, 1996; Jepperson et al., 1996; also, Kratochwil and Ruggie, 1986; Wendt, 1992; Wendt, 1994; Ruggie, 1998a; Finnemore and Sikkink, 1998; Risse-Kappen, 1995b).

Sociological institutionalism in European studies has begun to make inroads in the theoretical landscape once dominated by variants of inter-governmentalism and supranationalism (for a review of the literature see Wind, 1997: 24–32). Scholars have examined the enlargement of the EU and NATO (Fierke and Wiener, 1999), European citizenship (Wiener, 1998), regionalism and European integration (Christiansen, 1997) and domestic-European relations (Larsen, 1997; Holm, 1997; Laursen, 1997) among others. This literature, like the international relations scholarship before it, is concerned partly with how state behaviour is shaped or constrained in ways not captured by rationalist theories and partly with how identity is constructed. Thomas Diez, for example, drawing on Ole Wæver, asserts that 'Europe has become a reference point embedded in all national identity constructions' (Diez, 1999b: 10).

Constructivists have taken the notions of history, institutions, norms, ideas and culture well beyond the point to which historical institutional-ists are willing to go, problematising a number of key concerns that rationalists taken for granted. They are especially concerned with the construction of norms internationally, but also with the communication of norms through discursive practices (Diez, 1999a; Weiner, 1998). As Katzenstein argues, 'self-reflection does not occur in isolation; it is communicated to others' (1996: 21). This discourse tends to reify the exis-tence of the sovereign state, the power of economic interests and the 'belonging' of citizens as a whole. Language therefore helps to construct a normative context which then becomes a basis for action.

Some of the institutionalist research within this general category has not addressed the integration process but rather the distinctions between European states. It has examined the role of separate European state cultural traditions, which also produce 'institutions', though not neces-sarily in the sense intended by historical institutionalists. In this work culture has been implicitly defined as a state phenomenon, informing national actors in similar ways (Zetterholm, 1994). For example, studies of European political economy have noted the enduring differences between state traditions in Europe and the importance of them in deter-mining responses to change (see Crouch, 1993; Crouch and Streek, 1997; Kitschelt et al., 1999). The nature of domestic industrial relations arrangements, based upon distinct cultural traditions, separate modes of capitalism and differential state–society relations, have an important impact upon how actors respond to a variety of external challenges, including opportunities or demands for integration. Nationally-rooted cultural features 'establish a system of common reference' among actors, including their perceptions of the outside world, and they also establish a common identity rooted in both history and an anticipated future (Zetterholm, 1994: 4–5). This differentiation acts as a cross-cutting influ-ence to the system-wide influences of social democracy, neoliberalism, or some other motivating ideology.

One interesting issue raised by the sociological institutionalist approach is how these distinct national cultural settings change as liberalism and competitive practices gain legitimacy more widely. Indeed, the contested nature of legitimate practices in European capitalism means that socio-logical influences act at cross-purposes. More than one 'institutional environment' exerts an influence upon agents and organisations, sending them conflicting signals about legitimate behaviour. This contestation is underplayed by sociological institutionalism, which assumes the rise of a rational, purposive isomorphism (Finnemore, 1996b).

Therefore, from the sociological institutionalist perspective, integration depends on cultural and cognitive variation, and consequently the impact of values, beliefs, and identities on actors' responses to integrative chal-lenges. This variation may occur along professional lines, where groups of professionals from different EU member states begin to respond in similar ways to proposed or agreed policies; it may occur along organisational lines; it may occur along national lines; it may occur at the subnational level, where citizens in one part of a country may have different views of the appropriate nature of state-society relations than citizens in another part of the country (Putnam, 1993).

A key underlying assumption from the point of view of action is that breaching cognitive boundaries adds transaction costs to co-operation, whether these links are founded in language, faith, geography, 'epistemic professionalism', or some other bond which assigns common meaning and value to human experience. Cultural persistence may be the result of external pressure (functional need or the desire for rewards) or internali-sation of norms. Alternatively, it may be caused by transmission of 'an exterior and objective reality' in which those cultural meanings that have wide significance in society are 'enculturated' into succeeding generations (Zucker, 1991). These commonalties solidify over time, and so sociologi-cal institutionalism shares with historical institutionalism this important focus upon the temporal aspects of institutions. Moreover, as we move from historical institutionalism to sociological institutionalism, we see a tendency to assume that institutions become internalised and part of agent identity. Institutions become increasingly important independent causes of outcomes whether these are institutional design/change decisions or policy decisions.

Methodology and theory

We hope this volume represents a starting point for an understanding, if not a reconciliation, between the new institutionalisms as they are employed in the field of European studies. Sharp divisions still charac-terise the theoretical debate on regional collaboration, and much has been made of the differences between the methodologies of the different institutionalisms. The most important result of the rationalist agenda is arguably the rigorous demonstration that power in the EU is shared in a complex and often counterintuitive way between competing actors. The approach assumes that actors understand the possibilities and limitations that the diverse decision-making rules have created. More particularly, rational choice institutionalism suggests that actors adapt their behaviour to these institutions and use them strategically.

The methodology of rational choice institutionalism has mainly been deductive, formal and universalist. It has tended not to examine individual cases and this has led (as we stated earlier) to conflicting interpretations of the same events, such as the influence of the co-decision procedure. As Green and Shapiro (1994) point out, a major weakness of rational choice theorising is this lack of empiricism. This is compounded by the occasional tendency to engage in *post-hoc* theory adjustments when empirical data are found to contradict the model and by the lack of attention to competing theories (neither of these latter two tendencies is limited to rational choice theorists, of course).

The methodology of historical and sociological institutionalism in European integration studies has tended to be empirical and case-study oriented, engaging in 'analytical induction and historically grounded comparisons' (Evans et al., 1985: 348). This has led to a rich collection of descriptive analyses of events but with little theoretical generalisation and even less quantitative data manipulation.

Empirical case studies have the distinct advantage that they are descriptively rich and quite precise in their explanation of unique events. However, they suffer from the defect that the very detail may obscure the relative importance of causal variables. Moreover, one-at-a-time case studies do not permit valid generalisations as long as no causal model exists to assist in the inevitable task of counterfactual reasoning.[12] Researchers could potentially overcome this by gathering a number of case studies together. The EU is a unique institution, but this uniqueness should not undermine theoretical sophistication and methodological rigour. On the contrary, most institutionalist research questions on the EU refer to a selection of similar events and thus invite comparativist analysis across policy areas, across member states, or across time.

Close comparison suggests that the main differences are the basic goals and scientific orientations that separate the three research traditions. Historical and sociological institutionalism have enjoyed a comparative advantage in the area of 'thick' description, though quantitative studies have also begun to emerge. On the other hand, rational choice approaches have an inbuilt bias towards parsimonious explanation. The other differences between the approaches are a consequence of this basic epistemological division. For instance, divergent opinions on the feasibility and desirability of endogenising preference change are not one of the

major reasons why a theoretical convergence between the competing institutionalisms seems unlikely. It is simply an effect of profoundly different
research designs. Historical and sociological institutionalist typically
describe how such changes take place. Rationalists, by contrast, put much
greater emphasis on the establishment of a causal mechanism under which
an endogenous change of preference becomes more likely. If they cannot
come up with a convincing model, the topic disappears from their
research agenda.

What should we make of this methodological pluralism? One advantage of formal modelling, whether it involves fully or only boundedly
rational actors, is that it forces precision into an argument. In other
words, strategic rationality, broadly conceived, uncovers some of the
problems of inductive reasoning. The necessary complement to a convincing empirical strategy (Moravcsik, 1997b) is a model, rational or
non-rational, which establishes causal links between variables and from
which testable hypotheses are derived. While we agree with many rational
choice critics that only empirically grounded examinations allow us to
move further in the social sciences, we also believe that it is urgent to
establish a solid theoretical model before engaging in qualitative or quantitative tests (Green and Shapiro, 1994; King et al., 1994). Without a solid
grounding of the basic hypotheses, any empirical work remains incomplete and shaky.

Analytical models are indispensable in the development of institutionalist theories even if they are dealing with potentially unique
constellations. Yet, any model in an applied setting such as the EU
decision-making arena should be empirically informed and accompanied
by a sound test. Without testing and confirmation of hypotheses with
empirical data, these hypotheses must remain subject to question. We
believe that this merger between theoretical rigour and substantive tests of
the deduced hypotheses is the main comparative advantage of a revised
institutionalism.

Finally, we believe that it is crucial that theorists take into account
alternative theoretical explanations to the puzzles they are addressing,
and this applies primarily to rational choice theorists, who would be
forced to relax their universality claims. As two well-known institutionalists put it: 'It is not obvious that any one approach is superior to the
others in capturing the complexities of change. There are several stories to
be told and a necessary humility associated with the telling of any one of
them' (March and Olsen, 1998: 958).

Conclusion

How much explanatory value is contained in rationalist, historical, or
sociological approaches to institutions? Do actors engage in an egoistic

quest for gain, navigating their way through institutional mazes, or are they governed by an auto-pilot which steers them away from hazardous (non-conforming) behaviour? European studies, like international relations, has no final answer to this question. Yet we believe that degenerating into a new polarity between rationalism and constructivism would be a mistake; that the insights from each can feed into the others rather than simply being used as means for discrediting alternative theories. Means of reconciling the approaches have been suggested by scholars in the field of international relations more generally. One way is a division of labour – constructive approaches specialising in explanations of how preferences are formed; rational choice approaches specialising in determining how these preferences are acted on (Katzenstein et al., 1998). Alternatively, we might try to discern whether norm creation is an (un)intentional byproduct of rational behaviour.

We believe that the theoretical differences between the competing schools of thought are not an insurmountable obstacle to greater mutual understanding. Epistemological divergences, by contrast, have not yet played a major role in the debate (but see Ruggie, 1998a: 884–5; Finnemore and Sikkink, 1998: 909–15). We hope a more constructive dialogue based on a common research agenda can be reached. A methodological convergence, however, will only become likely under two conditions. First, rationalists have to give in to the historical and sociological institutionalists' demand for empirical precision. Without a meaningful referent in reality, any hypothesis remains, to quote David Singer (1968), an 'insight without evidence'. Second, non-rational choice research should also acknowledge that models, be they rational or non-rational, are an indispensable method to derive hypotheses. We believe that many case studies could be improved if they were more theoretically guided and more consciously seeking to detect those causal mechanisms that matter.

Our contributors are drawn from all three theoretical camps. A commentator from an opposing theoretical view follows each chapter, providing an alternative perspective on that chapter. Authors have investigated a variety of formal and informal institutional environments within two broad categories: institutional formation, maintenance and change; and the impact of institutions on decision-making. These broad categories reflect our collective concern both with the intentional design and creation (or unintentional evolution) of institutions, and also with their subsequent impact.

Notes

1 This introduction is largely based on Aspinwall and Schneider (forthcoming).
2 The economists include North (1981); the sociologists include Giddens (1976; 1984) and Berger and Luckmann (1967).

3 The label 'historical' is, in our view at least, a misnomer since every social phenomenon can be attributed to the influence of history. As social scientists we should specifically delineate between important and unimportant historical influences. We simultaneously recognise that many social scientists use historical institutionalism as an independent category and we follow this convention.

4 One basic distinction in the rationalist literature is between games *on* rules and games *within* rules. We will come back to this categorisation in the conclusion.

5 This is the reason why one of us labels rational choice institutionalism as the theory of strategic integration (Moser and Schneider, 1997b).

6 Although voting power studies were originally insensitive towards institutional aspects, some recent work tries to take legislative procedures into account. One problem with these revisions is that they implicitly assume an unambiguous impact of these rules on the actors' voting power. As the spatial voting literature has repeatedly shown, such a uniformity is, however, unrealistic if actors' preferences are allowed to vary. Three proponents of the voting power literature have also shown that these problems cannot be solved through the inclusion of ideological consideration since the voting power indexes are highly sensitive to small variations in the actors' preferences (Lane, Berg and Maeland, 1997).

7 Kaiser (1996) attributes Tsebelis' (1997) interpretation that the EP has lost influence under co-decision in comparison to co-operation to his failure to recognise that the European Commission matters in the second reading and that, consequently, the influence of the Parliament is more limited than he conjectures in his analysis of this decision stage. Scully's (1997a and b) attack on Tsebelis' interpretation raises similar points, but is unfortunately hampered by severe misinterpretations of strategic reasoning (Tsebelis and Garrett, 1997).

8 Pahre (1997) similarly demonstrates that different forms of parliamentary involvement can be used strategically and affect a country's behaviour at the international level.

9 These insights represent an implicit extension of the recent thinking by comparativists about state autonomy from domestic social forces (Skocpol, 1985).

10 This observation is, by the way, perfectly compatible with the rationalist literature on two-level games.

11 This has also been pointed out by Scharpf (1988) who would not consider himself a historical institutionalist.

12 The 'method' of counterfactual reasoning has recently been proposed as a means to overcome the small n-problem that characterises theoretical explorations of many interesting social phenomena. It is often forgotten, however, that the number of cases can be raised in most research designs.

Constructing European institutions[1]

Over forty years after the European project began, it is striking how little we know about its socialisation and identity-shaping effects on national agents. Indeed, prominent Europeanists are themselves deeply divided on this question, with some arguing that integration has led to a fundamental shift in actor loyalty and identity, while others claim the opposite (compare Wessels, 1998; and Laffan, 1998, for example). The basic premise of this essay is that both schools are right: constructing European institutions is a multi-faceted process, with both rationalist and sociological toolkits needed to unpack and understand it.

Put differently, much of European integration can be modelled as strategic exchange between autonomous political agents with fixed interests; at the same time, much of it cannot. Dynamics of social learning, socialisation, routinisation and normative diffusion, where fundamental agent properties change *during* interaction, are not adequately captured by strategic exchange or other models adhering to strict forms of methodological individualism. For these constitutive processes, the dominant institutionalisms in studies of integration – rational choice and historical – need to be supplemented by a more sociological understanding that stresses the interaction context through which interests and identities are formed.

After briefly addressing definitional issues and the literature on integration, I argue that social construction, a growing literature in contemporary international relations, can help students of integration to theorise and to explore empirically these neglected questions of interest and identity. Specifically, the chapter shows how a social constructivist cut at institution building explains key aspects of Europeanisation – social learning and normative diffusion – more completely than its rationalist competitors, with the practical goal being to elaborate the specific methods and data requirements for such work.

Before proceeding, three comments are in order. First, my analytic starting point is that research on integration should be problem, and not method, driven; the goal is to encourage dialogue and bridge-building between rationalists and social constructivists. By itself, each school explains important elements of the integration process; working together, or at least side-by-side, they will more fully capture the range of institutional dynamics at work in contemporary Europe.

Second, the constructivism favoured in this essay belongs to what has been called its modernist branch. These scholars, who combine an ontological stance critical of methodological individualism with a loosely causal epistemology, are thus well placed, within the integration literature, 'to seize the middle ground' – staking out a position between positivist and agent-centred rational choice on the one hand, and interpretative and structure-centred approaches on the other (Adler, 1997: 335–7; Checkel, 1998).

Third, the chapter's central focus is theoretical and methodological, and not empirical. My concern is how one could develop and apply, in a systematic manner, constructivist insights to key puzzles in the study of integration. Empirically, I seek only to establish the plausibility of such propositions, and do so in two ways: (1) by drawing upon arguments and evidence from a wide range of existing studies on European integration; and (2) by reference to my own work in progress.

Institutions and European integration

Of the many institutionalisms floating around these days in economics, political science and sociology, I need briefly to discuss three: rational choice institutionalism, historical institutionalism and sociological institutionalism (DiMaggio and Powell, 1991: Chapter 1; Longstreth et al., 1992: Chapter 1; Koelble, 1995; Kato, 1996; Katzenstein, 1996: Chapter 2; Finnemore, 1996b; Hall and Taylor, 1996). For rational choice scholars, institutions are thin: at most, they are a constraint on the behaviour of self-interested actors – be they interest groups or unitary states in international relations (IR). They are a strategic context that provides incentives or information, thus influencing the strategies agents employ to attain given ends. In this thin conception, institutions are a structure that actors run into, go 'ouch' and then recalculate how, in the presence of the structure, to achieve their interests; they are an intervening variable.

For historical institutionalists, institutions get thicker, but only in a long-term historical perspective. In the near-term here and now, they are thin – structuring the game of politics and providing incentives for instrumentally motivated actors to rethink their strategies; they are a constraint on behaviour (Immergut, 1992; and Pierson, 1994, for example). Over the longer term, however, institutions can have deeper effects on actors as strategies, initially adopted for self-interested reasons, get locked into and institutionalised in politics (Hattam, 1993; Goldstein, 1993). Thus institutions can be both intervening and independent variables.[2]

Sociological institutionalists are unabashedly thick institutionalists (DiMaggio and Powell, 1991: *passim*; Dobbin, 1994; see also March and Olsen, 1998: 948–58). Not only in the distant future, but in the near-term, institutions constitute actors and their interests. What exactly does it mean for institutions to constitute? It is to suggest they can provide agents with understandings of their interests and identities. This occurs through interaction between agents and structures – mutual constitution, to IR scholars. The effects of institutions thus reach much deeper; they do not simply constrain behaviour. As variables, institutions become independent – and strongly so.

In research and theorising about Europe, should one of these institutionalisms be favoured, serving as the baseline? The answer here is 'no,' for ultimately this is an empirical question. No doubt, there are many situations and aspects of integration where agents operate under the means-end logic of consequences favoured by rationalist-choice and some historical institutionalists – in other words, where actors leave an exchange largely as they entered it (meetings of the European Council or the hard-headed interstate bargaining that features prominently in inter-governmentalist accounts). At the same time, a less static perspective reminds us that social interaction also involves dynamics of learning and socialisation, where individuals leave exchanges different from how they entered (informal communications in working groups of the Council of Ministers, European-level policy networks centred on the Commission). Unfortunately, these latter processes, while equally compelling and plausible, have received little systematic theoretical attention in studies of Europeanisation.

I substantiate this claim by briefly examining the controversy between proponents of multi-level governance and historical institutionalists on the one hand, and intergovernmentalists on the other. Among the former, I include supranational institutionalists and some neofunctionalists; rational choice theorists, as well as neorealists, are grouped with the latter. The purpose is not to provide yet another review of this debate; others have done that much better than I could (Anderson, 1995: 443–51; Risse-Kappen, 1996: 55–7; and Marks et al., 1996: 343–7). Rather, my concern is the conceptualisation of institutions in these analyses.

Beginning with intergovernmentalists, their conception of institutions is clear, consistent and very thin. Because these scholars are self-conscious about their theoretical and methodological foundations, it is easy to comprehend immediately the brand of institutionalism on offer. Moravcsik's carefully argued work is a case in point. Institutions at the European level are an arena for strategic interaction and bargaining; by facilitating credible commitments and side payments, they help self-inter-

ested states attain efficient bargaining outcomes. Moreover, EU institutions – typically the Council of Ministers or European Council for
intergovernmentalists – have little or no autonomy; the preferences of the
large and powerful member states prevail. Thus, at most, institutions
shape the strategic environment of states (Moravcsik, 1991: 25–7, 1993:
496–517).

In more recent work, Moravcsik has added a theory of national preference formation to his earlier intergovernmentalist approach. Given this
move, an important question – for my purposes – is the role of domestic
institutions. Do they provide actors with understandings of their interests? Hardly, for the institutions here, at the national level, are as thin as
they are internationally. The preferences of social groups are 'aggregated
through political institutions'; the latter have no independent causal role.
This should come as no surprise as Moravcsik's domestic model simply
imports the rational choice microfoundations of neoliberal regime theory
(Moravcsik, 1994: 4–6, 14, 24–5, 43, 49, 59, 63; 1993: 481 [for quote];
also see Moravcsik, 1997a, 1998: Chapter 1).

The portrayal of EU institutions in game theoretic, rational choice,
principal-agent or neorealist work differs little from that sketched above.
Garrett, Weingast and collaborators, for example, draw upon theories of
incomplete information and incomplete contracting, as well as non-co-
operative game theory to offer a sophisticated analysis of the role played
by institutions in the construction of the internal market and of the relation between EU member states and the European Court of Justice (ECJ).
The use of such approaches addresses gaps in standard rational choice
models, which assume, unrealistically, that emergent co-operative
arrangements represent uniquely efficient solutions to the problems faced
by states; their use also contributes, in a systematic manner, to the
ongoing debate over the ECJ as 'servant' or 'master' to member states
(Garrett, 1992; Garrett and Weingast, 1993; Garrett et al., 1998; and, for
applications of principal-agent analysis to the EU, Pollack, 1997;
Franchino, 1998).

However, the rationalist foundation that undergirds their preferred
theories leads these scholars, like intergovernmentalists, to conceptualise
institutions in very thin terms. In nearly all cases, EU institutions – like the
ECJ – are viewed as entities with fixed preferences that do not change
through interaction. Neorealist work on the EU differs little on this score,
with Joe Grieco, for example, viewing its bodies as a strategic environment constructed by weaker states to constrain the choices and behaviour
of the more powerful (Grieco, 1995; 1996).

How do proponents of supranational institutionalism, multi-level
governance and historical institutionalists conceptualise EU institutions?
One would think quite differently – given the great amount of heat and
fire in their debate with intergovernmentalists. However, this often turns

out not to be the case. To begin, consider the work of Sandholtz. While he argues the need to endogenise interest formation, it is not at all clear that institutions play any meaningful role in this process. In his research on telecommunications, the Maastricht treaty and EU membership, he portrays EU organs as helping states overcome collective action problems and, more generally, affecting the calculations, behaviours and strategies of self-interested domestic actors.

Not surprisingly, given this thin conception of institutions, his three 'direct influences' of the EU on 'national interest formation' are all captured and explained by variants of rational choice institutionalism. In turn, this suggests Sandholtz is not so much analysing the impact of institutions on national interests, but how they affect the strategies employed by member states in the pursuit of given interests (Sandholtz, 1993a: 4, *passim*; 1993b; 1996; also see Stone Sweet and Brunell, 1998, which systematises, in an explicit and rigorous manner, the rational choice institutionalist insights implicit in much of the other supranationalist literature).

Proponents of multi-level governance, while adding a new and important institutional layer to neofunctionalist and intergovernmentalist arguments, do not challenge the rationalist microfoundations of either school (Risse-Kappen, 1996: 56; Moravcsik, 1993, 1994, respectively). Consistent with such an approach, these scholars typically argue that their perspective supplements the state-centred, high-politics focus of intergovernmentalism by considering subnational actors and other points in the policy process (Marks, 1993; Leibfried and Pierson, 1995: Chapter 1; Hooghe and Marks, 1996; Marks et al., 1996).

Through richly detailed studies, this literature has convincingly shown that multi-level governance is a reality in a variety of policy areas. However, it has not paid sufficient attention to the role of institutions in this process; moreover, the institutional analysis on offer is largely predicated on rational choice foundations. The dominant institutional metaphor and empirical focus is institutions as constraint; they induce actors to adopt certain strategies or shape their behaviour.

While early work by proponents of multi-level governance tended toward the descriptive, more recent studies are self-consciously theoretical. This analytic base, consistent with my observations, is solidly rational choice – theories of transaction costs and informational asymmetries, as well as principal-agent frameworks. In sum, the fight these scholars pick with intergovernmentalists is more about which institutions matter than about how they have effects (Marks et al., 1996: 347–56; Leibfried and Pierson, 1995: 28, 30–1, 38, 40).[3]

Finally, one has historical institutionalist work on the EU. This recent addition to EU studies is best exemplified by the work of Paul Pierson. As noted earlier, this branch of institutionalism sits, somewhat uneasily, between rational choice and sociological institutionalism. However, Pierson's version moves it decisively closer to rational choice scholarship; one result is a very thin conception of institutions. His discussion, within the context of the EU, of unanticipated consequences, adaptive learning, institutional barriers to reform, sunk costs and exit costs is entirely consistent with – and, in fact, premised on – rational choice. EU institutions are thus all about constraint and incentives. While Pierson should be commended for providing solid rational choice microfoundations to a largely descriptive historical-institutionalist/EU literature (Bulmer, 1994; Cram, 1997b; Alter, 1998; Armstrong, 1998, among others), the costs are significant.

Indeed, he essentially severs the bridge that links parts of that same literature to a sociological or thick understanding of institutions. Put differently, Pierson is entirely correct to assert that the 'path to European integration has embedded member states in a dense institutional environment'; however, he provides us with only a limited set of methodological tools for understanding exactly how that dense environment matters (Pierson, 1996: 158–9, *passim*; 1994: Chapters 1–2, where he elaborates this particular synthesis of rational choice and historical institutionalism; also see Pollack, 1996: *passim*).

In sum, what is wrong with all this institutional analysis on Europeanisation? Nothing. Rather, the proper question is 'What is missing here?'. In virtually all the foregoing, institutions are at best intervening variables. Missing is a thick institutional argument that demonstrates how European institutions can construct, through a process of interaction, the identities and interests of member states and groups within them.

Constructing European institutions

In this section, I develop an approach that addresses the above-noted gaps, and I do so by drawing upon a growing and vibrant body of international relations scholarship: social constructivism. As presently elaborated, the modernist constructivism of concern here is an argument about institutions, one which builds upon the insights of sociological institutionalism. It is thus well suited, in a conceptual sense, for expanding our repertoire of institutional frameworks for explaining European integration. In particular, it seeks to explain theoretically both the content of actor identities/preferences and the modes of social interaction – so evident in everyday life – where something else aside from strategic exchange is taking place (Adler, 1997; Checkel, 1998; Ruggie, 1998b: 35–6).

So defined, constructivism has the potential to contribute to the study of integration in various areas. Below, I consider two: learning and socialisation processes at the European level; and the soft or normative side of Europeanisation at the national level. In each case, I explore what a constructivist approach entails, how it could be carried out empirically and its value added compared to existing work on integration. I also address and counter the argument that my results cannot be generalised. The section concludes by noting how a constructivist approach to integration can build upon and systematise theoretical arguments and descriptive insights advanced by a growing number of Europeanists; I also argue that the whole exercise is not one of re-inventing the wheel.

Learning and socialisation

What does it mean for an agent to learn? In a very fundamental sense, rationalists and social constructivists answer this question differently. While it is true that rational choice analysis has come to accord a role of sorts to learning and socialisation, such work falls short of fully capturing the multiple ways they are causally important in social life. Most important, because of their adherence to methodological individualism, rationalists cannot model the interaction context during which agent interests may change. Indeed, when prominent scholars working in this tradition talk of 'social interactions', they are neither 'social' nor 'interactions' in any meaningful sense. Instead, in a manner that is rather puzzling, 'interactions' are collapsed into the utility functions of discrete agents (Becker, 1996: Chapters 8–9).[4]

A direct consequence of such a stance is to portray learning in highly individualist terms. For example, some rationalists talk of Bayesian updating, where, *after* each discrete interaction, individual actors update their strategies and – perhaps – preferences. Others discuss another type of updating, where agents come to learn new 'probability distributions'. Using different language to make the same point, many rational choice scholars emphasise so-called simple learning (Levy, 1994), where agents acquire new information as a result of interaction; at a later point, this information is used to alter strategies, which then allow these actors to pursue given, fixed interests more efficiently. Not surprisingly, all this rationalist theorising reduces communication and language, which are central to any process of *social* learning, to the 'cheap talk' of agents with fixed identities and interests. The result is to bracket the interaction context that constructivists, through theories of persuasion, learning and arguing, seek to understand (Calvert, 1995: 256–8, *passim*; Sargent, 1993: Chapter 1, *passim*; Finnemore and Sikkink, 1998: 909–15; and, for helpful reviews, Cohen and Sproull, 1996).

Specifically, the constructivist value added is to explore complex social learning, which involves a process whereby actors, through interaction with broader institutional contexts (norms or discursive structures), acquire new interests and preferences. Put differently, agent interests and identities are shaped through and during interaction. So defined, social learning involves a break with strict forms of methodological individualism; it thus differs significantly from the rationalist work surveyed above (again see Cohen and Sproull, 1996, *passim*).

Consider small group settings. It seems clear that there are times when agents acquire new preferences through interaction in such contexts. This is not to deny periods of strategic exchange, where self-interested actors seek to maximise utility; yet, to emphasise the latter dynamic to the near exclusion of the former is an odd distortion of social reality. Now, the perhaps appropriate response is 'so what?'. In an abstract sense, it can readily be appreciated that social learning takes place at certain times, but how can one conceptualise and empirically explore whether and when it occurs? Luckily, there is a growing literature in contemporary IR – by constructivists, students of epistemic communities and empirically oriented learning theorists – that performs precisely this theoretical/ empirical combination (DiMaggio and Powell, 1991: *passim*; Haas, 1990, 1992, Hall; 1993; Risse-Kappen, 1996; Checkel, 1997a: Chapters 1 and 5). More specifically, this research suggests four hypotheses on when social learning occurs; these could be translated to empirical work conducted at the European level:

Hypothesis H1   social learning is more likely in groups where individuals share common professional backgrounds – for example, where all/most group members are lawyers or, say, European central bankers;

Hypothesis H2   social learning is more likely where the group feels itself in a crisis or is faced with clear and incontrovertible evidence of policy failure;

Hypothesis H3   social learning is more likely where a group meets repeatedly and there is a high density of interaction among participants;

Hypothesis H4   social learning is more likely when a group is insulated from direct political pressure and exposure.

Clearly, these hypotheses require further elaboration. For example, can a crisis situation be specified *a priori*, and not in a *post-hoc* fashion as is typically done? When is the density of interaction among group participants sufficiently high for a switch to occur from strategic exchange to interactive learning? These are difficult issues, but they are only being raised because a first round of theoretical/empirical literature exists. Europeanists could build upon and contribute to this work – for example, by exploring and theorising the impact, if any, of different EU voting rules (unanimity, qualified majority voting) on these group dynamics.

The deductions also point to a powerful role for communication. However, in keeping with this chapter's attempted bridging function, it is a role between that of the rationalists' cheap talk, where agents (typically) possess complete information and are (always) instrumentally motivated, and the post-modernists' analyses, where communication and language create a discursive structure that often hides more than it reveals (see also Johnson, 1993).

Yet, this role itself requires further unpacking. Underlying these communication/learning arguments are implicit theories of persuasion and argumentation. Oddly, the non-rationalist learning literature (propositions H1–H4 above) has been largely silent on the latter, hinting at mechanisms of persuasion, socialisation, etc., through which agents learn new interests/identities, but failing to theorise them. This lacuna arose because much of the research, especially that by organisational theorists, failed to explore *social* interaction contexts; instead, the focus was often 'artificial interactions,' where no 'face-to-face' meetings occur (Cook and Yanow, 1996: 440–53, quotes at 449; Simon, 1996: 177; Levitt and March, 1996: 518).

To explore such mechanisms, constructivists and learning theorists should exploit a rich literature in social psychology, political socialisation and communications research on persuasion/argumentation (for example, Zimbardo and Leippe, 1991; see also Johnston, 1998: 16–25). At core, persuasion is a social process that involves changing attitudes about cause and effect in the absence of overt coercion; put differently, it is a mechanism through which social learning may occur, thus leading to interest redefinition and identity change. The literature suggests three hypotheses about the settings where agents should be especially conducive to persuasion:

Hypothesis H5   when they are in a novel and uncertain environment
    and thus cognitively motivated to analyse new information;
Hypothesis H6   when the persuader is an authoritative member of the
    in-group to which the persuadee belongs or wants to belong; and
Hypothesis H7   when the agent has few prior, ingrained beliefs that are
    inconsistent with the persuader's message.

This focus on persuasion highlights and begins to operationalise the patently obvious role of communication. Moreover, it restores a sense of agency to the social norms that may be central to learning. Norms are not just something out there, waiting to help actors learn; they are carried by individuals and organisations ('the persuader' in H6) who actively seek, through deliberation and argumentation, to promote learning.

While these deductions partly overlap with the first set, further work is still needed – for example, how to operationalise 'uncertain environments' and integrate political context. On the latter, my strong hunch is that persuasion will be more likely in less politicised and more insulated settings (also see Pierson, 1993: 617–18). All the same, both sets of hypotheses do elaborate scope conditions (when, under what conditions persuasion and social-learning/socialisation are likely), which is precisely the promising middle-range theoretical ground that still awaits exploitation by both constructivists and students of European integration (Checkel, 1998).

What are the data requirements for research based on the above hypotheses? Essentially, you need to read things and talk with people. The latter requires structured interviews with group participants; the interviews should all employ a similar protocol, asking questions that tap both individual preferences and motivations, as well as group dynamics. The former, ideally, requires access to informal minutes of meetings or, second best, the diaries or memoirs of participants. As a check on these first two data streams, one can search for local media/TV interviews with group participants. This method of triangulation is fairly standard in qualitative research; it both reduces reliance on any one data source (interviewees, after all, may often dissimulate) and increases confidence in the overall validity of your inferences (also see the excellent discussion in Zuern, 1997: 300–2).

For constructivists, is the process-oriented, micro-focus outlined here a feasible undertaking? Drawing upon my own work in progress, I suggest the answer is 'yes'. In a larger project, I am studying the evolution of new European citizenship norms; an important concern is to explain, at the European level, whether and how new understandings of citizenship are emerging – that is, the process through which new citizenship norms are created. To date, my focus has been on Strasbourg and the Council of Europe (CE), for this has been where the more serious, substantive work has occurred. When the CE is trying to develop new policy, it often sets up committees of experts under the Committee of Ministers, the intergovernmental body that sits atop the Council's decision-making hierarchy.

I have been examining the Committee of Experts on Nationality, the group that was charged with revising earlier European understandings of citizenship that dated from the 1960s. My interest was to describe and explain what occurred in this group as it met over a four year period – in particular, why it changed existing understandings on dual citizenship to remove the strict prohibition that had previously existed at the European level. To address such issues, I did the following. Extensive field work was carried out in Strasbourg; during these trips, I interviewed various individuals who served on the Committee – members of the Council Secretariat and experts. Then, I conducted interviews in several member-state capitals, meeting with national representatives to the committee of experts. Finally, as a cross-check on interview data, more recently I was granted partial access to the confidential meeting summaries of the Committee.[5]

This was a considerable amount of work, but the pay off was high.

Over time, particular individuals clearly shifted from what they viewed as a strategic bargaining game (for example, seeking side payments to advance given interests) to a process where basic preferences were rethought. This shift was particularly evident on the question of dual citizenship, where a growing number of committee members came to view the existing prohibition as simply wrong. Instead, they agreed on a new understanding that viewed multiple nationality in a more positive light.

Processes of persuasion and learning were key in explaining why individual members began to comply with this emerging norm, and such dynamics were facilitated by four factors. First, Committee members shared a largely common educational and professional background, being trained as lawyers who had for many years dealt with issues of immigration and nationality (H1). Second, the group was meeting at a time when there was a growing sense of policy failure: The number of dual nationals was climbing rapidly despite the existing prohibition (H2). Third, the shift from a bargaining to an arguing game was greatly facilitated by the committee's insulation from publicity and overt political pressure. Indeed, it benefited from the public perception of Strasbourg as a quiet backwater – with the real action occurring in Brussels (the EU's provisions for a 'European citizenship'). This allowed it to meet and work out revised understandings on citizenship prior to any overt politicisation of its work (H4).

Fourth and perhaps most important, the Committee contained three individuals – the Swiss, Italian and Austrian representatives – who were both highly respected by other group participants and renowned for their powers of persuasion. Indeed, several different interviewees, with no prodding by me, identified these same individuals as playing central roles in 'changing people's minds' – not through arm twisting, but by the power of arguments. That is, the Committee possessed effective persuaders who were authoritative members of the in-group (H6). These interviews, it should be stressed, were designed to minimise the introduction of unintended bias into my inferences. For example, I suggested four possible ways to characterise dynamics within the group: coercion, bargaining, copying/imitation, persuasion/arguing. Interviewees were then asked to rank order them; persuasion/arguing consistently came out on top. (Interviews: Horst Schade, former Secretary to the Committee, May 1994, June–July 1995, November 1998; GianLuca Esposito, current Secretary to the Committee, June–July 1995, April 1997, November 1998; and Ambassador Ulrich Hack, Head, Permanent Representation of Austria to the Council of Europe and former Chair of the Committee, November 1998; see also Council of Europe, 1993, 1994.)

At the same time, not all committee members complied with the emerging norm or learned new interests. Indeed, one national representative held deeply ingrained beliefs that were opposed to arguments favouring a relaxation of prohibitions on dual citizenship. Consistent with the above deductions (H7), there is no evidence that this individual was persuaded to alter his basic preferences. Instead, he consistently tried to steer group meetings toward an intergovernmental bargaining game, showing up with long lists of talking points that made clear his and his government's concerns – especially on the question of multiple nationality.[6]

The point of this example is not to dismiss rationalist accounts of strategic bargaining. Rather, it is to note the value added of a middle-range constructivist supplement to these more standard portrayals: it led me to ask new questions and employ a different set of research techniques. The result was to broaden our understanding of how and under what conditions new European institutions – norms – are constructed through processes of non-strategic exchange.

Whether one accepts my particular arguments, the basic point remains. In making claims about socialisation, learning, persuasion or deliberation promoted by, or conducted within, European institutions, students of integration must theorise these dynamics. In recent years, it has become almost a cottage industry to cite such processes as central, while simultaneously failing to elaborate their theoretical underpinnings. The result has been a near total disconnect between analytic claims and empirical documentation that such dynamics are at work (Wincott, 1995: 603–7; Kerremans, 1996: 222, 232–5; Oehrgaard, 1997: 15–16, 19–21; Cram, 1997b: *passim*; Joergensen, 1997: 174–5; Wessels, 1998: 227; Laffan, 1998: 242–3; Falkner, 1998: 6–7, 12, 17, *passim*). As one scholar has correctly noted in reference to the EU, 'what is needed is a decision-making theory which includes in its analysis the ways in which preferences, beliefs and desires are shaped by participation in the decision-making process itself' (Kerremans, 1996: 221; see also Olsen, 1998: 31–32).

Socialisation/diffusion pathways
Constructivists view norms as shared, collective understandings that make behavioural claims on actors (Katzenstein, 1996: Chapter 2). When thinking about norms in the EU context, two issues must be addressed: (1) through what process are they constructed at the European level; and (2) how do such norms, once they reach the national level, interact with and socialise agents. Now, the distinction between European and national levels is false, as multiple feedback loops cut across them; at the same time, the dichotomy can be justified analytically as it helps one unpack and think through different stages in the process of European norm construction. In what follows, I am less interested in formal legal norms developed and promulgated, for example, by the ECJ; a growing body of literature in both law and political science already addresses such understandings and their impact (Mattli and Slaughter, 1998, for example).

Rather, the constructivist value added comes from its focus on the less formalised, but more pervasive, social norms that are always a part of social interaction.

On the first issue – the process of norm development – constructivists have theorised and provided empirical evidence for the importance of three dynamics. First, individual agency is central: well-placed individuals with entrepreneurial skills can often turn their individual beliefs into broader, shared understandings. The importance of this particular factor has been documented in case studies covering nearly a 100-year period and a multitude of international organisations and other transnational movements. In the literature, these individuals are typically referred to as moral entrepreneurs; in the language of my earlier discussion, they are the agents actively seeking to persuade others (Nadelmann, 1990; Finnemore, 1996a; Florini, 1996; Finnemore and Sikkink, 1998; and, for a tough but fair-minded critique of this literature on supranational entrepreneurship, Moravcsik, 1999).

Second, such entrepreneurs are especially successful in turning individually held ideas into broader normative beliefs when so-called policy windows are open. This means the larger group, in which the entrepreneur operates, faces a puzzle/problem that has no clear answer, or is new and unknown. In this situation, fixed preferences often break down as agents engage in cognitive information searches. While the policy-window concept was first elaborated by public policy (agenda setting) and organisational theorists (garbage-can models), it was only more recently that constructivists applied its insights in the international realm to explain norm formation (for example, Haas, 1992; Checkel, 1997a: Chapter 1).

Third, processes of social learning and socialisation (see previous section) are crucial for furthering the norm creation first begun by individual actors exploiting open policy windows. The basic point is that individual agency is insufficient to create durable social norms. A brief example clarifies the point. In the mid-1980s, several close advisers to Soviet leader Gorbachev played the part of entrepreneurs seeking to advance new ideas about international politics. In the near-term, such individually held beliefs, which were influential in shaping Gorbachev's own preferences, were decisive in bringing the Cold War to a dramatic, peaceful and unexpected end. Yet, once the USSR collapsed and Gorbachev was swept from power, these ideas largely vanished, as many analysts of Russian foreign behaviour have noted. Put differently, absent social learning among a larger group of actors – that is, the development of norms – the particular ideas held by specific agents had no real staying power (Checkel, 1997a: Chapters 5–6).

When and if new European norms emerge, one must still theorise the mechanisms through which they diffuse to particular national settings and (perhaps) socialise agents. Here, constructivists, sociologists and students of international law have identified two dominant diffusion pathways: societal mobilisation and social learning. In the former, non-state actors and policy networks are united in their support for norms; they then mobilise and coerce decision-makers to change state policy. Norms are not necessarily internalised by the elites. The activities of Greenpeace or any number of European non-governmental organisations (NGOs) exemplify this political pressure mechanism (Koh, 1997; Keck and Sikkink, 1999: Chapter 1, *passim*; Risse and Sikkink, 1999; and, for discussion, Checkel, 1999a: 3–8).

A second diffusion mechanism identified by these scholars is similar to the process of social learning already discussed. In this case, agents – now national decision-makers – adopt prescriptions embodied in norms; they then become internalised and constitute a set of shared intersubjective understandings that make behavioural claims. This process is based on notions of complex learning drawn from cognitive and social psychology, where individuals, when exposed to the prescriptions embodied in norms, adopt new interests (Stein, 1994; Risse-Kappen, 1995b; Herman, 1996).

A key challenge is to develop predictions for when one or the other of these mechanisms is likely to be at work. To date, constructivists have been silent on this issue; however, my work on European citizenship norms suggests a possibility. I hypothesise that the structure of state-society relations – domestic structure – predicts likely diffusion pathways, with four categories of such structures identified: liberal, corporatist, statist and state-above-society. From these, I deduce and predict cross-national variation in the mechanisms – societal mobilisation and social learning – through which norms are empowered (Checkel, 1999b: 87–91).

A brief example highlights the utility of the approach as well as the attendant data requirements. In the project on European citizenship norms, I have explored whether and in what way they diffused to several European states, including the Federal Republic of Germany (FRG). Consider this German case. First I researched the basic structure of state-society relations in the country; like many others, I concluded that the polity is corporatist. That is, it possesses a decentralised state and centralised society, with a dense policy network connecting the two parts; both state and society are participants in policy-making, which is consensual and incremental.

Given this coding of the German structure, I next advanced predictions on the expected process whereby norms would have constitutive effects, arguing that societal pressure would be the primary and (elite) social learning the secondary mechanism empowering European norms in Germany. The logic is as follows. In a corporatist domestic structure, state decision-makers play a greater role in bringing about normative change than in the liberal case, where policymakers are constantly pressured by social actors; however, this does not mean that they impose their preferences on a pliant populace. A hallmark of corporatism is the policy networks connecting state and society, with the latter still accorded an important role in decision-making. In this setting, I thus hypothesise that it is both societal pressure (primary) and social learning (secondary) that lead to norm empowerment.

With these predictions in hand, I then conducted extensive field work in the FRG. To date, this research has confirmed my working hypotheses: emerging European norms on citizenship are diffusing and being empowered in Germany primarily via the mobilisation of societal pressure from below; social learning at the elite level has been secondary. More specifically, these norms are connecting to a wide variety of social groups and individuals: NGOs favouring the integration of Germany's large resident foreigner population; activists in the churches and trades unions; and immigrant groups. At the decision-making level, one finds isolated evidence of elites learning new preferences from the norms – for example, a small group of Christian Democratic Bundestag deputies (Checkel, 1999b: 96–107).

Two streams of evidence are important for establishing the presence of these diffusion mechanisms, as well as their relative weighting. Most important were structured interviews with a wide range of actors – both societal and state. As at the European level, these discussions were designed to probe the degree to which agent preferences were changing and the motivations for such change. However, as the rationalists remind us, talk is cheap. Therefore, as a cross-check on the interview data, I consulted a wide-range of primary documentation – official summaries of Bundestag debates, media analyses and interviews given in newspapers or on television.

What is the value-added of this work? It convincingly demonstrates that a rational-choice institutionalist understanding of the role norms play in social life (norms as constraint) missed an important part of the story in the FRG. I indeed found instances where domestic agents simply felt constrained by the European norms (for example, a number of officials in the Federal Interior Ministry); yet, in many other cases, I uncovered evidence of non-strategic social learning where agents, in the norm's presence, acquired new understandings of interests. Clearly, much theoretical work remains to be done – in particular, elaborating scope conditions for when norms have constraining, as opposed to constitutive, effects.

Extending the argument
Perhaps, though, my constitutive analysis of European institutions only works because of the particular organisation and policy area from which I drew examples: the Council of Europe (CE) and human rights. Such arguments are largely irrelevant for the EU – a special type of institution

with very different policy domains. Two responses counter such a critique.

First, there are well-established theoretical reasons for suspecting that Europe, especially Western Europe, is a most likely case for international institutions to have constitutive effects. Most important, it is an institutionally dense environment, one where theorists predict high levels of transnational and international normative activity. This logic, precisely because it is a particular way of viewing the social world, is in principle equally applicable to a variety of European institutions (Weber, 1994, for example; see also Risse-Kappen, 1995a: Chapter 1; Adler and Barnett, 1996: 97, *passim*) – whether their focus is human rights (CE) or political and economic affairs (EU).

Second, assume, despite the foregoing, that differences in policy domains do matter. That is, arguments about social learning or the constitutive effects of European norms just do not work when applied to the EU. After all, the process of European integration has largely been about market integration, where national and transnational business interests have played key roles. Such groups are quite different in structure and goals from the actors of civil society – domestic NGOs, churches – highlighted in several of my examples. However, if the institutional (enhanced role of EP) and substantive (third pillar of justice and home affairs) innovations of Maastricht and Amsterdam continue to evolve, new actors and policy issues are increasingly likely to make themselves felt (Obradovic, 1997; see also Hooghe and Marks, 1996). Moreover, the current interest in Brussels, London and elsewhere for moving the EU away from a strict regulatory role to one emphasising standard setting and so-called 'soft law' (Barber, 1998; and Parker, 1998) plays to the strength of social actors like NGOs: it is precisely the promotion of such informal practices and norms where they are most influential.

In fact, human rights pressure groups have begun utilising the EP as a means for generating precisely the sort of normative pressure-from-below documented in my CE example (Khalaf, 1997; Tucker, 1997; *Economist*, 1998). Moreover, immigration, which is now on the third pillar agenda, is an issue where previous studies have documented the extensive degree to which European state interests are constituted by broader international norms (Soysal, 1994). On the related issues of citizenship and racism, recent work establishes that the 1996–97 Intergovernmental conference (IGC) saw extensive mobilisation by NGOs and other transnational movements, and their qualitatively different, when compared to the past, interaction with EU institutions, as well as the IGC itself (Favell, 1998: 5–6, 10–14). Thus, even if differences in policy domains are important, these are presently being blurred if not erased.

Summary

My purpose in the foregoing was constructive. The goal was not to dismiss rational choice or historical institutionalist work on integration; those literatures are rich and offer many insights. Yet, because of their adherence to variants of methodological individualism, certain analytic/ empirical issues – interest and identity formation, most importantly – are bracketed. A more sociological and constructivist understanding of institutions as constitutive allows one to address such questions. Constructivism, however, need not and, indeed, should not be viewed as *terra incognita* to Europeanists. In fact, a constructivist cut at integration is already evident, albeit implicitly, in both theoretical and empirical/descriptive studies.

Theoretically, one has the recent work of Olsen, Kohler-Koch and Fligstein. Olsen's writing, including that on the EU, has been concerned with broader institutional environments – how they provide the very basis of action for political agents, how they lead to rule-governed behaviour, which may supplant instrumental, strategic calculation and how they promote learning. Yet, he has failed to explicate, in a theoretical sense, the processes through which such institutional dynamics occur (Olsen, 1995, 1996, 1998). The constructivist work reviewed above suggests a number of ways that these micro-macro linkages could be developed in a specifically European context.

Much of the analysis in recent work by Kohler-Koch and Knodt is also premised on sociological assumptions – in particular, their exploration of the domestic normative impact of EU institutions, where they do not simply constrain, but rather constitute agents and their preferences. Unfortunately, this argument is much less clear about the process through which, and the conditions under which, EU norms have such effects (Kohler-Koch and Knodt, 1997; see also Conzelmann, 1998: Part IV, *passim*). Here, constructivist hypotheses on the mechanisms through which national-level socialisation and social learning occur might be relevant.

Fligstein is also interested in constitutive dynamics, but in contrast to Kohler-Koch and Knodt, the focus is on Brussels. In his work on the Commission, he argues that, under certain conditions marked by crisis and uncertainty, it can play an entrepreneurial role helping culturally construct political action. Less clear, however, are the specific processes through which such construction takes place, as well as his theoretical understanding of agency's role (Fligstein, 1998: *passim*; see also Oehrgaard, 1997; and Cram, 1997b, where similar problems arise). All the same, this analytic move hints at rich possibilities for a dialogue with those social constructivists who theorise the role of individual agency, entrepreneurs and policy windows in their work on normative change.

Empirically, the last decade has seen an explosion of work on institutional fusion, policy networks, comitology and informal communication patterns centred upon and generated by EU institutions. While this research is extraordinarily rich in a descriptive sense, it is often undertheorised. To be fair, solid empirical work is often a prerequisite for theory building. All the same, more attention to theory would help these scholars systematise their implicitly sociological view of institutions – and constructivism has much to offer here.

Consider three examples. Wessels, Rometsch and their collaborators have made a powerful and well-documented case for institutional fusion within the EU context, where the density of interaction between European and national institutions is such that old distinctions between the two levels no longer hold. These analysts ascribe an important symbolic and identity-shaping role to institutions – to constructivists, a constitutive role. Yet, they are silent, theoretically, on when, how and why such identity formation occurs, which leads them to advance an underspecified convergence thesis, where 'the constitutional and institutional set-up of [EU] member states will converge towards one common model' (Rometsch and Wessels, 1996: Preface, Chapters 1–2, 14 [quote at 36]). Given that constructivists have already begun to specify scope conditions regarding institutions and identity change, the potential for theoretical cross-fertilisation would seem significant.

In a second example, recent work by Beyers and Dierickx on the EU Council and its working groups suggests that informal communication is the key for understanding their operation. Yet, this research, despite its empirical richness, neglects a crucial theoretical question: under what conditions – if at all – does this communication lead political agents away from situations of strategic exchange and into those marked by social learning, socialisation and communicative action? For both theoretical (debates over the consequences of integration) and policy reasons (explaining when and why member-state interests change), this issue is fundamental. However, because of their reliance on a methodologically individualist ontology, Beyers and Dierickx seem simply unaware that they are in fact well placed to address it (Beyers and Dierickx, 1997, 1998; see also Beyers, 1998; Hooghe, 1998: 5–6, 8–9). The point is not that they get the story wrong; rather, it is incomplete. And constructivism, with its concern for modelling modes of social interaction beyond strategic exchange, could provide analytic tools for filling out the picture.

Research on so-called comitology represents a third example where constructivist theorising and empirical integration studies could profitably interact. Comitology refers to the complex set of committee rules that have evolved to implement EU policy and procedures (for example, Pedler and Schaefer, 1996; Dogan, 1997); the system stems from a 1987 European Council decision in which member states made clear their unwillingness to lose control of the implementation process – in particular, by ceding too much power to the Commission. These committees, by member-state dictate, are composed of governmental representatives and, occasionally, additional experts; yet, the growing empirical literature on them notes how these representatives must often turn elsewhere for information and, more important, interpretation. Indeed, two analysts argue that 'scientific evidence' is accepted as the most valid currency for 'effecting convincing arguments' in comitology (Joerges and Neyer, 1997b: 617).

The last point suggests a link to my earlier hypotheses on small groups, communication and social learning. On the one hand, discursive argumentation, committee-level learning and its accompanying preference change do not necessarily lead to a reconstitution of member state interests, for comitology, after all, involves only implementation; yet, on the other hand, it is well known that implementation is often the making of policy by other means. Moreover, learning and deliberative arguing of this sort cannot be captured by standard strategic exchange models. Constructivist deductions on the role of common backgrounds, crisis, density of interaction, etc., could thus be readily exploited by Europeanists (for example, Pedler and Schaefer, 1996: 47; and, especially, Joerges and Neyer, 1997a: 291–2, 1997b: 618) to explore more systematically the conditions under which European committees do indeed, through learning and argumentation, socialise their participants.

A final issue is not so much one of new theoretical directions for analyses of integration, but, instead, a look back. Simply put, is my call for bringing constructivist insights to bear on the study of the EU a short-sighted reinventing of the neofunctionalist wheel? After all, over thirty years ago, Haas and others were writing about the identity-shaping effects of the European project. Indeed, collective identity was to emerge via a 'process whereby political actors in several distinct national settings are persuaded to shift their loyalties, expectations and political activities towards a new centre, whose institutions possess or demand jurisdiction over the pre-existing nation-states' (Haas, 1958: 16).

While references to social learning and socialisation are evident in the work of many early neofunctionalists and regional integration theorists, the differences with constructivism are significant. Most important, the latter is not a general substantive theory that predicts constant learning or a growing sense of collective identity; rather, its aspirations are more modest. As it is currently developing, it is a middle-range theoretical approach seeking to elaborate scope conditions for better understanding precisely when collective identity formation occurs. Constructivism is thus agnostic as to whether the endpoint of social interaction is greater common interests and identity. Neofunctionalists, at least implicity, were not neutral on this question; there was a clear normative element to their scholarship (Caporaso, 1998: 6–7).

In addition, despite the strong allusions to identity formation and change, neofunctionalists failed to develop explicit microfoundations that moved them beyond an agent-centred view of social interaction. In fact, there is a strong element of rational choice in their research (Burley and Mattli, 1993: 54–5; and, more generally, Pollack, 1998: *passim*). While considerable work remains, constructivists are attempting to elaborate such alternative foundations – their stress on social learning and communicative action, for example.

Conclusions

Two points can be made, the first of which is that a central challenge for both rationalists and constructivists is to develop scope and boundary conditions for explaining when social interaction is best captured by their preferred model of it. Nothing in this chapter should be read as dismissing rationalist work on integration, or proclaiming the superiority of constructivist methods. Rather, I have suggested a number of different scope conditions that should help us think more systematically about the role of both rationalism and constructivism in explaining the European project. This stress on dialogue intersects with a growing trend in IR theory, where there is a pronounced move away from an 'either/or' orientation (either rational choice or constructivism) to a 'both/and' perspective. This shift is seen in forums as diverse as the flagship journal of German IR, regime analysis, the 50th anniversary issue of *International Organization* and the work of prominent rationalists (Risse, 1998; Underdal, 1998; the essays by Katzenstein/Keohane/Krasner, Finnemore/Sikkink, Kahler and March/Olsen, all in *International Organization* 52 [Autumn 1998]; and Laitin, 1998, respectively; also see the concluding section of Bernard Steunenberg's commentary on this chapter).

Second, my arguments throughout this chapter were based on an obvious but too often neglected truism about our social world: the most interesting puzzles lie at the nexus where structure and agency intersect. The real action, theoretically and empirically, is where norms, discourses, language and material capabilities interact with motivation, social learning and preferences – be it in international or European regional politics. Research traditions such as rational choice, postmodernism and, more recently, parts of constructivism, which occupy endpoints in the agent-structure debate, have life easy, for they can ignore this messy middle ground. Yet, the true challenge for both rationalists and their opponents is to model and explore this complex interface (Hix, 1998: 55–6; Checkel, 1997b); the foregoing has suggested several ways in which this could be done.

Notes

1   An earlier version of this chapter appeared as 'Social Construction and Integration,' *Journal of European Public Policy*, Vol. 6, No. 4 (September 1999).
2   Consistent with my near/long-term distinction, the analysis in Immergut and Pierson is contemporary, while that in Hattam and Goldstein spans decades.
3   I am indebted to Gary Marks and Liesbet Hooghe for discussion on these points.
4   Thanks to Gerald Schneider and Bernard Steunenberg for discussions on the points raised here and in the following paragraphs.
5   My Strasbourg/CE field work was conducted in four rounds: May 1994, June–July 1995, April 1997 and November 1998.
6   This individual was the German representative, whom I interviewed on two separate occasions.

Bernard Steunenberg[1]

Comment: 'Constructing European institutions'

Two friends are walking in the mountains. When they leave the woods and stop to admire the view, they notice someone coming down a hill. 'Wow, that guy is really running fast down the hill', says one. 'No', replies the other, 'he's falling'. This disagreement between the two friends illustrates the basic differences between the two approaches that are central to Jeffrey Checkel's chapter on 'Constructing European institutions'. The first approach is *institutional rational choice*, which takes the individual as the starting point and argues that behaviour is based on individual intentions. Institutions are regarded as human-made constructs that constrain behaviour. The runner in the example may have miscalculated the steepness of the hill, or the difficulty of the track, leading to a higher speed than he had expected. Nevertheless, his running has to be regarded as an *intentional* act. The other approach is *sociological institutionalism*, or social constructivism, which presumes that structure shapes behaviour. In terms of the example, the hill pushes the runner down the slope. Running is now regarded as a *consequence* of being on the hill.

Each approach – rational choice and sociological institutionalism – adopts a different perspective concerning the way in which institutions, conceived as sets of rules, may affect human behaviour. The rational choice approach presumes that institutions are external to the individual and constrain his or her behaviour. Individuals only have preferences, which are mostly regarded as given or exogenous to the analysis. The sociological approach suggests that institutions, which are often conceived as norms, are internalised by the individual and therefore shape his or her view of the world. Institutions therefore constitute actors and their interests and thus are made endogenous to the analysis. Checkel's main argument is that the sociological approach has been mistakenly neglected in the literature on European integration, although it can 'explain key aspects of the European project – social learning and normative diffusion – better than its rationalist competitors.'

My comment will focus on the question of whether this claim is justified in Checkel's chapter. I first focus on the current research in rational choice on European institutions. I then discuss the approach advocated by Jeffrey Checkel. Finally, I conclude by pointing to a basic challenge to both approaches.

Rational choice: the circle of preferences

The extensive rational choice literature on political and social institutions can be broadly divided into two kinds of analyses. On the one hand, there are studies that focus on the selection of a policy within the context of a given set of institutions. Institutions are then conceived as sets of rules, which constrain the behaviour of actors. This kind of analysis can be labelled *policy analysis*, since its main purpose is to analyse the choice of policy as a result of the complex interaction of different actors in some institutional setting. When Checkel typifies rational choice institutionalism as 'thin', since 'at most' institutions constrain behaviour, he refers only to this type of analysis. Another type of rational choice analysis, which also focuses on institutions, is absent in his account.

The second type of rational choice analysis concentrates on the choice of institutional arrangements or institutional change. Institutions are then no longer exogenous to the analysis: they are part of the choice problem that is faced by a group of actors. These actors have to decide whether they are willing and able to introduce new institutions to replace the current ones. This is what I call *constitutional analysis*, which differs from policy analysis. Nevertheless, with the broad category of constitutional analysis, different kinds of analyses exist, which vary to the extent that they claim some 'other' institutions as given in the analysis. On the one hand, there exists very abstract and theoretical work, which focuses on the basic institutions of political systems (see, for instance, Rawls, 1971). On the other hand – and this fits better with reform debates in the EU – there are partial analyses in which the choice of some institutional arrangements are analysed within the context of some 'other' institutions. While constitutional analysis concerns the *choice of institutions*, policy analysis focuses on the *consequences of institutions*.

Clearly, preferences are the key notion in both types of rational choice analysis. In a policy analysis, individual preferences determine the choice of strategies, which are constrained by institutions, leading to a decision or outcome. In a constitutional analysis, preferences are central to the choice of institutions, which structure future decision-making processes. Thus, in rational choice, preferences play a role in the choice of institutions and, at the same time, are constrained by these very institutions. This relationship between preferences and institutions, which I call 'the circle of preferences', has been noted by Riker (1980), who regards institutions as 'congealed' preferences. The existence of transaction costs, or a higher level of inertia because of decision-making arrangements at the constitutional level, may temporarily induce institutional stability, which allows one to consider institutions as given in policy analysis.

Both types of analysis inform research on the EU. Policy analysis is perhaps the most popular type, typically analysing the possible outcomes of the European decision-making process. Common European legislative procedures, such as the co-operation and the co-decision procedures, have been studied by several scholars (for example, Crombez, 1996, 1997a; Garrett, 1995; Garrett and Tsebelis, 1996; Moser, 1997a; Schneider, 1995b; Steunenberg, 1994, 1997; Tsebelis, 1994; Tsebelis and Garrett, 1997). The different models of these procedures have led to several academic disputes concerning such questions as whether the role of the Commission has been correctly taken into account,[2] or how the co-decision procedure may best be represented.[3] Other studies focus on the way in which the European Commission has discretion in implementing European law. Steunenberg, Koboldt and Schmidtchen (1996, 1997) have modelled the comitology procedures in the EU and show how the Commission is constrained by various procedural requirements in setting measures.

A growing number of studies employs the constitutional perspective in rational choice. Examples include analyses of the political structure of the EU (Mueller, 1997a), the search for alternative institutional arrangements for governing Europe based on the notion of functional overlapping and competing jurisdictions (Frey and Eichenberger, 1997) and the contents of the principle of subsidiarity (Vanberg, 1997). Recently, much attention has been given to *a priori* assessments of voting power under the current and possible future structures of the EU. Based on insights from co-operative game theory, König and Bräuninger (1998b) and Berg and Lane (1999), analyse the extent to which voting rules allow for policy change. Their key insight is that the more a procedure allows for policy change, the greater is the potential that political actors are able to reach some desirable outcome. As a result, actors are expected to select new decision-making procedures that allow for more change.

Institutional rational choice thus takes different views on social and political institutions. Institutions can serve as constraints to behaviour in a policy analysis; however, they are the objects of analysis in a constitutional analysis.

Sociological institutionalism: the circle of structure

Like institutional rational choice, sociological institutionalism also focuses on human interaction. Checkel advocates a constructivist approach that reintroduces the 'agent' or actor. This may make the two approaches more similar. What is less clear is the role of institutions in

Checkel's analysis. The basic idea is that institutions shape the views of actors. Institutions, as Checkel states, provide actors with 'new understandings of interests regarding a particular policy issue.' Nevertheless, the approach needs to avoid actors becoming 'the slaves of structure', i.e., the theoretical position that human behaviour only follows structure. Institutions are, of course, social constructs, which are human made. So the problem arises of how the very same actors, who understand the world through institutions, are able to change these institutions.

The constructivist 'answer' to this problem is a dual relationship between institutions and behaviour. On the one hand, institutions shape interests. On the other hand, interests also shape institutions and therefore allow for change. This relationship, which characterises institutions as independent as well as dependent factors in the analysis, can be called 'the circle of structure'. Like rational choice, where preferences shape and are constrained by institutions, social constructivism presumes that institutions shape and are affected by behaviour. The question is then whether social constructivism is able to disentangle both processes.

Unfortunately, Checkel does not provide a clear answer to this question. In his discussion of social learning, Checkel points to a number of research hypotheses, in which the occurrence of learning is, among other things, related to the extent to which a group 'feels itself in a crisis' or when they are 'in a novel and uncertain environment'. As Checkel already admits, these hypotheses are far from clearly formulated, since it will be difficult to specify *a priori* the conditions of a crisis situation or a novel and uncertain environment. A similar problem occurs in his discussion of norm development or the change of social structures. Here, Checkel points to moral entrepreneurs, that is, well-placed individuals who are able to 'turn their individual beliefs into broader, shared understandings', in order to allow for change. Again, this solution is troublesome, since *a priori* it is not clear who will be able to have this impact on norms. In addition, the success of moral entrepreneurs is made conditional on the existence of 'policy windows.' A 'policy window' can be regarded as an opportunity that arises; one that is by its very nature coincidental and unanticipated. This implies that 'policy windows' can only be identified retrospectively. Thus, only when some 'puzzling problem' has been used by 'moral entrepreneurs' to introduce new norms can a 'policy window' be said to exist. This conceptual framework is highly problematic as a basis for a *predictive* theory about social or political interaction. It does not identify the conditions under which agents can be influential as initiators of institutional change.

More generally, social constructivism is in need of a well-developed theory of human behaviour and social interaction. Checkel seems to agree with this position when he concludes that '[c]learly, much theoretical work remains to be done – in particular, elaborating scope conditions for when norms have constraining as opposed to constitutive effects'. The 'circle of structure' is a muddling process in which causality flows in both directions. I am therefore very sympathetic to Checkel's plea for further theory development. Nevertheless, social constructivism can perhaps be characterised as still being 'under construction'. It does not yet present a satisfactory explanatory framework for European integration issues.

The challenge to both approaches: towards a new behavioural model

At the same time, my criticism of social constructivism may obscure the basic problems of both approaches. Both approaches share the goal of analysing and explaining human interaction, whether this is part of decision-making within political or social groups. The main problem of the constructivist agenda is the absence of a clear theoretical framework that concentrates on social learning. The main challenge of the rational choice agenda is the limits of the traditional model of economic man. In this model, learning does not play a role since individuals are assumed to have perfect foresight. More recent modifications of this model introduce uncertainty by assuming that the consequences of individual behaviour follow some probability distribution. However, the classical information requirements of the traditional model are now pushed one step back to the level of these distributions, which are assumed to be given. But how do we know our behavioural alternatives, their consequences or the likelihood that these consequences will indeed occur in the future? In other words, if uncertainty about future events and contingencies is indeed taken seriously, the social sciences, including the institutional approaches discussed in this comment, are in need of a new behavioural model. According to Elinor Ostrom, such a model may view 'all humans as complex, fallible learners who seek to do as well as they can given constraints that they face and who are able to learn heuristics, norms, rules, and how to craft rules to improve achieved outcomes' (1998: 9). Both approaches may share the goal of developing a new and explicit model that takes these elements into account. This model may form the basis of the analysis of social and political interaction. The main challenge to sociological institutionalism and institutional rational choice is to develop such a model.[4] However, this does not imply that both approaches need to work in close co-operation. Competition and rivalry between the different 'schools of thought', which may lead to alternative formations and substantial criticism of each others attempts, can be very beneficial to this enterprise.

Notes

1   I wish to thank Karen Anderson and Willem Trommel for helpful suggestions and comments.

2   See the dispute between Tsebelis and Moser on the role of the Commission in the co-operation procedure. According to the Treaty, the Commission has the right of initiative and therefore drafts the initial proposal. Parliament, which only has conditional veto rights (i.e., it can only veto the proposal under the condition that the Council is not unanimously in favour of the proposal), seems to have a rather limited impact. Tsebelis (1994), however, presents a rather different model in which the interactions are reduced to a game between the Council and Parliament only. Based on this model, he claims that the European Parliament has much more power, which claim was questioned by Moser (1996).

3   See the dispute between Garrett and Tsebelis on the one hand, and Scully on the other, on the modeling of the co-decision procedure. Garrett and Tsebelis reduce the procedure to a game in which the Council can make a take-it-or-leave-it offer to Parliament (Garrett, 1995; Garrett and Tsebelis, 1996; Tsebelis and Garrett, 1997). This model is based on the third reading stage of the co-decision procedure. Scully (1997a; 1997b) argues that this model presents an incomplete account of the strategic interactions, since, according to the available data, the Council and Parliament mostly reach agreement at an earlier stage. See also Crombez (Chapter 5, this book).

4   Heiner (1983) has proposed an interesting new model of behaviour. This model, which differs substantially from the traditional economic model of optimising behaviour, allows for adaptive, rule-following behaviour.

Thomas Bräuninger, Tanja Cornelius, Thomas König and
Thomas Schuster

3

The dynamics of European integration: a constitutional analysis of the Amsterdam Treaty

Research question: how to explain the choice of European voting rules?

For more than forty years, the dynamics of European integration have promoted a voluntary and peaceful co-operation throughout Western Europe. The integration process, characterised by a stepwise but continuous Treaty reform, has considerably widened the former European Communities' scale of jurisdiction by transferring competencies for many policy areas from the national to the European level (König, 1996: 553). Today's EU has also increased its scope by enlarging its membership from six to fifteen countries with a population of more than 320 million people. In terms of scale and scope, the dynamic feature of European integration, compared to other transnational processes, is its continuous intergovernmental rule-making (Moravcsik 1993: 473). Initiated and adopted by a growing number of member-state governments, intergovernmental conferences have established and strengthened a set of organs and complex voting rules for binding European legislation (Bednar et al., 1996; Pollack, 1997). After the Single European Act (SEA) in 1987 and the prominent reform by the Maastricht Treaty on European Union in 1993, the 1997 Amsterdam Intergovernmental Conference again modified the EU's rules.

Important changes in the EU's institutional framework are necessary for guaranteeing proper functioning of European legislation, particularly in the case of further enlargement. The reform of the rules is especially concerned with two topics, the extension of majority voting and the degree of parliamentary participation. The EU's growing membership, and particularly the forthcoming accession of rather dissimilar Eastern and Southern European countries, requires relaxing the unanimity voting quota in the Council of Ministers in order to decrease the danger of gridlock in European legislation (König and Bräuninger, 1998a). While the European Parliament (EP) already participates in the co-operation and assent procedure (1987) and the co-decision procedure (1993), these procedures are modestly applied to European legislation: only about fifteen per cent of all articles and about ten per cent of all binding proposals are presently provided for EP participation. Regarding proper functioning of the EU the crucial question is to what extent the Amsterdam Treaty reforms the rules of Council majority voting and parliamentary participation in European legislation.

To predict the outcome of Treaty reforms, previous studies have successfully applied an actor-orientated view stressing the role of member-state governments for institution-building and transformation. According to Milner (1997: 203) the governmental preferences on the Maastricht Treaty were completely determined by the Economic and Monetary Union (EMU) dimension, while Garrett (1992) emphasises an economic and institutional dimension of the main governments on the Maastricht draft Treaty. Moravcsik (1991: 27) proposes an intergovernmental approach, suggesting investigation of the preferences of Germany, France and Britain in order to explain the Maastricht Treaty. In his recent publication (1998), he extends this perspective to previous events, such as the Rome Treaties (1958) and the SEA (1987). He claims that 'from the signing of Rome to the making of Maastricht, the EC (EU) has developed through a series of celebrated intergovernmental bargains, each of which sets the agenda for an intervening period of consolidation' (Moravcsik 1993: 473). Garrett and Tsebelis support his findings but add that 'if Moravcsik is correct and if the signatories of treaties are strategically rational, one must explain why the signatories of a Treaty selected one set of institutional arrangements over another' (1996: 270). According to them, one must analyse the policy consequences of different constitutional choices of rule-making.

We follow this idea of a policy-seeking constitutional choice of rule-making by considering the Amsterdam delegations' policy preferences and deriving their expected utilities from alternative voting rules – Council unanimity or qualified majority as well as the participation of the EP in the (new) co-decision procedure. We consider the long-term implications of voting rules when transforming the delegation's policy preferences to preferences regarding the Council's voting quota and the participation of the EP. To specify actors' expected utilities from future decision-making we refer to the amount and the relative distribution of coalition gains under standard and modified co-decision procedure. Our concern is to test empirically whether the rule-making reforms of the Amsterdam Treaty improve all member states and, if so, how this criterion is fulfilled. Does rule-making require individual benefits on each issue or is, allowing for commitments, an overall improvement for all member states sufficient to change the Union's rules? We accordingly check whether more status quo-orientated member states could successfully threaten more integrationist governments by their veto power (Schneider and Cederman, 1994).

The remainder of the chapter first provides an introduction to our policy-seeking concept of constitutional choice. We use tools of co-operative game theory for measuring constitutional preferences and raise hypotheses that specify the parameters of constitutional choice. In order to present our data, we then introduce the debate on the 1997 Amsterdam Intergovernmental Conference, describing the main issues and actors involved. Finally, we apply our policy-seeking concept to the analysis of the Amsterdam Treaty, concentrating on the reasons for the choice of the Council's voting quota and parliamentary participation.

Model and hypotheses: the analysis of constitutional choice on rules

Studies of the introduction and change of political institutions rely either on evolutionary concepts of spontaneous emergence and social selection at the system level, or the intentional design of purposeful acting entities (Knight and Sened, 1996: 3). The historical institutionalist analysis of European integration, however, mixes both concepts when stressing that 'actors may be in a strong initial position, seek to maximise their interests, and nevertheless carry out institutional and policy reform . . . in ways that are unanticipated and/or undesired' (Pierson, 1996: 126). In our view, the second sentence is not a derivation from a precise set of assumptions but rather an imprecise statement of the assumptions. But if the historical meaning were that (unanticipated and/or undesired) outcomes are shaped – perhaps but not necessarily – by previous events, then a nontrivial theory might be articulated to explain how actors' behaviour – or a system's development – is influenced by which previous events. In this chapter, we follow the idea of institutional rule-making by individualistic intentional design, but we scrutinise the historical perspective when testing which member states best explain the puzzle of the Amsterdam Treaty reform.

Since Buchanan and Tullock (1962: 96), individualistic theory of the constitution assumes consensus as a norm. For the analysis of constitutional choice from an actor-orientated view, it is therefore useful to start with a conceptual distinction between two types of rules: voting rules as institutional settings for deciding on policies and higher-order rules for constitutional matters – including decisions on voting rules. Voting rules are fixed parameters of policy-making, but their introduction and change depends on higher-order rules, as any institutional framework is nested in higher frameworks that define how the institutional setting can be changed (Ostrom, 1990: 52; Tsebelis, 1990: 113). Accordingly, we distinguish between the choice within and the choice on rules, the latter being higher-order decisions on the institutional constraints for future decision-making. These constitutional choices are characterised by actors' uncertainty of future outcomes, generating the question of how to study actors' constitutional preferences for different rules. To examine constitutional preferences, we start from the assumption that rules are not valued on their own merits, but states favour rules that are likely to provide the policies they prefer (Mueller, 1996: 62). Of course, states may prefer different rules and they may even favour rules for other than policy reasons when relying on consistency with their own idea of (democratic) government, particularly in the case of EP participation. We therefore separate the two objects of choice, the Council voting quota and parliamentary participation, and develop a policy-seeking view of actors' constitutional preferences, assuming that the distribution of (non-)integrationist policy positions independently determines actors' rule-making preference on the Council's voting quota and EP participation for any issue. Compared to extreme versions of constitutional analysis assuming a veil of uncertainty in terms of an ignorance of actors' own and others' policy positions, we base this assumption on the rather detailed application of procedural settings to European policy areas, indicating that member states primarily expect rather issue-specific gains from future legislation. This allows us to distinguish between policy and constitutional preferences, the latter to be derived from the former under the uncertain policy impact of different voting rules on future legislation.

The uncertain policy impact raises the major problem in deriving actors' constitutional preferences. Their constitutional choice precedes policy choice, and constitutional actors are often considered to know *ex ante* neither their (one- or multidimensional) policy preferences nor the preferences of the other actors involved in future decision-making processes (Steunenberg, 1998: 3). In analysing the introduction or change of voting rules, however, we do not stress actors' uncertainty of their and others' policy preferences but their uncertainty of policy outcomes that can be obtained under different voting rules. Hereby, we specify actors' constitutional preferences by their expected utilities from future decision-making which are determined by the amount and the relative distribution of coalition gains.

Applying our expected utility concept to derive the Amsterdam delegates' constitutional preferences, we are able to assess the EU's higher-order rules for constitutional decisions on voting rules. Formally, the EU's higher-order rules for introducing and modifying voting rules are repeated in Article 14,1 of the Amsterdam Treaty: the 'Treaty shall be ratified by the High Contracting Parties'. This is based on the legal principle of state sovereignty implying that unanimity is the formal default rule for constitutional decisions of member states as 'masters' of the treaties (Everling, 1997: 290). Consequently, all member states must formally agree on any transfer of their national powers to the EU, including the right to decide on their own, which is limited to their 'voting power' under different rules in the case of a European competence. Such agreement on a Treaty by rational, self-interested member states can only come about by beneficial expectations from rule enforcement, while consent should not be feasible if one or more expect to be worse off (Mueller, 1997b: 126). If consent is impossible, the former voting rules are assumed to remain, or, if there are no voting rules, another status quo will prevail including member states' right to act on their own. Applied to the topics of the Amsterdam Treaty, the first hypothesis is:

Hypothesis H1   The change in the status quo rule of Council unanimity or parliamentary exclusion by the Treaty can only come about if all member states expect to be better off.

In the words of contracting theory, the Amsterdam agreement requires Pareto-superiority of the Treaty as a whole. Some member states may expect to be worse off on some issues but make commitments to be compensated with expected gains from voting rules for other issues. However, it is not easy to make credible commitments on political markets, particularly in the case of rule-making implying a high degree of uncertainty for future decision-making: actors must share their expectations about future decision-making and find a clearing system to compensate for expected losses. By contrast, a more restrictive criterion would be that member states exclude expected losses on any issue, resulting in the maintenance of the corresponding status quo rule. In order to examine both criteria, we formulate two further hypotheses. Our second hypothesis concerns the number of member states which are required to introduce or change the Council's voting rule and parliamentary integration for each issue:

Hypothesis H2   The more member states prefer Council majority voting or parliamentary participation for a specific issue, the more likely the status quo rule of Council unanimity or parliamentary exclusion is to change.

If fifteen member states are indeed the best predictor for the issue by issue adoption of Council majority voting and parliamentary participation, the commitment assumption has to be rejected. Otherwise, a majority threshold would indicate to which extent the EU's constitutional level allows for compensation – provided that the Treaty as a package promises benefits as a whole.

In addition to overall benefits, previous studies have argued that some member states are more important than others in the EU's constitutional decision-making (Cameron, 1992; Dinan, 1994; Pollack, 1997; Schneider, 1994b). Garrett (1992: 546) states that on the negotiations of the SEA in 1986 neither a southern coalition plus Ireland that preferred resorting to simple majority rule in the Council of Ministers, nor the United Kingdom and Denmark which favoured continuing with unanimity rule, could prevail against the French-German preference on qualified majority voting. According to Moravcsik (1991, 1993, 1998), European constitutional politics reflect the positions of the three most powerful member states: France, Germany and the United Kingdom. Including Italy, the four largest states with ten votes in the Council of Ministers finance more than three-quarters of all net contributions. Member states that contribute to transfer payments within the EU, and large contributors in particular, may thus have a stronger bargaining position with regard to their smaller and poorer partner states. As a result, both the relative and absolute economic power of member states may enhance their bargaining position.

Diverging interests of southern and northern member states are another observation in the course of Treaty reforms (Lane and Maeland, 1995; Widgrén, 1995; Closa, 1995; Wallace, 1992). Hosli (1996) refers to a differentiation regarding external trade policy between the northern 'free traders' and an opposed southern group, whereas Ireland and Greece were in a intermediate position. She argues that the latest accession of Austria, Finland and Sweden shifted the equilibrium both between larger and smaller member states and between northern and southern member states as the new members are all relatively small and belong to the group of richer countries. A further differentiation concerns membership duration, which may lead to a distinction between original and new member states, where the former not only have divergent attitudes towards the process of integration but can also refer to their seniority in order to steer the political debate (König and Schulz, 1997: 9). According to these findings, the third basic hypothesis on the different importance of member states for constitutional decisions is:

Hypothesis H3 The more the 'important' member states prefer Council majority voting or parliamentary participation, the more likely the status quo rule of Council unanimity or parliamentary exclusion is to change.

In sum, we take actors' constitutional preferences to be a key variable, but also consider that the Amsterdam Treaty may reflect the constitutional preferences of some member states more than others. Before testing our hypotheses, we will introduce our data on the Amsterdam Treaty and the technique for deriving constitutional preferences from actors' policy positions.

Data and measurement: the Amsterdam Treaty

European integration has advanced considerably since its re-launch in the mid-1980s: most of the measures which were deemed necessary to complete the Single European Market have not only been adopted but also extended in both scale and scope, as seen for example in structural and monetary politics, which had often been considered fundamental to the continuous existence of the nation-state. And even more remarkable, there have been crucial institutional changes stemming from the introduction of the SEA in 1987 and the Maastricht Treaty on European Union in 1993, which have modified the decision-making system of the EU. The most notable of these changes have been the more frequent provision for qualified majority voting in the Council of Ministers and the increased legislative powers of the EP (Nugent, 1996: 1). Only five years after the latest integrative step in Maastricht, the Amsterdam Treaty again revises the EU's framework. To understand the reasons for the new revision, we briefly introduce the 'history' of the Amsterdam Intergovernmental Conference.

The Maastricht Treaty on European Union already provided for an intergovernmental conference (IGC) to be convened in 1997. The official reason for establishing an IGC was to review the provisions introduced in 1993. Unofficially, the review gave assurance to both European integrationists and non-integrationists, who believed that either insufficient or too much integration had been made at Maastricht. Compared to previous IGCs, the European Council decided at its June 1994 Corfu meeting to establish a preparatory Reflection Group, consisting of sixteen delegates of the member states, two representatives of the EP and one of the Commission. Before the group published its report in December 1995, the non-intergovernmental organs – the Commission, the EP and the European Court of Justice (ECJ), which had been invited by the Corfu summit – produced their own reports. Unsurprisingly, the ECJ moderately expressed some concern about legal problems arising from different jurisdictions under the three pillars, and the Commission largely confined itself to analysis supporting the simplification of decision-making. In contrast, the EP's report strongly recommended reducing the number of legislative procedures and the extension of qualified majority voting in the Council of Ministers and its parliamentary rights.

Regarding the problems of the Amsterdam IGC, the dissenting votes listed in the Reflection Group's report already indicated the difficulties in formulating a common draft text. The group still identified the main issue of the IGC as making Europe more relevant to citizens – even in external matters – by increasing the EU's competencies, improving the functioning of the EU by extending Council qualified majority voting and parliamentary participation (Nugent, 1996: 9). However, there was consensus on neither the EP's proposal to reduce the number of procedures nor on the extension of qualified majority voting in the Council of Ministers.

After marathon negotiations the European Council succeeded in reaching agreement in many areas at the Amsterdam Intergovernmental Conference. In addition to the draft Treaty of Amsterdam, the delegates decided on the completion of Economic and Monetary Union (EMU) and the proceedings for further enlargement. They agreed on the regulations making up the Stability and Growth Pact and confirmed the start of Monetary Union in January 1999. They also opened the way for launching the enlargement process by instructing the Commission to present its opinion on ten candidates. The fifteen member-state delegates of the European Council, as well as the Commission and EP representatives, expressed their policy positions concerning 236 issues.[1] The order of the issues follows the order of subjects set out in the conclusions of the Presidency of the Turin European Council of 29 March 1996, supplemented by a number of other areas referred to in the resolutions of the EP. The issues are divided into nineteen chapters including Citizen Rights, Third Pillar Policies, Common Foreign and Security Policy (CFSP), matters on Subsidiarity and Organs, etc.. For analytical purposes, we categorise the set of issues into three types: 116 provisions for the functioning of institutions, 50 issues on procedural settings and 70 regulations of issues. The first category contains rather general institutional provisions, such as the introduction of new instruments or committees. The second category encompasses general procedural provisions, such as the extension of the Commission's agenda-setting power or a strengthening of parliamentary rights. Together, these 166 issues of both categories deal with institutional settings that may influence the general expectations regarding further integration, but they do not directly affect the distribution of policies. For this reason, the following analysis focuses on those 35 of the 70 issues which have been included in the draft Treaty and integrated in the Treaty of Amsterdam.

The left-hand columns of Table 3.1 summarise our data on actors' policy positions. The first column lists the numbering, the second column the policy domain of the thirty-five issues. Columns three to five show the policy positions[2] of the actors involved – the fifteen member-state governments, the Commission (C) and the EP. It also indicates the location of the legal status quo (+). Over all issues, we find a rather polarised distribution of policy positions, with actors either opposed to (0) or in favour of (1) these policies; but only a few positions are in between. For most issues, about two-thirds of member states support a modification of the status quo, while they are reserved in the area of citizens' rights and even more reserved regarding the introduction of new policies. In almost all cases, the EP has a pro-integrative policy position and the status quo is located at the non-integrative position. However, there is no clear pro- or anti-integrative tendency in the distribution of member-state policy positions.

These policy positions are the basic element for the analysis of the constitutional preferences that we assume to affect the expected outcome of the thirty-five issues when allowing unanimous or majority voting in the Council of Ministers and for parliamentary participation or abstinence. How actors' policy positions are transformed into constitutional preferences and whether their choice of voting rules is determined by

Table 3.1 Policy and rule preferences of Amsterdam delegations regarding 35 policies

No	Issue	Policy preferences			Constitutional preferences			
		0 (No integration)	0.5	1.0 (Pro integration)	Unanimity	QM voting	No participation	EP participation
1	Citizenship	2+	1	12,C,EP	2	13,C,EP*	2*	13,C,EP
2	Citizenship	1+		14,C,EP	1	14,C,EP*	1	14,C,EP*
3	Citizenship	4+		11,C,EP	4	11,C,EP*	4*	11,C,EP
4	Citizenship	8,C+		7,EP	8,C+	7,EP	8,C	7,EP*
5	Citizenship	15,C,EP+			15,C,EP*		15,C,EP*	
6	Citizenship	7,C*		8,EP	7,C*	8,EP	7,C*	8,EP
7	Citizenship	4*		11,C,EP	4*	11,C,EP*	4	11,C,EP*
8	Citizenship	8,C+		7,EP	8,C*	7,EP	8,C	7,EP*
9	Interior/judicial co-operation	+		15,C,EP		15,C,EP*		15,C,EP*
10	Interior/judicial co-operation	3+	2	10,C,EP	3	12,C,EP*	3	12,C,EP*
11	Interior/judicial co-operation	+	2	13,C,EP		15,C,EP*		15,C,EP*
12	Interior/judicial co-operation	+	3	12,C,EP		15,C,EP*		15,C,EP*
13	Interior/judicial co-operation	+		12,C,EP		15,C,EP*		15,C,EP*
14	Interior/judicial co-operation	1+	2	12,C,EP	1	14,C,EP*	1	14,C,EP*
15	Interior/judicial co-operation	3+	5	7,C,EP	3	12,C,EP*	3	12,C,EP*
16	Interior/judicial co-operation	10+	2	3,C,EP	10*	5,C,EP	10*	5,C,EP
17	Employment	2+		13,EP,C	2	13,C,EP*	2	13,C,EP*
18	Employment	+		15,C,EP		15,C,EP*	*	15,C,EP
19	Employment	+		15,C,EP		15,C,EP*		15,C,EP*
20	Employment	3+		12,C,EP	3	12,C,EP*	3	12,C,EP*
21	Employment	2+		13,C,EP	2	13,C,EP*	2	13,C,EP*
22	Employment	4+		11,C,EP	4	11,C,EP*	4	11,C,EP*
23	Employment	10+		5,C,EP	10	5,C,EP*	10	5,C,EP*
24	General provisions	4,EP		11,C*	11,C*	4,EP	11,C*	4,EP
25	Environment	1+		14,C,EP	1	14,C,EP*	1	14,C,EP*
26	Environment	+		15,C,EP		15,C,EP*		15,C,EP*
27	Environment	1+		14,C,EP	1	14,C,EP*	1*	14,C,EP
28	Environment	3+	1	11,C,EP	3	12,C,EP*	3	12,C,EP*
29	Transparency	2+		13,C,EP	2	13,C,EP*	2	13,C,EP*
30	Crime	10+		5,C,EP	10	5,C,EP*	10	5,C,EP*
31	New policies	7,C+		8,EP	7,C	8,EP*	7,C	8,EP*
32	New policies	8,C+		7,EP	8,C*	7,EP	8,C*	7,EP
33	Foreign/Security	4+	3	8,C,EP	4*	11,C,EP	4*	11,C,EP
34	Foreign/Security	15,C,EP+			15,C,EP*		15,C,EP*	
35	Foreign/Security	1+	1	13,C,EP	1*	14,C,EP	1*	14,C,EP

Abbreviations: 1–15 Number of member states with corresponding policy preference; C Commission; EP European Parliament; + Status quo; * adopted by the Amsterdam Treaty.

Source: European Parliament (1997). Summary of the positions of the member states and the European Parliament on the 1996 Intergovernmental Conference, JF/bo/290/97, Luxembourg, 12 May.

intergovernmental consensus, or by the authority or veto power of some member states, will be examined empirically. Before that, we present our approach to constitutional preference formation and how to construct the matrix of constitutional choice, which is the starting point of our empirical analysis of the Amsterdam reform of the EU's institutional framework.

Approach: the formation of constitutional preferences

When modelling the transition from policy positions to constitutional preferences, we use a co-operative game-theoretical approach assuming the existence of external and internal mechanisms that make policy outcomes binding and enforceable. This is not an outlandish assumption, given the binding character of European legislation and the instruments of the ECJ to make outcomes enforceable. We also assume that, when bargaining at IGCs, constitutional actors know their own and other actors' current policy positions and the current location of the status quo, which serve them as 'best estimates' for their future policy positions and the future status quo. However, actors are uncertain about future coalition formation and the policy outcomes that future coalitions will produce. While they have complete information about the procedural settings, the future number of decision-making actors and the policies preferred by this actor set, we assume that they do not know exactly which outcome will finally be realised, but that they do have expectations about possible outcomes and benefits of future European legislation.

Under these assumptions, the formation of constitutional preferences can be explained by expected benefits from future policies regulated by specific voting rules. In accordance with constitutional analysis, we first suppose that constitutional actors lack knowledge about which coalition will finally be formed in the future (Buchanan and Tullock, 1962: 78). Therefore, they consider all feasible coalitions but, in contrast to constitutional analysis, we secondly assume that coalitions are not equally probable – as actors with similar policy positions are more likely to collaborate than actors with dissimilar policy positions. Hence, when deriving their expected utilities from future decision-making, they consider homogeneous coalitions (with actors having similar policy preferences) more likely to form than heterogeneous coalitions (with actors having dissimilar policy preferences). (See appendix to this chapter, equations 2–4.) To measure the impact of voting rules on coalition formation, we take account of two rule-making properties, inclusiveness and conditional decisiveness. The former measures the actor's chances of being included in future winning coalitions, the latter the probability of deciding the outcome – which is conditioned, as it depends on whether the actor is included in the winning coalition or not.

In general, the high status quo bias of the unanimity rule results from all actors' interest in high inclusiveness, while majority rules decrease the status quo likelihood by offering the exclusion of some actors. Hence, when constitutional actors decide on the voting quota, they trade their individual risk of being excluded against their collective capacity to act in the future. Their collective capacity to act can be measured as the ratio between the number of winning coalitions (able to alter the status quo) and all feasible coalitions (Coleman, 1971: 278) – where coalitions are weighted to their likelihood of occurrence. At the individual level, inclusiveness is expressed by the (weighted) number of times an actor participates in winning coalitions in relation to the (weighted) number of all feasible winning coalitions (see appendix, equation 5). Unanimity thus guarantees every actor a veto-player position with the maximal inclusiveness of 1.0 as no actor can be excluded from the single favourable winning coalition. Conversely, if an actor can be excluded from building any feasible winning coalition, the inclusion of its policy position is determined only by luck (Barry, 1989: 287). Thus, if all coalitions have the same likelihood, an actor's inclusiveness index ranges between 0.5 and 1.0.

Compared to the inclusiveness trade-off, decisiveness has already been studied in many relative voting power analyses (Brams and Affuso, 1985; Hosli, 1996; Lane et al., 1995). In order to measure an actor's relative decisiveness, almost all voting power indices calculate the actor's relative ability to be decisive in transforming a losing into a winning coalition. When measuring the distribution of relative decisiveness with respect to a *single* winning coalition, these values can be interpreted as actors' probabilities of determining the policy outcome. We calculate Shapley–Shubik indices (Shapley and Shubik, 1954) but with respect to *each* winning coalition because different winning coalitions may have different sets of decisive members with different policy positions (see appendix, equation 6). These values indicate the probability with which an actor is able to determine the policy outcome according to his policy position under a specific voting rule. Excluding strategic behaviour, each actor may thus have expectations on possible policy outcomes (see appendix, equations 7–8).

A special feature of our expected rule utility model for the formation of constitutional preferences is that it takes into account actors' utilities for all possible outcomes – maintenance of the status quo, policy change with and without the actor's support. When deriving an actor's constitutional preferences from a policy-seeking rationality, we consider both the expected utilities from possible outcomes and their likelihood, i.e., q_j as the probability of status quo maintenance and $1-q_j$ as the probability of policy change (see appendix, equation 10). In the actor's view, successful coalition-building under the constraints of a specific voting rule j occurs with probability $1-q_j$ and yields outcomes $x(S)$. In this case, an actor is either a member of the winning coalition S and then has an opportunity to determine the policy outcome, or he is not a member so that his preference is at best reflected by chance (see equation 11). For any voting rule *j*, each actor also assesses the status quo maintenance to its individual utility function U^i and the corresponding status quo probability q_j. Since outcomes are uncertain, we have the expected utility $EU^i_{j,t}$ of each actor *i* for any feasible rule *j* regarding any issue *t*.

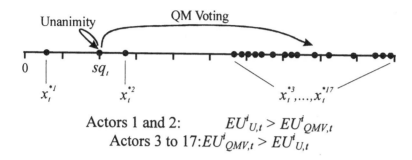

Actors 1 and 2: $EU^i_{U,t} > EU^i_{QMV,t}$

Actors 3 to 17: $EU^i_{QMV,t} > EU^i_{U,t}$

Figure 3.1 Formation of preferences regarding Council voting rules

Figure 3.1 exemplifies our measurement concept of constitutional preferences on voting rules. Regarding the issue *t* the status quo is located somewhere left of the centre of the policy space. The preference distribution shows a configuration with one actor favouring a position left of the status quo, one actor right but close to the status quo and all other fifteen actors being to the right of, and far from, the status quo. Under unanimity, only the single winning coalition of all actors can change the status quo, resulting in expected utility almost entirely determined by the status quo location. Under qualified majority rule, a large number of winning coalitions often leads to outcomes in between the policy positions of the majority. As a result, expected utilities from qualified majority rule are determined by both the status quo and the expected outcomes at the right side of the policy space. Therefore, both actors 1 and 2 will favour unanimity since they have to expect losses from a change in the status quo to the majority position; conversely, actors 3 to 17 will prefer Council qualified majority voting as they gain more from policy change. They will exclude the EP when it is located at the policy position of actor 1 or 2.

In general, there exist *n* actors and *m* different rules for any issue *t*. Assuming that an actor tries to maximise his expected utility, we predict that for any issue *t* an actor *i* will prefer rule *j* to rule *k* if, and only if, the expected utility $EU^i_{j,t}$ from rule *j* is greater than the expected utility $EU^i_{k,t}$ from *k*. This enables us to arrange expected utilities for each issue *t* in our matrix of constitutional choice:

$$\Delta EU_t = \begin{pmatrix} EU^1_{1,t} - EU^1_{ref,t} \cdots EU^1_{m,t} - EU^1_{ref,t} \\ \vdots \qquad \ddots \qquad \vdots \\ EU^n_{1,t} - EU^n_{ref,t} \cdots EU^n_{m,t} - EU^n_{ref,t} \end{pmatrix}$$

In this matrix, the ith row depicts the expected surplus of actor i under the change from the current rule *ref* to the different rules in question; the jth column of *EU* denotes the expected surplus for actors when the current setting *ref* is changed to rule j, i.e., whether a voting rule satisfies the criterion of Pareto-superiority with respect to issue t. Hence, for each issue t the matrix of constitutional choice ΔEU_t sums up actors' individual policy-seeking assessments of voting rules. It is the starting point of our empirical analysis of the Amsterdam Treaty which introduces or modifies the voting rules for many issues.

Results: the constitutional determinants of the Amsterdam Treaty

The expected rule utility model of the formation of constitutional preferences offers insight into two general aspects. The first aspect concerns the impact of voting rules on the probability of outcomes. The second refers to the consequences of changing a voting rule for the actors' expected utilities. Both can be used to test criteria under which the Amsterdam delegates selected one out of many voting rules. Two topics were particularly important for the Amsterdam rule reform: the extension of qualified majority voting in the Council of Ministers and EP participation. In order to raise parliamentary involvement, the modified co-decision procedure (Art. 2, 44 Treaty of Amsterdam) was considered the most promising voting procedure, requiring not only the consent of the EP, but also giving an agenda-setting function to parliamentary delegates in the conciliation committee. The Amsterdam Treaty proposes to apply the standard and the modified co-decision procedure extensively, while the assent procedure is to be used for legislation on external relations (CONF/4001/97, 119). We therefore investigate the procedural settings of the standard and modified co-decision procedure (with Council qualified majority voting or unanimity) as ideal types for reforming the EU's framework. In order to delineate delegates' constitutional preferences regarding the Council voting quota and parliamentary participation we compare their expected utilities from:

- Council qualified majority voting versus unanimity in the standard procedure, both including the Commission as part of any winning coalition, and
- standard procedure versus modified co-decision procedure, with qualified majority voting in the Council, the latter defined by winning coalitions of the Council and the EP.

The constitutional preferences regarding the Council's voting quota and the participation of the EP are listed in the right-hand columns of Table 3.1. Obviously, the two member states favouring the status quo of the first issue on citizenship prefer unanimity rule enabling them to maintain the status quo, while all other pro-integrative actors will profit from Council qualified majority voting allowing the status quo to be altered. The same holds true for issue 24 where the majority of actors can only preserve the pro-integrative status quo location by unanimity rule. Except for two issues, the EP always prefers to alter the status quo leading to a high similarity between preferences for Council qualified majority voting and EP participation. The asterisks indicate the rule that has been adopted by the Amsterdam Treaty. For most of the issues, we find a majority of member states favouring the Council's qualified majority voting rule. The EP almost always prefers qualified majority voting, while the Commission partly supports member states' unanimity. With respect to the participation of the EP, we find a similar picture: a majority of member states, often the Commission, and nearly always the EP prefer the extension of parliamentary rights.

For hypothesis H1, total net utilities are important from a change of the current rule to the final settings provided in the Amsterdam Treaty.[3] Table 3.2 shows total net utilities of the Amsterdam delegates over all thirty-five issues as derived from our expected rule utility model of constitutional preference formation in the second column. Columns 3 to 6 list total net expected utilities for four other settings providing for either standard procedure with qualified majority voting, standard procedure with unanimity, co-decision procedure with qualified majority or co-decision procedure with unanimity for all thirty-five issues. According to column 2, all member states as well as the two supranational actors may expect gains from the reform of rules by the Amsterdam Treaty. Confirming hypothesis H1, the delegates' constitutional decision is Pareto-superior to the status quo rule of no integration. Actors' expected utilities, however, vary to quite an extent with the supranational actors, the Benelux countries, having a net value of more than 0.4, whereas France, Germany, Ireland and UK have less than 0.2.

Comparing the reform of the Amsterdam Treaty with the four other possible settings reveals that Council unanimity would also fulfil the criterion of Pareto-superiority, but delegates' expected utilities are only marginally greater than zero due to the high status quo bias. Conversely, Council qualified majority would offer higher gains from more likely policy change of the (mostly non-integrationist) status quo to the (mostly integrationist) policy position of a majority of member states. Again, as majorities are changing from issue to issue and none of the constitutional actors fears being outvoted permanently under majority rule, all delegates have a positive assessment of future benefits. Since all total net expected

Table 3.2 Expected utilities from voting rules

Actor	Amsterdam Treaty	Standard/ QM voting for all issues	Standard/ unanimity for all issues	Co-decision/ QM voting for all issues	Co-decision/ unanimity for all issues
			Net expected utilities over 35 issues $\sum_{t=1}^{35} \Delta EU_{j,t}^i$		
Commission	.431	.736	>0	.373	>0
France	.173	.268	>0	.128	>0
Germany	.108	.254	>0	.116	>0
Italy	.413	.842	>0	.433	>0
UK	.199	.250	>0	.115	>0
Spain	.342	.649	>0	.329	>0
Belgium	.441	.823	>0	.423	>0
Greece	.415	.784	>0	.403	>0
Netherlands	.411	.734	>0	.371	>0
Portugal	.247	.529	>0	.265	>0
Austria	.433	.808	>0	.415	>0
Sweden	.335	.473	>0	.231	>0
Denmark	.301	.392	>0	.193	>0
Finland	.349	.614	>0	.311	>0
Ireland	.197	.329	>0	.156	>0
Luxembourg	.429	.764	>0	.389	>0
EP	.449	.926	>0	.483	>0
Standard deviation	.110	.230	>0	.134	>0

utilities from qualified majority voting in the standard procedure are greater than from the Amsterdam Treaty's rules, the question arises as to why delegates did not provide for this procedure for all thirty-five issues. One answer might be indicated by the standard deviation (last row of Table 3.2), showing that the distribution of actors' expected utilities is even more asymmetric with qualified majority voting under standard procedure (0.230) and under the co-decision procedure (0.134) than under the Amsterdam outcome.

On closer inspection, hypothesis H2 asks for commitments of member states to adopt Council majority voting and parliamentary participation over the issues. To test this hypothesis we use logit probability models estimating different thresholds of the number of member states (T^1 to T^{15}) as predictors for the choice of the Council's voting quota (VQ) and the EP's participation (PP) on thirty-five adopted issues.[4] We also consider the impact of the Commission's preference (C) while we must exclude the constitutional preferences of the EP because of its non-discriminatory attitude to both rules. The logit model estimates probabilities of the two possible events of the dichotomous dependent variables using the cumulative logistic probability function. The probability that the constitutional actors will choose qualified majority voting ($VQ_t=1$) for an issue t, e.g., is given by:

$$P(VQ_t = 1) = \left(1 + \exp(-(\beta_0 = \beta_1 T_t^8 + \beta_2 C_t))\right)^{-1},$$

where the independent variables are the Commission's preference and the eight member-states' threshold variable. A high positive value in a beta coefficient indicates that the variable contributes to a higher probability for Council majority voting and parliamentary participation, while a negative value shows a decreasing likelihood for any issue.

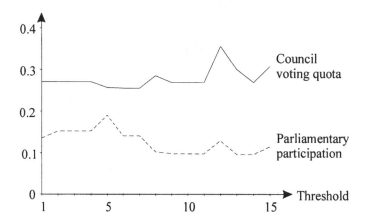

Figure 3.2 Predictive quality of threshold models (Pseudo-R^2)

In order to test hypothesis H2, we look for the most appropriate threshold model to explain the final settings of the Amsterdam Treaty. Figure 3.2 portrays our threshold model findings with the number of member states on the horizontal and their predictive quality on the vertical axis.[5] Due to the distribution of rule preferences, the null-model of fifteen member states plus Commission is worse than the twelve member-state plus Commission threshold model. This means that the probability of an issue by issue adoption of Council qualified majority rule significantly increases when at least twelve member states favour this quota. It is interesting to note that the significance of the Commission's influence increases when the number of member states decreases. However, the twelve member-state threshold model correctly predicts 82.9 per cent of all cases and proves to be the best predictor for the introduction of Council qualified majority voting. In contrast, none of the threshold models sufficiently explains the participation of the EP. Consequently, we can only reject the hypothesis that member states have to consent regarding each single issue for their constitutional choice of Council voting rules. Here, commitments may allow for the adoption of qualified majority voting as twelve of fifteen member states have the highest significance in predicting the Amsterdam outcome. This generates the question of which member states' preferences best predict the Amsterdam choice of voting rules.

This question is the conjecture of hypothesis H3 referring to the different relevance of member states for constitutional decisions. In order to reveal the impact or 'power' of one delegate to realise his rule preferences against other delegates, ideally we should correlate the delegate's preferences with the final outcome *controlling* for the preferences of all other delegates. However, several delegates have quite similar rule preferences making it difficult to differentiate powerful and lucky actors. Besides, the number of thirty-five cases is small so that a sophisticated analysis using a multivariate logit model is not possible. For this reason, Table 3.3 lists how often actors' rule preferences coincide with the final outcome and shows the corresponding association coefficients: a high coefficient thus indicates either high power to get one's preferences through or simply luck to have preferences similar to a powerful actor.

Table 3.3 Correlation between rule preferences and Amsterdam Treaty outcomes

	Number of policies where preference coincides with outcome (%)					
Actor	Unanimity (N=10)	QM voting (N=25)	Association[a]	No particip. (N=12)	EP particip. (N=23)	Association[a]
Commission	0.60	0.92	0.313***	0.42	0.87	0.105*
France	0.40	0.56	0.001	0.25	0.49	0.068
Germany	0.50	0.60	0.008	0.50	0.61	0.011
Italy	0.20	0.88	0.011	0.25	0.91	0.049
UK	0.80	0.72	0.225***	0.67	0.70	0.121**
Spain	0.30	0.92	0.081*	0.17	0.87	0.002
Belgium	0.40	0.96	0.216***	0.42	1.00	0.319***
Greece	0.30	0.88	0.047	0.33	0.91	0.096*
Netherlands	0.50	0.88	0.167**	0.42	0.87	0.105*
Portugal	0.30	0.68	0.000	0.42	0.74	0.025
Austria	0.40	0.92	0.147**	0.42	0.96	0.221***
Sweden	0.90	0.84	0.479***	0.67	0.78	0.195***
Denmark	0.90	0.80	0.417***	0.67	0.74	0.155**
Finland	0.50	0.80	0.090*	0.33	0.94	0.006
Ireland	0.70	0.68	0.120**	0.58	0.65	0.051
Luxembourg	0.50	0.92	0.225***	0.42	0.91	0.153**
EP	0.10	0.96	0.014	0.17	1.00	0.116**

Notes: [a] Goodman and Kruskal (1954) (? = $(N_c-N_d) / (N_c+N_d)$, where N_c and N_d are the number of concordant and disconcordant pairs in the 2 by 2 table of rule preferences and treaty outcomes). * significant at 10% level; ** significant at 5% level; *** significant at 1% level.

From the total of thirty-five issues, the Amsterdam Treaty provides for Council QMV on twenty-five issues and for parliamentary participation in twenty-three cases. We find a high coincidence between outcomes and a preference for Council majority voting for both supranational actors, the Benelux countries and also the three Southern European countries Greece, Italy and Spain. Conversely, there is high coherence between the preference of the United Kingdom, Sweden and Denmark for unanimity and the introduction of that rule in the Treaty. As a result, both the Commission and the Benelux countries, as well as the United Kingdom, Sweden and Denmark, have a strong and highly significant correlation between their rule preferences and outcomes. Compared to them, France and Germany were powerless or out of luck at the Amsterdam Intergovernmental Conference. For parliamentary participation we also find evidence for our third hypothesis, positing the different relevance of member states: although the correlation between preferences and outcomes is weaker, the effect of the EP seems to be much higher on this question. As for lowering the Council's voting quota, the support of the small Benelux member states is always positive for parliamentary integration, and some three member states may be responsible for holding on to the status quo rules.

Conclusion: Europe towards a majority system?

Regarding proper functioning, the crucial question was to what extent the Amsterdam Treaty provides Council majority voting and parliamentary participation for reforming the European legislature. The answer is important for the proper functioning of the present and future EU when five or ten applicant countries will have joined the club. For 25 and 23 of the thirty-five adopted issues, the Amsterdam Treaty includes the participation of the EP and applies Council qualified majority voting. When Council unanimity has to be applied, the EP participates in only three of seven issues, while parliamentary participation is fixed in twenty out of twenty-five issues with Council qualified majority voting. We correctly predict the rulemaking outcome for twenty-three of twenty-five issues with Council qualified majority voting, but only six of ten issues providing for Council unanimity. Concerning parliamentary participation we miss half of the twelve policies excluding the EP, while we correctly predict twenty-one of twenty-three policies with parliamentary participation. We are able to predict the EU's move towards a (parliamentary) majority system, but we underestimate its international character of safeguarding state sovereignty by Council unanimity without EP participation.

Besides Pareto-superiority, the pattern of the Amsterdam constitutional choice, especially the choice of the Council's voting quota, can be explained by the commitments of a twelve-member state majority plus Commission, the latter increasing its importance when the number of member states preferring Council qualified majority voting decreases. We found evidence for our first hypothesis (H1) on the consensus requirement of Treaty reform, but also for the hypotheses on the higher number of member states (H2) and on the different importance of member states (H3). To underpin our results, a possible extension might be a two-step estimation which first predicts whether the European regulation of an issue will be adopted and then determines the likely voting rule. Moreover, the empirical preference structure revealed our difficulty in measuring actors' policy positions. We had to reduce our analysis to the member states' and Commission's role because the EP exclusively voted for more Council qualified majority voting and parliamentary integration. Even though we were able to collect *ex ante* policy preferences of the negotiating actors and to derive their constitutional preferences, a higher quality of data is needed for the (spatial) location of actors' policy positions.

In spite of some empirical shortcomings, the analysis showed a significant pattern of constitutional choice when twelve member states are in favour of introducing or changing the voting rules. Member states take into account their individual expected gains from future policy-making when deciding on the Council's voting quota for future decision-making. The Commission also proved to be influential, but its impact is limited, particularly when the twelve members make commitments on qualified majority voting. This result certainly indicates why policy-seeking member states do not change the Commission's role. The Commission's impact can be drastically reduced when a qualified majority of twelve member states has the same preferences. Compared to the findings on the Council's voting quota, the results on the EP's participation indicate different reasons for its choice. Commitments of a certain number of member states do not sufficiently explain the participation of the EP. We suspect that policy-seeking delegations may be guided by different 'central ideas' when deciding on both voting rules. However, the EU is moving towards a majority system and Pareto-superiority of the Treaty as a whole is enough for further integration.

In sum, our results confirm the basic premises of constitutional analysis, namely actors' policy-seeking view of constitutional matters and the Pareto-superiority requirement of constitutional change. However, our empirical analysis on the Amsterdam Treaty does not confirm previous research on Treaty reforms. Our findings suggest that the introduction of QMV is likely induced by the support of the Benelux countries, Spain, Greece and Italy, while the maintenance of unanimity is due to the extreme policy preferences of the United Kingdom, Denmark and Sweden. This may challenge the insight of intergovernmental institutionalism concluding that European 'bargaining tends to converge towards the lowest common denominator of large state interests. The bargains initially consisted of bilateral agreements between France and Germany; now they consist of trilateral agreements including Britain' (Moravcsik, 1991: 26).

In addition, our findings suggest that the Commission's impact is high in general but limited when twelve member states agree on constitutional changes. This may qualify the view of supranational institutions as autonomous and powerful actors who are necessary for constitutional change. The Commission only has an important and independent causal role in the integration process if member states disagree on the terms of integration.

Appendix

Calculation of inclusiveness and conditional Shapley–Shubik indices
Formally, an arbitrary voting rule can be depicted as a simple game which is a map v_j with $v_j(S)=1$, if S is a winning coalition with respect to the rule, and $v_j(S)=0$, if S is losing, where S is a subset of the player set N. By definition, S is winning if there is a subset T of S that is winning. For any rule v_j, we denote its corresponding set of winning coalitions by

$$1 \quad W_j = \{S \subseteq N \mid v_j(S) = 1\}$$

Given the knowledge of policy preferences, we assume that the likelihood that actors α and β will collaborate in a coalition is related to their spatial proximity of their policy preferences.

Let x^{*i}_t be the ideal point of actor i regarding issue t in the (multi-dimensional) policy space $\Omega_t \subseteq CR^n$ and denote the dispersion of policy references by

$$2 \quad diam_t(N) = \begin{cases} \max\limits_{\mu,\nu \in N} \{s^\mu_t s^\nu_t |x^{*\mu}_t - x^{*\nu}_t|\} & \text{if } \max\limits_{\mu,\nu \in N} \{s^\mu_t s^\nu_t |x^{*\mu}_t - x^{*\nu}_t|\} \neq 0 \\ 1 & \text{if } \max\limits_{\mu,\nu \in N} \{s^\mu_t s^\nu_t |x^{*\mu}_t - x^{*\nu}_t|\} = 0 \end{cases}$$

where s^i_t is i's salience regarding issue t. The homogeneity of a coalition S can thus be defined as the mean similarity of all pairs of coalition members

$$3 \quad h_t(S) = \frac{2}{s(s-1)} \sum_{\substack{\alpha,\beta \in S \\ \alpha<\beta}} 1 - \frac{s^\alpha_t s^\beta_t |x^{*\alpha}_t - x^{*\beta}_t|}{diam_t(N)},$$

where s denotes the number of actors in S. Accordingly, the likelihood $\pi_t(S)$ that a coalition S actually will form depends on how homogeneous it is compared to other coalitions

$$4 \quad \pi_t(S) = \frac{h_t(S)}{\sum\limits_{S \subseteq N} h_t(S)}.$$

Using the concept of simple games, we define the *inclusiveness* ω_t^i of an actor i regarding an issue t as its probability of participating in a winning coalition

$$5 \quad \omega_t^i(v_j) = \frac{\sum\limits_{S \subseteq N, i \in S} \pi_t(S) v_j(S)}{\sum\limits_{S \subseteq N} \pi_t(S) v_j(S)}.$$

If all coalitions are equally probable, inclusiveness of an actor is the number of times it participates in winning coalitions in relation to the number of all feasible winning coalitions (Bräuninger, 1996: 42).

To derive conditional Shapley–Shubik indices with respect to an arbitrary winning coalition S (i.e., $v_j(S) = 1$), we consider subsets T of S. According to the concept of simple games, we let $v_j(T) = 1$ if T is winning, and $v_j(T) = 0$ otherwise. Our conditional Shapley-Shubik indices for all actors i with respect to the coalition S are

$$6 \quad \phi_s^i(v_j) = \sum_{T \subseteq S} \frac{(t-1)!(s-t)!}{s!} [v_j(T) - v_j(T \backslash \{i\})]$$

where s and t denote the number of elements of the sets S and T, respectively.

Calculation of expected outcomes x(S)
To assess expected outcomes in a policy area t and actors' expected profits from outcomes, we distinguish between the status quo (sq_t) and the outcomes, of all feasible winning coalitions. If the coalition supporting a policy proposal is losing, the status quo remains. In contrast, if the supporting coalition is winning, the policy proposal is the decision-making outcome. Formally, we assign every coalition S an expected outcome $x_t(S)$ in the space of all feasible outcomes $\Omega_t \subseteq \mathbf{R}^n$:

$$7 \quad x_t : S \rightarrow x_t(S), \text{ where } x_t(S) = sq_t \quad \forall S \notin W_j.$$

Given the knowledge of preferences, we assume that decisive actors are able to realise their first preference in the corresponding winning coalition. Then, the expected outcome of a specific winning coalition S is a linear combination of the first preferences of coalition members where actors' conditional decisiveness indicates how often they are able to realise their own preference within S. Let x_t^{*i} be the ideal point of actor i regarding issue t, then actors expect the following policy outcome:

$$8 \quad x_t(S) = \sum_{i \in S} \phi_s^i(v_j) x_t^{*i} \quad \forall S \in W_j.$$

where the conditional Shapley–Shubik indices of all coalition members sum up to unity:

9 $\sum_{i \in S} \phi_s^i (v_j) = 1 \forall S \in W_j.$

Calculation of expected utilities of rules

The status quo is maintained if the supporting coalition does not succeed within the setting defined by rule v_j. Since the probability that a coalition will form depends on its homogeneity, the probability of the status quo in issue t is

10 $q_t = \sum_{S \notin W_j} \pi_t(S).$

As a consequence, the actor's probability of being in one out of all winning coalitions is its individual inclusiveness:

11 $\sum_{S \in W_j, i \in S} \pi_t(S) = \omega_t^j(v_j).$

We now consider a general utility function $U^i = U^i(x)$ with x as a potential outcome in the policy space and $U^i(x)$ as the resulting utility of actor i. Actors behave as expected utility maximisers, i.e. actors try to maximise their expected utility function. Since rules can be depicted as risky lotteries, we have the expected utility $EU^i_{j,t}$ of each actor i for any feasible rule v_j regarding any issue t:

12 $EU^i_{j,t} = \sum_{S \subseteq N} \pi_t(S) \, U^i(x_t(S)) = q_t U^i(sq_t) + \sum_{S \in W_j} \pi_t(S) \, U^i \left(\sum_{k \in S} \phi_s^k (v_j) x_t^{*k} \right).$

Notes

1 The positions of the seventeen participating actors were collected by the EP's Task Force on the IGC. The EP itself has utilised these positions in its regular work (see Parliament's White Paper on the IGC, Vols. I and II, and the briefings on the IGC). The following data stem from the sixth, final update drawn up by memorandums, press reports, etc.. The Task Force emphasises that, despite their provisional nature, the tables of positions 'offer a reasonably reliable summary of the present situation as regards the IGC and should improve understanding of the Conference' (JF/bo/290/97, 12/5/1997, 1). The issues of these tables have been coded as one-dimensional issues with positions on ordinal scales. In addition to the seventeen positions on each issue we coded the status quo, the Amsterdam bargaining result, and the provided institutional settings.

2 Policy positions are conceived as single-peaked utility functions where the ideal point or position indicates the alternative with the highest utility. For the empirical analysis we use the following functional form:

$U^i(x) = 1 - | x_t^{*i} - x |$, where x_t^{*i} is the position of actor i regarding issue t.

3 For all thirty-five issues the current rule is 'no integration' allowing for no policy change; the final settings in the Amsterdam Treaty are indicated in Table 3.2.

4   Dependent variables are coded: $VQ_t=1$ [$PP_t=1$] if the Amsterdam treaty provides for Council qualified majority voting [parliamentary participation] regarding issue t, $VQ_t=0$ [$PP_t=0$] otherwise. Independent variables are coded: $C_t=1$ if Commission prefers Council qualified majority voting [parliamentary participation] regarding issue t; $C_t=0$ otherwise; $T_t^x=1$ if at least x member states prefer Council qualified majority voting [parliamentary participation] regarding issue t; $T_t^x=0$ otherwise.

5   We report Pseudo R^2 as indicators for the predictive quality of the models: $R'^2 = 1 - L_1/L_0$, where L_0 and L_1 are the negative log-likelihoods of the initial and the current model (McFadden, 1974: 21). R'^2 compares the negative log-likelihood of the threshold model to the negative log-likelihood of the model where the constant is the only independent variable. Thus R'^2 approaches 1, if the predictive quality of the threshold model increases and therefore L_1 is much smaller than L_0. If the independent variables T^x and C do not provide any further information to explain the choice of rules, L_1 equals L_0 so that R'^2 is zero.

Mark Aspinwall

Comment: 'The dynamics of European integration'

This chapter sets out to explain constitutional change in the EU, a crucially important subject, and it tries to get to the bottom of the question why, and under what conditions, member states agree to change voting rules. The authors apply co-operative game theory to an examination of the creation of new voting rules (comprising voting quotas and EP participation) in the Amsterdam Treaty. Institutions are the end product and they do not influence behaviour, at least not overtly. The study is, to use the distinction elaborated elsewhere in this book, *on* rather than *within* rules. The institutional rules for achieving constitutional change, of course, revolve primarily around unanimity voting (with a few preparatory events like the Reflection Group report contributing a small level of agenda setting). The 'power' of member state actors is the same in the sense that they all have veto power over constitutional change and so their preferences are of primary importance. However, the authors raise the possibility of member state power differing according to size, budgetary contribution and similar features, which I address below. Supranational actors (the EP and Commission) also express preferences on constitutional change, but of course they do not have a vote in the IGC.

Where do preferences come from? The authors painstakingly assemble a matrix of preferences on thirty-five substantive policy areas and the corresponding location of the status quo, which is the basis for a modelling exercise in which these preferences are transformed into preferences on how to change voting rules. Member states have expected utilities based upon an uncertain and risky assessment of coalition possibilities, given their present knowledge of their own and other member states' preferences on substantive policies and the location of the status quo. In accordance with constitutional analysis, they assume the lack of constitutional actors' knowledge about which coalitions will be formed in the future, but more realistically they assume that coalitions are not equally probable – as actors with similar policy positions are more likely to collaborate than actors with dissimilar policy positions. The chapter builds a formal model of constitutional change in which all actors behave strategically, within the bounds of uncertainty, to achieve set goals, namely to maximise the chances of a substantive policy outcome they can support. Following Garrett and Tsebelis (1996), the authors assert that preferences over substantive policies are the independent variable leading to preferences over the shape of constitutional rules.

Accounting for constitutional change then becomes a matter of accounting for the mix of constitutional preferences. Hypotheses are constructed which follow from the knowledge about these preferences. The first hypothesis posits Pareto-superiority for all member states as a necessary condition for rule change. The second indicates that the greater the number supporting change, the more likely it will be. The third states that distinctions between member states on the basis of power or socio-economic characteristics explains some variation in outcomes. I concentrate on these latter two hypotheses here.

The authors find strong correlation between the number of member states supporting rule change to qualified majority voting and its success. To my mind, one of the most interesting of the empirical findings in this chapter is that support by twelve member states (out of fifteen) is the best predictor for change in the voting quotas. Two potential implications flow from this: one, small states matter (contra many studies that concentrate only on larger states); second, veto power is being sacrificed by three member states in many cases. But for what? This awaits further empirical study and would be a useful follow up to the chapter. Furthermore, the study finds that France and Germany were comparatively uninfluential in the selection of voting rules, a counter-intuitive and remarkably significant finding given the near universal focus on these two states by theorists interested in the grand bargains. In fact, net Pareto changes were lower for the big three member states than for the smaller states.

The effort to distinguish between member states on the basis of various domestic characteristics is more troubling. On the one hand, the bigger member states may have greater bargaining power by virtue of their economic position, net budget contributions and similar features, and this is why hypothesis three focuses on the 'important' member states. Ironically, the findings appear to reject this claim conclusively by showing that twelve states correlate to adoption of qualified majority voting rules. On the other hand, preferences may diverge because of differences between northern free trade orientation and southern protectionism, new members and old members, as well as wealthy and poor members.

There are several possible problems here. Do these distinctions lead to differences in bargaining power or differences in preferences? If the former, on what basis would, for example, northern free trade orientations lead to greater bargaining power? One could posit that the growing importance of liberal ideas, possibly augmented by clever persuasion, would lend free traders more bargaining power, but the authors are not asserting this, and if they did it would lead them directly into the constructivist realm.

If the latter is true, then certain domestic characteristics lead to initial preferences in a predictable way. For example, the original members of the European Communities may hypothetically have convergent preferences because the older member states have had a longer period to adjust to each other and to membership, giving a common outlook. But this would mean that German–Italian preferences would be closer than German–Austrian; and Danish–Irish preferences would be closer than Danish–Swedish, which is not obvious *a priori*. In fact, on the voting quota changes, the empirical findings appear to disconfirm all socioeconomic variables, since successful change to Qualified Majority Voting (QMV) correlates to support by Benelux, Spain, Greece and Italy; and successful change to unanimity correlates to support by the UK, Denmark and Sweden.

But even if we accept the point, then long-term co-operation leads to a socialising effect whereby member state preferences are altered to resemble each other more closely. This may occur through learning, mimicking, persuasion or some other mechanism, and it would be worthwhile discovering how it occurs. Rational choice scholars have begun to model preference change, but we may also be led to sociological institutionalism for the answers.

This is not to suggest that hypotheses on the grounds of domestic variation should be abandoned, but that they may present an opportunity to bridge the gap between the new institutionalisms. If we infer preference variation on the basis of entrenched institutionalised behaviour, then we necessarily pry into the inner workings of the unitary non-temporal rational actor. A separate set of institutional variables, historically derived and internal to the member states, may 'intervene' between policy preferences and constitutional choice, or even precede and determine preferences. An exploration into the basis for actors' different preferences, as well as into their experience during membership, may show that preferences over substantive policies are a product of experience. So the question remains, why did these groups of member states consistently support certain types of rule change?

Some of the differences between member states may be the sort that condition preferences in a 'rational choice' manner, such as the level of economic development. Alternatively, some differences may exert normative or cultural claims upon preference formation and may therefore affect whether member states consider certain policy outcomes to be 'appropriate.' Examples include the Scandinavian countries' often-cited preference for openness and transparency in decision-making, or the southern countries' tendency to resist curtailment of bureaucratic involvement in the economy.

These important issues suggest avenues of research, whereby both rational and 'non-rational' motivations are explored. Case study empirical work may uncover some hidden variables and could supplement the data analysis of the authors. We may find that institutions are not only the target of conscious design by states but that they have become 'internalised' within the actor and help to shape preferences, which later feed into further constitutional change. Is it possible that preferences over policies do not lead to preferences over constitutional design? To what extent are member states motivated by symbolic politics, by pan-European cohesion values or by some alternative logic of appropriateness (to borrow from March and Olsen) in making constitutional decisions? If these are important, we have more probing to do to uncover the reasons why voting arrangements are what they are.

One further issue relates to the correlation between certain member states and rule change. The correlation is high in some cases, but is there causality? The Benelux countries are closely associated with rule change to more EP involvement in decision-making. The Benelux and southern member states are closely associated with increased QMV. Britain, Denmark and Sweden are closely associated with unanimity voting. But causality remains unclear. If these countries *always* support certain types of rules, we would expect to see them associated with successful cases where these rules are instituted. Ironically, France and Germany may provide the answer. The authors interpret them as 'powerless or out of luck' at the Amsterdam IGC, but further empirical work may reveal whether they made sacrifices on some institutional questions to achieve other aims.

Finally, one of the most interesting findings is the impact of the Commission on changes in voting rules. The Commission appears to have little influence where member states are of a single mind, but does reinforce the view of a majority of member states when its preferences coincide with the majority. This is worth pursuing since a number of historical institutionalists (as well as neofunctionalists before them) have suggested that the supranational institutions have consequences that go well beyond their initial *raison d'etre* of overcoming informational, enforcement and contracting inadequacies. Further insights here would help answer the question of how important these institutions are in subsequent change.

The 'Europeanisation' of central government: the UK and Germany in historical institutionalist perspective[1]

As European integration has widened and deepened over the post-war period, so the terrain of study has grown. Institutionalist analysis has largely concentrated on EU-level phenomena, such as inter-institutional relations and policy evolution. Applications to relationships between the EU and its member states have been rather thinner on the ground, and yet these relationships are of fundamental importance to our understanding of EU governance. At one and the same time member state policies retain importance to the process of policy-making in the EU, even under qualified majority voting in the Council; and, as integration has deepened, so it has had an increasingly pervasive impact upon the study of the political process in the member states themselves.

This chapter is concerned with the ways in which governments have adapted their domestic arrangements for EU policy-making: one of the principal consequences of what has been termed 'Europeanisation'. How is this subject-matter to be examined from the institutionalist menu? Those seated at the rational choice institutionalist 'table' – to use the editors' analogy – would most likely be concerned with examining a series of iterative impacts: a sequence of snapshot-analyses of the EU's impact upon the institutional arrangements for policy-making in the member states. We would expect such studies to have three characteristics. They would model the causality associated with the EU's impact on domestic institutional change. They would understand the national government's response as designed to optimise its bargaining position in EU arenas. (For Coasians, ensuring an efficient domestic policy-making machinery would reduce the internal transaction costs of co-ordination.) Finally, they would regard the wider context of national governance, including institutional culture, as exogenous to the explanation, which would be actor-centred.

For those seated at the historical institutionalist 'table', by contrast, the analysis would be of a continuous nature over a long time horizon, emphasising path-dependency. In line with historical institutionalists' characteristic methodology of the case-study approach, the modelling of causality would be relaxed in order to capture less quantifiable independent variables, such as informal rules and norms. Thus institutional change at the national level might be seen as having less to do with rational solutions designed to reduce transaction costs in the formulation of national European policy than with incrementalism following existing tradition and with potentially unintended consequences.

The sociological institutionalist would share some of these concerns but would factor in the analysis a much greater cognitive and cultural component. Institutional response at the national level would again be seen over the long term. However, the character of that response would be defined with rather different emphases. It would be seen as reflective of perceptions of the state's culture. Intrinsic to this cultural dimension would be the state's collective identity as defined in the history of its relationship with the integration process. Domestically, the important thing about the institutions would not be 'that they enhance efficiency but that they offer a normative context that constitutes actors and provides a set of norms in which the reputation of actors acquires meaning and value' (Katzenstein, 1997: 12–13). Those analysts seated at this 'table' would be especially concerned with culture, cognition and constructivism.

Before proceeding with our analysis we should declare where we are seated. The title of our chapter suggests that we are at the historical institutionalist 'table', and this is certainly how we see things. However, we see the historical and sociological 'tables' as linked. We are conscious of the cultural dimension and that the adaptation of EU policy-making machinery within member states is conditioned by constructivist interaction with the integration process. Nevertheless, our methodological approach is historical, and for that reason we locate ourselves at the HI 'table'.[2] Our view is that the adaptation of central government to Europeanisation has to be seen as part of a continuous process, and one in which informal institutional features, along with norms, are of considerable significance. A further observation to make is that we use institutionalism as a heuristic device in what follows; we are not engaged in theory-building. What, then, of our empirical material, namely the Europeanisation of central government?

On the face of it the impact of membership of the EU on the member states is both substantial and wide ranging. Areas of policy have been removed from the domain of the national state to that of the EU. European issues are a central feature in party and public debate in all member states. Large numbers of national politicians and bureaucrats are now engaged in European policy-making and large parts of the political agenda of each member state are now set in an EU context. The consequence is that the flow of business to and from Europe that governments, at all levels, have to handle is now considerable. While there can be no doubt that the impact of the EU on the member states' politics has been great, the effect on their governmental systems has been far less evident. There is a puzzle here as to how the Europeanisation of both politics and policy has been possible without dramatic changes in the structures and processes of national governments. Given that member states have been subject to similar pressures, why has there not been a convergence in governmental systems? Why has national diversity survived to the degree it has? Indeed, the impact of membership of the EU on state institutions and practices seems to have been to renew national traditions of administration rather than to confound them.

Part of the answer to this puzzle lies in the fundamental power structure of the EU. It is one in which the national governments hold a privileged position. The balance between the intergovernmental and the supranational features of EU politics is changing, but critical cards still remain in the hands of national governments. Another part of the answer, however, lies in the resilience and adaptability of national institutions. It is this feature that we consider in this chapter. Historical institutionalism provides a way of explaining both institutional change and continuity. The emphasis is on working with the known and established and the way in which new developments emerge from and are shaped by existing formats. To do this we need to be clear about not only what historical institutionalist analysis entails, but also what is involved in the concept of Europeanisation. This, as we attempt to show, is a highly interactive and iterative process. We then look at the development of national approaches in the case of the UK and Germany using these analytical tools. We look predominantly at central government and its adaptation to the EU. Of course, other parts of the political system may have been changed more significantly as a result of EC/EU membership and any explanation is likely to be the poorer as a result of the neglect of these features.

Europeanisation and institutionalism

We use Europeanisation in this chapter to characterise the impact of the European integration process upon the national level and specifically upon the domestic institutions of government. On the face of it Europeanisation might appear a loose construct. However, Europeanisation is distinct in that one can identify it with a political process, namely integration, and a system of government, namely the EU.

In working towards a detailed dissection and definition of Europeanisation for the purposes of this chapter, we need to consider the following questions.

- What is the scope of Europeanisation as concerns member states?
- What is our understanding of 'institutions'?

- Above all, is Europeanisation simply one-way causality: of the integration process and the EU stimulating responses in the member governments; or is it interactive?
- How can we analyse institutional change in examining how governments adapt to EU membership?

The scope of Europeanisation

If national political life consists of politics, polity and policy, it is likely that all three of these domains are affected by Europeanisation. A study of the impact of integration on member state *politics* in these terms would be typically concerned with the effect on parties and interest groups but also upon public opinion. For parties and interest groups Europeanisation poses the dual challenge of organisational adaptation and the ability to exploit the new EU channels of action. The term 'Europeanisation' is prone to being used more loosely when examining the impact of the EU upon member state *policies* because of the difficulty of isolating an 'EU-effect'. Nevertheless, the EU has had an important effect across the whole policy spectrum of member states, especially on agriculture and trade policy, where competences have been transferred to a significant extent to Brussels. The growth of EU policy competences, such as through treaty reforms in the Single European Act (SEA) or the Maastricht Treaty, may also be seen as a key dimension of Europeanisation. In passive terms, policy adaptation consists of making domestic policy compatible with the requirements of EU policy. There is, however, a more active manner in which adaptation can take place: through seeking to 'export' domestic policy models, ideas and detail to the EU.

Europeanisation of the *polity* also comprises a variety of impacts. If we interpret 'polity' widely, to encompass the constitutional order, the legal dimension needs to be taken into account. European Community (EC) legal doctrine may have a major impact upon domestic practice (as it did upon the English Common Law system). The concerns of this chapter are with a narrower notion of the polity: how governments handle European policy. Thus, Europeanisation impacts upon the political and administrative responsibilities for policy, on executive-legislative relations and on the territorial distribution of power within the state. Within the institutions of government, too, Europeanisation entails a passive response, namely an organisational one designed to recognise the extent to which domestic governance is a response to prompting from Brussels or needs to be compatible with EU rules. But there is also the need to ensure that national policy positions are reached and then presented fully and effectively in EU policy-making arenas.

We have identified the scope of Europeanisation and where our concerns with the institutions of government fit in with that. If our concerns appear to be with a small part of the subject, it is worth mentioning that the institutions of government occupy a key role in political life. They are, of course, responsible for policy. And they play an important intermediating role with political forces. Hence, even if Europeanisation has much wider scope than the empirical focus of our chapter, the impact upon governmental institutions is of crucial importance. But how do we see 'governmental institutions'? To answer that question, we need to make a preliminary inspection of the institutionalist toolkit.

Defining the character of government institutions
The institutional universe we are dealing with can be defined in terms of a particular task – the handling of EU policy at central government level in EU member states and out into Brussels. We are concerned with the activities of the agencies engaged in this task over their period of engagement with the EC/EU. In doing this it is essential to look at change both in the formal features of the institution and in the informal operations that take place within it. We examine four institutional levels or components at which analysis can be applied:

1 *The systemic level*: the constitutional framework of state and government;
2 *The organisational level*: the offices and networks and the positions within them (including the powers, resources and skills attached to them), delineating who are the key players and the nature of the connections between them;
3 *The regulative level*: the rules and guidelines about who should do what and the extent to which there is a strategic capacity to ensure tasks are fulfilled and to think ahead;
4 *The procedural level*: the processes shaping how business is handled – including information systems and policy processes.

These four components are not wholly distinct – they overlap somewhat – but for analytical purposes it is useful to treat them as separate. There is, however, an added component which needs to be taken into account: the *cultural* dimension. This cultural dimension concerns the norms and values that are prevalent within the institution and how these are inculcated. This dimension is slightly different from the other four because it is present at all four levels. At the systemic level, culture could refer to overarching issues, such as the understanding of national sovereignty or national identity. At the organisational level, it could refer to understandings about who is eligible to fill a position and what they are expected to do. At the procedural level, it could refer to the traditional Whitehall value of sharing information between ministries. At the regulative level, it could refer to values concerning when officials in a ministry should take legal advice on a matter. Our general point is that this cultural dimension is present at all of the four levels.[3]

Over time these components of central government institutions adjust, reflecting the iterative nature of EC/EU change and member state response. This process of interaction between national and EU institutions is open to mutual constitution.

The interaction between EU and national institutions
In examining the scope of Europeanisation we have already suggested that integration engenders a passive response, which we term 'reception', and an active one, which we term 'projection'. Reception entails institutional adaptation so as to grasp within government the full ramifications of EU membership, EU decisions and proposals. It corresponds most closely to Ladrech's formulation of Europeanisation as a 'process reorienting the direction and shape of politics to the degree that EC political and economic dynamics become part of the *organizational logic of national politics and policy-making*' (Ladrech, 1994: 69 – our emphasis). However, Europeanisation involves more than this; it entails an ability to participate in integration so as best to 'project' national governmental concerns into the EU decision-making process. European integration is not just 'out there' as some kind of independent variable; it is itself to a significant degree the product of member government's wishes. Given that the EU has its own organisational logic, it is necessary for national political actors – here the institutions of government – to accommodate some of that logic if the opportunities afforded by the EU are to be exploited.

To dissect Europeanisation as reception and projection highlights our view of the relationship between the EU and member-government institutions as *iterative and interactive*. It is difficult to try to conceive of the relationship in conventional, positivist social science terms, i.e., with independent and dependent variables and simple causality, if analysis is to capture incrementalism and continuity. This situation has clear implications for theoretical questions, such as 'which institutions matter?'. Is it the EU's institutions that matter since they provide the defining context for the European policy-making machinery in member governments? Or is it the particular national government's institutions that matter, since they may shape that state's effectiveness at articulating its European policy in Brussels? In reality, national institutional arrangements are subject to challenge as the EU's structure itself evolves over time.[4] So, how does the dynamic, interactive relationship between the EU and the institutions of the member states operate in practice?

The institutions of the EU set the context for European policy-making within the institutions of government in the member states. This is most clearly the case when one compares the dynamics of European policy within the national context with those of domestic policy. The most obvious distinction is that the former are driven by a Brussels timetable. While purely domestic business can often be deferred, to attempt postponement of a national response to an EU proposal is simply to risk exclusion from the Brussels debate. What then are the key characteristics of the EU institutions and of the integration process more generally that shape (but do not determine) responses at the national level?

- A first, general point to make is that the EU style of policy-making and administration, inasmuch as there is one, has only recently become institutionalised. We can perhaps characterise its general features as fluid, open, network-based, rule-guided, sectorised and subject to significant inter-institutional bargaining (for a useful review see also Wright, 1996: 150–3).
- The policy process is fluid in the short or medium term because it is characterised by 'uncertain agendas, shifting networks and complex coalitions' (Mazey and Richardson, 1996: 54). It is also fluid in the long term because of episodic constitutional change within the EU, such as that following through from the SEA, the Maastricht Treaty or the Amsterdam Treaty. Similarly, potential alliances have shifted as successive enlargements have taken place.
- The policy process is open in that the Commission is surprisingly receptive to external thinking in comparison to national executives. It draws heavily upon the ideas and expertise of national officials and of interest groups. It is a multinational institution and thus a 'melting pot' of different national outlooks. The Commission is also a vertically disjointed institution. While officials in the 'services' hold formal responsibility for specific policy areas, the ability of the political level – the Commissioners and their all-important *cabinets* – to seize the reins on detailed policy issues is remarkable. Finally, the policy process is open and potentially unpredictable in the sense that the EU institutions have some autonomy of action.
- The EU policy process is network-based. Aspects of the openness outlined above have as their consequence the need for national governments to forge contacts with key officials. They may also establish close links with 'their' commissioner(s) and his/her *cabinet*. Networking places an emphasis upon inter-personal skills, including language ability and problem-solving. These skills will not necessarily be the ones most needed and most developed within the national political systems.
- The EU policy process is particularly rule-bound. Its legalism follows the continental tradition. In addition, there are strong imperatives for regulation because of the lack of shared institutional culture and trust in an immature, multinational polity.
- The EU policy process is sectorised. Horizontal co-ordination between directorates-general (DGs) of the Commission is poor, and they often operate according to different 'missions'. Between the different func-

tional Councils of Ministers co-ordination is also poor, with different decisional rules, procedures etc.. The introduction of three different pillars of activity under the Maastricht Treaty introduced further differentiation into the policy rules.

- Inter-institutional rules have become increasingly complex. Voting rules depend on a legal base and political circumstance. In addition, resort to voting may simply form a last resort, with consensus being the preferred mode of decision-making. Where the EP's co-decision powers apply, complex games may be played between that institution and the Council. Alliance-building is potentially both inter-state and inter-institutional in character.

The way in which member governments respond to the policy-making challenges of EU membership follows no single pattern. While there is a common challenge posed by EU membership, the EU presents 'no single pattern of practices, style or culture likely to spread with increased inter-action' (Olsen, 1995: 25). In Johan Olsen's view national administrative diversity has co-existed with ever closer European political integration. This view is borne out by the findings of three surveys of member-state response to EU membership (Rometsch and Wessels, 1996; Hanf and Soetendorp, 1998; Wright, 1996). Rather than European integration prompting major convergence of governmental structures, it may simply be incorporated into the existing national structures. These national structures are deeply embedded, and the costs of organisational change may be high. European integration's diffuse and evolutionary character – i.e., across the totality of governmental institutions and over time – rarely triggers a critical moment at which to ask: 'are we effectively organised for pursuing national objectives in the EU?' Accession to the EC/EU might be one such critical moment. Major reform, such as the Maastricht Treaty, might be another. However, if these opportunities for change occur at inconvenient moments in domestic politics, they may not be opportunities at all.

A further factor that is particularly pertinent, especially to 'projection', is the congruence of national and EU institutions. If the rules and institutional models of the domestic political game are so distant from those operative in the EU, it may be particularly difficult to shape the institutional character of the latter in the EU's periodic reform debates. The degree of congruence reflects the EU's fit with national traditions of government. Congruence may reflect the extent to which a state has been able, through early membership and thereafter, to shape EU institutions. And it is this ability of member states to shape the EU which reveals the interactive nature of stimulus and response between the two levels of government.

Europeanisation and institutional change
The difficulty of pursuing an interactive approach in empirical analysis is one which rational choice institutionalists would quickly alert us to. If one direction of flow is not isolated, it is difficult to locate causality in a situation of circularity. Thus, in what follows we seek to understand the impact of membership of the EC/EU on the internal workings of member-state governments. However, we will make occasional contextual references to the flow from member-governments to the EU. In examining the impact of integration we adopt a historical institutionalist approach. In particular we draw out and develop three propositions.

First we hold, along with other historical institutionalists, that in settled and stable societies, pressures for change, whether generated externally or internally, usually lead to the adaptation of existing institutions rather than the creation of new ones (Thelen and Steinmo, 1992: 16–8; Skowronek, 1982: 12; Ikenberry, 1988: 194–5; March and Olsen, 1996: 256): *incremental change*. Significant transformations may occur, though these tend to be infrequent (Krasner, 1988; Collier and Collier, 1991): *radical change*. However, there is a third way of understanding change. That is when the outcomes of incremental change have accumulated and crystallised to such an extent that what has become established is something distinctly and qualitatively different from that which previously existed (see Bulmer and Burch, 1998; Thelen and Steinmo, 1992: 13–18): *incremental-transformative change*. We hold that while institutional change is usually incremental it is useful to distinguish moments of qualitative change within the incremental pattern.

Second, historical institutionalists also hold that institutions change not only in line with existing institutional formats, but that past choices also restrict subsequent actions (Armstrong and Bulmer, 1998: 55; Pierson, 1998). Change is thus often referred to as path-dependent in that initial choices determine later developments and once a particular pathway is selected alternatives tend to be ruled out thereafter. We are concerned to explore the extent to which institutional change has been path-dependent.

Third, like other historical institutionalists, we find it useful to concentrate on key points of institutional choice and change when departures are made from established patterns (Thelen and Steinmo, 1992: 27). These are the moments when new patterns and processes are set. Collier and Collier (1991: 29) use the term 'critical juncture' which they define 'as a period of significant change ... which is hypothesised to produce distinct legacies.' Indeed we go further, by distinguishing a critical moment from a critical juncture. A 'critical moment' is when an opportunity arises for significant change. Such opportunities may not be realised and exploited but, if they are, the outcome is a 'critical juncture' at which there is a clear departure from previously established patterns. Critical junctures create branching points at which institutional development moves on to a new trajectory or pathway which is then followed incrementally until a new critical moment arises and (potentially) a new critical juncture follows and a new direction is taken. In theory, at each critical moment the opportunities for institutional innovation are at their widest.

In the next part of the chapter we look at the experience of Germany and the UK, two large member states, and the impact of membership on government in each country. We provide a historical analysis of the ways both have adapted to EC/EU membership. We isolate the critical moments and junctures involved from the point of early engagement with the integration process through to the present day. In doing this we provide an indication of the manner in which, and of the pace at which, institutional components have emerged and the extent to which these conformed to a traditional, national format. To summarise our objective in terms of a hypothesis: it is that Europeanisation entails change at each of the four institutional levels identified earlier, as well as in the cultural dimension.

The development of European policy-making in Britain and Germany: initial observations

From the creation of the European Coal and Steel Community (ECSC) to the Amsterdam Treaty, the character of supranational governance has been in evolution: sometimes snail-like, sometimes much more rapid. Supranational competences have grown, as have the volume and complexity of policy activity. In line with our understanding of Europeanisation, so all member states have had to contend with growing demands upon their own response in terms of reception and projection.

Before detailed analysis we need to note the different circumstances in which governments in the two countries adapted to integration.

- (West) German participation in the integration process was as a founder member. The Federal Republic (FRG) had experienced twenty years of integration, from the ECSC onwards, before the UK acceded. Europeanisation of government in the FRG had a twenty-year head start.
- The circumstances of accession were quite different. The FRG was not a sovereign state and was able to gain sovereignty through the integration process.[5] It was also a new state: one which lacked embedded institutions because of the need to build a new political system in the post-war era. For the UK, by contrast, the voluntary surrender of national sovereignty as part of joining the EC created controversy that recurs to some degree with every step to deepen integration. The relationship of national sovereignty to European integration has worked in quite different ways in the two states.
- The political context has been quite different. In the FRG all the main

political parties had accommodated European integration by the early 1960s. In British politics European integration has been a 'poisoned chalice'. There have been persistent divisions on integration within the two main parties. Labour's policy has been contorted, favouring withdrawal in the early-1980s; the Conservatives have been more consistently supportive but of a limited form of integration.[6] The partypolitical debate on Europe has consequently had a quite different character in the two countries.

- The FRG is a federal state, while the UK was a unitary and centralised one until devolution came into effect in 1999. The FRG has been used to the vertical sharing of power in a federal system (and, for that matter, horizontal sharing within coalition governments), whereas both became features of the 'new Britain' from May 1999.

- The above circumstances have contributed to a situation where the FRG's governmental system tends towards consensus and co-operative federalism. Historically, the UK system has been directed more towards adversarialism and centralism. This contrast has considerable importance to the comparative congruence of the two states with the character of the EU.

United Kingdom

The UK approach to handling EC/EU business was established prior to entry in 1973. Indeed the origins of the British approach can be traced back at least as far as the first, failed, application for entry in 1961–63 when the rudiments of the structure which is now in operation were first brought into play. That centred on a tiered system of cabinet committees, one ministerial and two levels of official committees, which brought together and co-ordinated the business for negotiation across Whitehall; a co-ordinating responsibility (located in the Treasury); a staff carrying out the negotiations in Brussels supported by UKDel, the UK delegation to the Communities, but with close liaison back to the inter-departmental committees; and involvement of a high powered legal team (Tratt, 1996; Ludlow, 1997). The same structure emerged at the time of the second application to join in 1967 except that responsibility for the co-ordination of the UK approach was moved from the Treasury to a special unit or secretariat in the Cabinet Office[7]. Also, by this time the early manifestations of the pattern of intradepartmental organisation for Europe were beginning to emerge in those Departments most affected by EC membership: the Ministry of Agriculture, the Department of Trade, the Treasury and the Foreign Office.

After the negotiations were successfully completed, effectively by the summer of 1971, the government reviewed its approach to handling the EC. The approaches of other member states were investigated, with the French being judged to have the best model of co-ordination. Also examined was the possibility of creating a Ministry for Europe and, briefly, allowing the Foreign and Commonwealth Office (FCO) to take the lead on Community matters across Whitehall (Wallace and Wallace, 1973: 254). All these options were rejected and Prime Minister Heath laid down the dictum that 'Departments should think and act European'. He endorsed a system for handling business, in keeping with that used in the negotiations, which entailed co-ordination and light supervision by the Cabinet Office. The main change was in the purpose of the machinery which was now switched to deal with membership as opposed to entry. This led to some enhancement in the number of personnel involved, but the mechanisms and the approach were not substantially altered. Here was a critical moment, but not a critical juncture. The institutional format had already emerged and it was in keeping with UK traditions and not simply at the organisational level, for the procedures, processes and guidelines for handling business that were adopted, and later built on, were those operative in Whitehall. Even the underlying values whereby the system operated were traditional Whitehall ones reflecting established practices of departmental lead, tempered by the requirement of sharing information and decision-making across departments.[8]

How do developments since entry relate to the five institutional components or levels of analysis? Institutional development since 1973 can be summed up under the themes of expansion, refinement and disaggregation.

The basic structure and framework which emerged in the 1960s and was brought into play fully upon accession has been further developed at each level, but *systemic* adaptation has been confined to the constitutional-legal order and the modification of arrangements to reflect the devolution of power, introduced in 1999.

At the *organisational* level, expansion has taken place in the number of departments involved. This reflects an EC/EU effect but the response has been in keeping with Whitehall traditions. Nowadays every central government department is drawn into EU business to some extent and has developed some institutional capacity to handle it. This has involved growth in the network of participants throughout Whitehall who have access to the relevant information flows – principally the Cabinet Office and FCO networks – and who may, depending on the nature of the business, be drawn into the shaping of policy and negotiation stances. Coupled with growth there has been a gradual refinement of the offices and agencies involved in EU policy-making, especially the Cabinet Office Secretariat (COES), the UK Permanent Representation in Brussels (UKRep) and the FCO's European departments. As the network has expanded and business has become more complex so the system has become more disaggregated. Matters concerning the second and third pillars of the EU, the Common Foreign and Security Policy (CSFP) and

Justice and Home Affairs (JHA) co-operation, are nowadays developed within subsidiary networks centred on the FCO and Home Office respectively. Similarly, policy regarding EMU has tended to be centred on the Treasury.

At the *regulative and procedural* levels, refinement is also evident as the processes for handling business have been more fully developed, especially so as to ensure an agreed line to pursue in Brussels. Brought into play here have been a number of devices including a regular Friday morning meeting bringing together the heads of COES, FCO European divisions, the Permanent Representative and relevant officials from the departments to agree positions on items coming up on the EU agenda in the weeks ahead. Expansion and refinement are also evident in the gradual development of guidelines concerning the handling and financing of EU policy both at Whitehall level, by COES, and independently within the departments. A measure of dissaggregation is also evident in the extent to which an increasing volume of business is handled largely by the departments and directly out into Brussels.

The *cultural* dimension has been influenced by persistent political dispute over British sovereignty within the EU. On the one hand, there has been a gradual emergence of a substantial cadre of EU-aware officials who have been brought together through sharing a common task and, through training and practical experience, have developed appropriate skills and to some extent shared values about the nature and handling of European policy (Buller and Smith, 1998). On the other hand, the political climate has made a positive engagement with integration very intermittent. As a consequence, the defining attitudes have been less concerned with adapting Whitehall to the EU than with adapting EU business to fit traditional Whitehall methods of operation.

The pivotal positions on the official side in the contemporary UK approach to handling EU matters in general are centred on COES, the three European sections of the FCO and UKRep. Also important are personnel in the Prime Minister's Office, and the relevant European sections of the Treasury, the Department of Trade and Industry (DTI) and the Ministry of Agriculture Fisheries and Food (MAFF). In particular the head of COES, the European Director in the FCO and the Permanent Representative constitute what is sometimes referred to as the 'Troika'. In ensuring the formulation of a consistent Whitehall response to the EU, COES is central. Its head is in effect adviser to the Prime Minster on European matters and the nine senior staff in the secretariat have co-ordination, monitoring and policy galvanising functions. Notably the staff is as small as it always has been (Bender, 1991). Key players at ministerial level are the Prime Minister and Foreign Secretary, the latter having the lead on EU institutional matters and the chair of the cabinet's ministerial committee on European issues ((E)DOP), which may occasionally feed up to the Defence and Overseas Policy (DOP) committee, chaired by the Prime Minister, or to Cabinet itself. Beneath this hierarchy of ministerial committees is the two-tiered system of official committees – designated EQS and EQO (though the former has fallen into infrequent use – since 1997 under the designation EQO*), and occasional ad hoc committees set up to deal with a particular issue. All these committees are serviced by the Cabinet Office (Bulmer and Burch, 1998). In order to understand how the system works it is essential to note that these formal devices are under-pinned by a great deal of informal contact. Nearly all the principal players are located within easy walking distance of each other, personal contact is frequent – a very evident feature of the characteristic Whitehall 'village' approach to politics (Heclo and Wildavsky, 1974: 8–11; Bruce-Gardyne, 1986: 2–4).

What are the key characteristics of the Whitehall system of making European policy? Principal amongst them is the highly co-ordinated approach. EU business has become so diverse since 1973 that it is difficult to have a central channel of communication between Brussels and London at both reception and projection stages of the policy cycle. Thus, much business is handled within the relevant lead-ministry, and at the lowest possible level. However, informal arrangements – at the procedural and regulative levels – exist to co-ordinate policy where it cuts across depart-mental responsibilities. When combined with the strong Whitehall culture of sharing information, the system offers strong support to ensure that UK officials and ministers 'sing from the same hymn sheet'. On cross-cutting matters of European policy the COES sees its mission as ensuring that government usually reaches an early agreed position – before engaging with negotiations in the EU – even though the co-ordinating machinery itself appears to be under-resourced. This well established practice of sharing information across departments and with the central machinery is the key to the operation of the system. However, the co-ordinated approach comes at a cost. It risks inflexibility at later stages of EU policy-making, a situation that has been exacerbated when governments have pursued an inflexible political approach to European policy, most notably with John Major's non-co-operation policy in 1996 over the ban on British beef exports. The approach reflects a long-standing culture of centralism in the British state. It is also better attuned to the reception of EU policy in Whitehall than to the effective pursuit of British policy in the EU, where greater adaptation to the norms of the EU would have to predominate over the present, Whitehall-dominated culture of the system.[9]

As the reference to John Major's government highlights, however, our concentration on the administrative arrangements in Whitehall must be linked with two other problematic aspects of EU policy-making. First, the fraught political circumstances have often hampered the UK from making a positive contribution to the EU. An effective administrative operation needs some direction. As one senior civil servant put it to us, 'there is no point having a Rolls Royce machinery if the driver's a lunatic.' It has arguably only been during Mrs Thatcher's middle phase as prime minister, when she was advocating neoliberal economic integration through the single market programme, and more recently under Tony Blair, that such direction has been provided. Secondly, the matter of congruence is pertinent as the UK has constitutional and legal traditions, which are quite distinct from the 'continental' traditions of the founder member states. Consequently, the fit between the UK and the EU is particularly poor.

Overall, since 1973 expansion, refinement and disaggregation have made the Whitehall system larger, more complex and less focused. What has taken place is a deepening institutionalisation on the basis of the structure which emerged prior to entry and in keeping with traditional Whitehall approaches and administrative values. If there was a critical juncture, it can be traced back to the first set of negotiations, i.e., twenty years before membership. In terms of our hypothesis, therefore, Europeanisation has resulted in change across all five institutional dimensions. However, for much of the period since 1973, the contested political nature of European integration has hampered government officials' ability effectively to project British interests at the supranational level.

Federal Republic of Germany

The handling of European policy within the German government has had a quite different history. The two most critical junctures concerning the handling of business came at the outset of integration and then with the Maastricht Treaty. For the FRG, established only in 1949, the political system was new. Owing to limits on sovereignty there was no separate foreign minister until 1955, and the Foreign Office had only been established in March 1951 (Taussig, 1970; Bulmer, 1986: 55).[10] How was the creation of the ECSC handled? Politically, Chancellor Adenauer provided the foreign-policy lead, while the Federal Ministry for Economics (BMWi), under Ludwig Erhard, was in charge of the essentially economic substance.[11] It was decided in 1951 to set up in the BMWi a sub-division for handling ECSC business.[12] Subsequently, the Interministerial Committee for ECSC Affairs was established, chaired by the BMWi. Its purpose was to co-ordinate with other ministries – notably the Foreign Office (AA) and the Federal Finance Ministry (BMF) – ahead of intergovernmental meetings of the ECSC in Luxembourg.

Although 1951 was a critical juncture in giving the BMWi an unparalleled centrality in European policy co-ordination, no formal decision had been taken. With the widening of integration to the European Economic Community and the European Atomic Energy Community, formal arrangements were needed. Adenauer exercised his chancellorial powers to set policy guidelines but Erhard was also a formidable force, with the Foreign Minister, von Brentano, seeking to stake a claim for the AA. Disagreements between Adenauer's political and Erhard's trade-oriented views of integration were intense (Koerfer, 1988; Nicholls, 1994: 343–6). Formal resolution came in 1958; Adenauer's policy views prevailed but the BMWi was entrusted with the co-ordination of day-to-day policy, including the chairing of inter-ministerial committees (Koerfer, 1988; Hesse and Goetz, 1992). The BMWi set up a full European Division for these tasks.[13] The AA was assigned responsibility only for integration policy. In effect other federal ministries would take charge of EC business according to their domestic responsibilities. The 1958 decision may be seen as a critical moment but the division of responsibilities was largely in keeping with the ad hoc arrangements of 1951.

A number of further characteristics deriving from wider institutional and normative aspects of German politics deserve attention. First, chancellors set policy guidelines and they may place a very high priority on European policy, as was the case with Adenauer and Kohl. The Chancellor's Office has a small staff monitoring European policy, reinforced by the establishment of the European Council in 1974. Second, all post-war governments have been coalitions. Ministerial positions are shared between coalition partners. Some empire-building may ensue, including over European policy. For instance, coalition agreements of an inter-party nature settle policy lines, including over Europe, and are held outside the governmental machinery. Senior officials may be party-political appointments, made by 'their' minister. Third, ministerial autonomy is a constitutional principle (Article 65). Sectorisation is strong in German European policy; a reflection of circumstances generally within the federal government. Collective cabinet government and information-sharing are weak; departmental norms prevail over collective ones. Fourth, the Federal Bank has been independent since its creation in 1957. Until the advent of the single currency it had autonomy over important aspects of European monetary policy. Fifth, it is worth noting that any federal election or new federal coalition accord, particularly with a change of coalition partners, is a critical moment in the handling of European policy. At the time of the federal election in 1994, for example, the Social Democrats gave a strong indication that they would create a ministry for Europe, but Chancellor Kohl was re-elected. However, with the election of a Red-Green coalition in 1998 the change of government led not only to a critical moment, but also to a critical juncture, in EU policy-making – see below.

From the 1950s to the 1990s the early organisational principles of handling European policy developed incrementally as the scope of European business gradually extended across the whole of the federal government by the time of the Maastricht Treaty, but four ministries

(BMWi, AA, BMF and the Federal Ministry for Food, Agriculture and Forestry (BML) were the most affected. There had also been a creeping impact upon the Länder. Unlike earlier, more incremental developments from the European level, this treaty prompted a second critical juncture, largely characterised by new constitutional provisions for consulting Länder governments (Article 23, Basic Law) and the Bundestag (Article 45) but accompanied by others.[14] The principal changes were in three areas. First, the Maastricht Treaty's creation of JHA co-operation increased the number of affected Departments to include the federal interior and justice ministries, as well as authorities in the Länder. Second, prompted by the Maastricht Treaty, including its aim to upgrade foreign policy co-ordination in the post-Cold War era, the AA set up a new European Division. Previously European business – apart from foreign policy co-operation – had been located in the Foreign Economic Policy Division. Third, the widening of EC/EU activity had a profound impact on the federal system, with the Länder governments facing an uphill task to get their views articulated in Brussels, where *federal* government negotiators held a privileged position. The Maastricht Treaty gave the Länder governments the opportunity to demand better consultation with Bonn as a condition of their ratification in the Bundesrat (Knodt, 1998). The critical juncture was embodied in the wider revision of the German Basic Law subsequent to German re-unification. Also included in the reform was the creation of a European Committee in the Bundestag, designed to give better machinery for parliamentary scrutiny of EU policy.

The arrival in office of Gerhard Schröder's Red–Green coalition in autumn 1998 prompted a further major change to European policy machinery, confined to within the federal government. The cause on this occasion did not emanate from Brussels but rather from the dynamics of the coalition agreement. The coalition negotiations were heavily influenced by Oskar Lafontaine, in his capacity as Social Democrat party chairman. As part of his wish to secure a portfolio of policy responsibilities to match his seniority, he had the co-ordination responsibilities of the BMWi's European Division transferred to the Finance Ministry, where he would be minister. As part of the deal the AA took over the chairing of key co-ordinating committees, again at the cost of the BMWi. Given the patterns of sectorisation within the federal government, the question was raised as to whether the new arrangements, combined with Lafontaine's political clout, would further weaken the coherence of German European policy. In the event his resignation in March 1999 defused this concern, but his enduring legacy is the new shape of the machinery arising from the critical juncture of 1998.

How do these developments coincide with the five institutional components of analysis? At the *systemic* level it is central to note that European integration went hand-in-hand with the foundation of the FRG.

Integration was factored into German constitutional development, and clashes of a constitutional nature have been infrequent and confined to the juridical sphere and relations with the Länder. The German constitution was Europeanised in its infancy (see also Goetz, 1995).

The horizontal *organisational* principles concerning the federal government's handling of European policy were formally defined in 1958. The new relationship between the federal and Länder governments was formalised after the Maastricht Treaty. And the Finance Ministry's new role was agreed in 1998. At the *regulative* and *procedural* levels the arrangements are a mixture of the old and the new. Since late-1998 the BMF and the AA share the co-ordinating functions. In practice other ministries and the Länder have independent sources of information from Brussels and are responsible for policy on their own 'turf'.

Finally, as regards the *cultural* dimension it is important to note that the strong elite consensus on integration within the FRG has facilitated Europeanisation. However, this consensus has had to compete with notions of 'house policies' (Ressortpolitik) and a culture of legalism that have often resulted in poor projection of German European policy in Brussels.

In contemporary Germany two federal ministries are involved in co-ordination. The AA is responsible for issues of integration (e.g., institutional developments, IGCs, Agenda 2000); the CFSP; foreign trade; and chairing the Committee of State Secretaries for European Affairs, at state/permanent secretary level. The last of these functions has been conducted by a junior AA minister with responsibility for European policy, a post dating from 1972. The BMF also has co-ordinating functions, including sharing with the AA the preparation of the Committee of Permanent Representatives (COREPER), liaison with the Bundesrat and the Länder. In addition, it has key functional responsibilities, especially for the EC budget. Finally, the Federal Chancellor's Office (BKA) has been involved from the ECSC onwards. Its European policy staff was expanded under Kohl, assisting his strong input into the Maastricht Treaty preparations (Gaddum, 1994: 73–4). The BKA's involvement is dependent on the individual chancellor's commitment to European policy. The FRG has a much weaker cabinet committee system than the UK. A committee for European policy was initially used by Kohl but was abolished by the Schröder government, with informal meetings or full Cabinet the preferred means of co-ordination at this level.

These and the other ministries are involved in the reception and projection roles. The tendency is to receive and process EU-sourced material within individual ministries until an EU decision is imminent, whereupon reconciliation of ministerial views begins in earnest. Lack of early co-ordination, to the embarrassment of the Permanent Representation (StV), is often very apparent at the projection stage, such as in Council working groups. Until 1998, and in line with the peculiar history of co-ordination in Germany, the StV, an embassy, formally received instructions from both the BMWi and the AA (Hoyer, 1998: 79). Since 1998 the StV is given instructions by either the AA or the BMF according to the formation of COREPER.[15] Unlike in the UK the Permanent Representative only infrequently attends inter-ministerial meetings in Bonn, and is less of a key player in formulating strategy. However, where a chancellor seizes a European initiative there is considerable scope within the BKA and the AA to develop influential policy ideas, backed up by supportive elite and public opinion.

Overall, the German federal government's handling of routine European policy is de-concentrated, handled by specialist officials, with inter-ministerial co-ordination occurring late.[16] This situation has the disadvantage of discordant German positions in Brussels but the advantage of flexibility in endgame negotiations. One German diplomat characterised his country's approach in terms of dependability, reliability and stability (Trumpf, 1988). Academic commentators have been more critical, suggesting – before the coalition change in autumn 1998 – various reforms designed to make Germany more effective (Bulmer, Jeffery and Paterson, 1998; Janning and Meyer, 1998). What is clear is that Germany is very effective in two respects: projecting ideas into the EU arena; and exporting its domestic institutional arrangements, like the Bundesbank, to the EU level. In these respects it is helped by a high level of institutional congruence with the EU (see Bulmer, 1997). Thus, European integration has brought change in all five institutional dimensions but the pattern of institutional adaptation has been quite different from that experienced in Whitehall.

Conclusions

We set out to show how historical institutionalism could help explain the response of national governmental systems to the common challenge of EU membership. By way of conclusion we summarise our empirical findings and then consider how they fit in with institutionalist analysis.

At a general level, we established that Europeanisation resulted in change in all five institutional dimensions. Our more detailed empirical findings concern three areas: the contrasting responses in the two states; the significance of the contrasts; and how they demonstrate different understandings of being effective in Brussels. In the first of the three, we have shown that the responses of British central government and of the German federal government to the common challenge of EU membership have been quite different. In both states Europeanisation has been compatible with resilient national traditions of government.

Second, looking beyond the causality of Europeanisation of the two member governments, these differences matter. They are significant, since the institutional arrangements in the two states affect the patterns and effectiveness of their EU diplomacy. For British governments, the highly co-ordinated arrangements in Whitehall have reinforced a policy where London has often been at odds with its EU partners. Whether the European policy machinery can be as effective in pursuing a policy of strategic engagement with the European idea remains largely unproved, although Tony Blair's European policy may provide evidence over the longer term. What is clear is that the UK's influence on the shape of the EU at the projection stage has been hampered by: the need to attend to the divisiveness of integration in British party politics; the political resistance to Europeanisation on the part of some ministers; and the lack of institutional congruence with both the continental mainstream and the EU itself. For German elites, by contrast, the normative commitment to integration came hand-in-hand with the establishment of the Bonn Republic: a point at which Germany was much more open to Europeanisation than the UK has ever been. Thus, finding European solutions to troublesome policy problems has provided opportunities for successive chancellors and foreign ministers, together with their officials, to place their imprimatur on integration. German institutional export, whether of central banking arrangements or of patterns of multi-level governance, has been a striking feature of European integration. On some of the less glamorous policy decisions, by contrast, Bonn has been at sixes and sevens. German efforts to reduce budgetary contributions during the Schmidt and Kohl chancellorships often foundered on the resistance of its own agriculture ministry. Strikingly, it was Chancellor Schröder who ensured greater consistency between these policies in his negotiating approach to the Agenda 2000 reforms by pursuing a policy couched more in terms of national interests.

For both Whitehall and the German federal government Europeanisation has followed a similar course with the incremental development of integration. However, the critical junctures have instilled quite different dispositions in the respective machineries. These dispositions can help us with the conundrum of evaluating national EU policy machineries: which model is best? Does co-ordination matter? Yes, but not as much as is often thought in Whitehall. It is most effective where a defensive policy is being pursued under conditions of unanimity in the Council. Can an approach giving greater priority to the strategy of integration make a successful European policy? Yes, but only on key decisions relating to the EU's development. In fact, these decisions may be highly visible but they represent only a small part of EU decision-making. Thus, some balance is needed between tactical co-ordination and a strategic approach. And history is important here. The UK's difficulty with developing a strategy towards integration has derived from the failure to embrace a new, regional, political role in the post-war era. Its centralised policy machinery seems better suited to an external relations context of realism, and an internal context of centralism. We suggest that the Blair government is addressing both these contexts by pursuing a more European strategy externally, and with its constitutional reforms, notably devolution. We would also suggest that devolution is likely to lead to major change – most likely a critical juncture – in the formulation of UK European policy (see Bulmer and Burch 1998). By contrast with the UK, the horizontal and vertical decentralisation of European policy responsibilities in Bonn/Berlin are the product of deliberate institutional design of the FRG to avoid the overt pursuit of national interests following the excesses of the Third Reich. This diffusion of power seems more attuned to the post-Westphalian world of the EU and a pattern of multi-level governance.

What are the analytical insights offered by institutionalism?

- In our analysis of German and UK responses to Europeanisation we have argued that historical and cultural context matter. The design of central government institutions for handling European policy has been strongly influenced by these circumstances: so much so that we believe they must be regarded as endogenous to the explanation. The 1971 review of European policy-making in the EC rejected the more centralised French approach because it did not fit in with the traditional institutional patterns and norms within British government. In the FRG, by contrast, such institutional traditions had not developed so strongly but the dispersal of executive power was a key characteristic of the Basic Law. In addition, the arrangements for the ECSC reflected much more the politics of the situation, i.e., Adenauer's relations with Erhard, and the weakness of the AA because of semi-sovereignty. The legacies of these early institutional choices are still evident today. In this sense our analysis takes account of longer-term institutional trends and the cultural dimension in a way which would pose problems for rational choice institutionalists.
- We have tried to offer a way of categorising institutional change in EU member-state relations: as incremental, radical or incremental-transformative. In our two cases Europeanisation has never engendered radical change; rather, it has been incremental. However, over time it has *transformed* the character of government both in Bonn/Berlin and Whitehall. In that sense the experiences display similarities. For example, Wessels estimates that some 40 per cent of higher civil servants from the German federal government are 'directly . . . involved in one segment or other of EU policy cycles as part of their everyday duties' (Wessels, 1997: 281). Our own research on Britain indicates that the official-level policy community on EU business is more extensive than any other in Whitehall, with an exceptional number of

horizontal connections. Over the longer term the impact of European integration has been incremental-transformative in nature. If change has been incremental or incremental-transformative, this finding suggests that 'snapshot' analyses of the impact of Europeanisation may not identify underlying trends that solidify over time in an accretive manner. We would argue that the typical case-study methodology of historical institutionalism is well placed to identify these trends.

- We have also tried to depart from the often deterministic character of historical institutionalism by addressing the circumstances under which change takes place. Institutional change does occur! It happens most obviously at the branching points associated with critical junctures. Our empirical work has suggested several conditions where critical junctures may occur in institutional design: at times of major European policy change; as a response to step-changes in European integration; in connection with a domestic government or coalition change; and – more speculatively – as a result of domestic constitutional reform.[17] Critical junctures alter the disposition of institutions and an interesting test for this will be the German Finance Ministry's new role. Will it accelerate the end to German cheque-book diplomacy in the EU? These findings also indicate that wider contextual circumstances are of crucial importance: critical junctures are not simply consequent upon Europeanisation and may thus present a challenge for rationalist analyses.

- The new institutionalism's contribution to political science has been to seek to depart from mere configurative studies of the polity to include 'softer' aspects of institutions. In our fivefold disaggregation of institutions – into their systemic, organisational, regulative, procedural and cultural components – we have suggested a possible taxonomy for use in measuring gradations of institutional change.

- Our empirical findings have highlighted one of the characteristic findings of historical institutionalism. Both machineries of policy-making reveal weaknesses, although they also both reveal strengths. Where the German weakness is on the tactical side, the British weakness is on strategy. Our historical institutionalist insight is to highlight the predominance of historical inefficiencies of institutional evolution over rational institutional designs geared to maximising governmental interests in the EU. But we recognise that there is an alternative, rationalist explanation. It is that the contrasting systems are efficient in the sense that they have kept the costs of domestic adjustment to Europeanisation low. The different national patterns of government have simply provided 'translator devices', appropriate to their national context, for managing the European dimension of policy.[18]

- Finally, our findings included a strong cultural component. This represents a point of contact with sociological institutionalists. They would doubtless wish to give greater stress to the cognitive and cultural – to the culture and belief-systems of post-war elites in the two states and the embeddedness in these of the institutional arrangements.

Notes

1   This chapter is based upon empirical research funded by the UK Economic and Social Research Council under its Whitehall programme, award no. L 124251001. We are grateful to the ESRC for financial support, and to the serving and retired officials and politicians who were willing to be interviewed (on a non-attributable basis). We are also grateful for their comments to the editors, other project participants, including Philipp Genschel who acted as conference discussant, and to Andreas Maurer for information on the 1998 changes in German arrangements.

2   We will note those areas of our analysis that are amenable to sociological institutionalism.

3   This observation is one which might be shared with sociological institutionalists.

4   This agency–structure relationship suggests a structurationist conception of EU member-state relations: both levels of institution matter but our analytical efforts are devoted preponderantly towards the member states. On structuration, see Giddens (1984).

5   Specifically, it gained sovereignty over its coal and steel industries, previously under allied control.

6   For more on this complex story, see Baker and Seawright (1998).

7   This reflected general changes in the distribution of co-ordination responsibilities in Whitehall which took place throughout the 1960s, this change was UK and not European driven (see Lee, 1990; Burch and Holliday, 1996: 22).

8   These practices derive from the central constitutional conventions of individual and collective responsibility both of which emerged in the nineteenth century (see Marshall, 1989: 1–13; Burch and Holliday, 1996: 51–2).

9   We should emphasise that this observation is a generalisation. In some policy areas, such as the internal market, the British have been effective operators in the Brussels system.

10 Chancellor Konrad Adenauer also took responsibility for foreign affairs.

11 A Schuman Plan Secretariat was created in the Chancellor's Office during negotiations ahead of the ECSC (Hesse and Goetz, 1992: 186).

12 The ECSC came into being in July 1952, the product of the Schuman Plan of May 1950. The Treaty establishing the ECSC was signed in 1951.

13 This was reportedly the decision of second state (permanent) secretary, Müller-Armack, who wished to strengthen his position in the BMWi (Taussig, 1970: 61).

14 The 1986 SEA largely expanded existing policy provisions or codified them. Only for the Länder governments were there major changes, and largely through confirming transfers of power. The SEA was a critical moment but, because the Länder chose not to demand constitutional reform, it did not amount to a critical juncture.

15 Meetings of COREPER II to service the General Affairs and Development
    Councils, are prepared under Foreign Ministry responsibility for co-ordina-
    tion and sending instructions. For COREPER II, which services all other
    formations of the Council, and for COREPER II meetings preparing Budget
    and Ecofin Councils, the Finance Ministry plays these two roles. This agree-
    ment was confirmed in December 1998.

16 There is also the need in several policy areas to co-ordinate with representa-
    tives of the Länder governments, which are also key players not examined in
    detail here.

17 This observation is on the presumption that devolution in the UK has the
    consequence of placing some limits on the UK's government's traditional
    ability to pursue a highly co-ordinated EU policy in the way we expect it to.

18 We are grateful to Philipp Genschel for this observation.

Philipp Genschel[1]

Comment: 'The "Europeanisation" of central government'

The core of the historical institutionalism is the idea of 'institutional friction' (March and Olsen, 1989: 106). Institutions, according to this idea, are inert, rigid and change-resistant. They tend to preserve their shape in the face of fluidity. They stay in place when everything else disappears. They impose continuity and structure on a constantly changing world and, thus, bring the past to bear on the present. Old institutions survive even though they do not fit present conditions, cross-national differences persist despite common challenges.

Simon Bulmer's and Martin Burch's chapter on 'The "Europeanisation" of central government' is firmly in this intellectual tradition. It asks why the process of European integration has not led to dramatic changes in the structures and processes of national governments and, more specifically, in the administrative structures and processes which handle European affairs. 'Given that member states have been subject to similar pressures, why has there not been a convergence in governmental systems?' For the historical institutionalist, the answer is obvious. It lies in 'the resilience and adaptability of national institutions'. The chapter develops this answer in fascinating terminological twists and theoretical diversions on the basis of very rich empirical observations. I cannot possibly do justice to the complexity of the argument here nor to the empirical wealth the authors manage to assemble. I will therefore limit my comments to two fundamental theoretical issues that are raised in this chapter as well as the broader literature it represents. I will question the standard against which the process of institutional adjustment is evaluated and discuss the theory of institutional change, which informs the analysis.

Why expect convergence?

The chapter starts from a prediction that historical institutionalists love to disprove: similar external pressures lead to similar institutional responses. Given that the process of European integration presents all member states with the same challenge, should there not be a convergence of 'how governments handle European policy'? The premise sounds intuitive, but is it also true? There are at least three reasons to believe that it may not be.

First, the premise implies that for every external challenge there is only one best institutional response. Yet, in many instances there may be a range of alternative structures which can deal with a given challenge equally well. As it is well known from systems theory and comparative research, similar external demands often result in dissimilar, but 'functionally equivalent' structures.[2] Hence, even if institutional change was instantaneous, frictionless and efficient, there is no reason to assume that the same external pressure – European integration – will result in institutional convergence – the same set up of government institutions for the handling of European affairs.

Second, the premise assumes that the best response – or set of best responses – to a common external challenge is the same across member states and that therefore convergence would be efficient. However, there is reason to believe that convergence would be inefficient. Indeed, efficiency may require the preservation of diversity. As Bulmer and Burch show, the government institutions for the handling of European policy have the character of translator devices: they translate EU requirements into domestic laws and regulations in order to make domestic policy compatible with EU policy, and they translate domestic policy models into proposals for EU action in order to keep the costs of domestic adjustment low. While it is true that, at the European end, all these translator devices speak the same 'language' – the language of the EC legal and institutional system – the same is not true at the domestic end. Here, the British translator has to speak the language of a unitary regime with a first-past-the-post system, while its German counterpart has to speak the language of a federal regime with proportional representation, etc.. It is hard to believe that efficiency would be enhanced if the various country-specific translator institutions were replaced by a uniform Euro-translator, which speaks the average of all national political idioms. Hence, the finding that European integration did not prompt a 'major convergence of governmental structures' but was simply 'incorporated into the existing national structures' does not necessarily prove that national structures are deeply embedded and difficult to change. Preserving diversity may simply have been the most efficient way to adapt to European integration.

Third, the premise supposes that the structures of national governments were actually under adaptive pressure. However, the evidence presented in the chapter suggests that the challenge of integration was mild at best, or even non-existent. As Bulmer and Burch show, a country with a fairly poor administrative apparatus for handling European affairs – Germany – consistently outperformed a country with a comparatively well-organised apparatus – the UK – in the Brussels negotiation arena. Apparently, the internal organisation of government was largely irrelevant for the external negotiation success. Yet, if the organisation of government is irrelevant to how a country fares under integration, why expect that country to adjust?

Institutional change

The chapter is also true to the historical institutionalist gospel in framing its analysis in terms of Stephen Krasner's (1988), by now classical, model of discontinuous institutional change: 'In settled and stable societies, pressures for change . . . usually lead to the adaptation of existing institutions rather than the creation of new ones . . . Significant transformations may occur, though these tend to be infrequent: radical change'. Institutions create order, the increasing returns to order induce institutional inertia and institutional inertia, in turn, produces an ever increasing mismatch with a changing environment until a 'critical moment' of historical crisis and drama offers the opportunity to shake off the institutional past: a 'critical juncture'. Implicit in this imagery of discontinuous change is the assumption that an efficient adjustment to new circumstances requires new institutions, i.e., radical change, whereas attempts to deal with them on the basis of old institutions, incremental change, is a comparatively less efficient fall-back option. Again, I find this assumption not very plausible.[3] The effect of institutions is more ambiguous than this assumption seems to appreciate. Bulmer and Burch focus almost exclusively on the constraining effects of institutions, as indeed most historical institutionalists do. Institutions are conceived of as restrictions on actors' opportunity sets, as media through which 'past choices . . . restrict subsequent actions'. This is, no doubt, true. Institutions limit choice sets. But what tends to get lost from sight is that these limits may have a very liberating and enabling effect on actors: they reduce the number of options that actors have to reckon with and thus help them to act in complex environments; they provide typified accounts of decisions and decision contexts, which make it easier for them to decipher the world and decide how to relate to it; they supply identities and second-order preferences which assist actors in defining who they are, what they want and what is appropriate for them to do; they reduce behavioural uncertainty and increase the chances of successful co-ordination; they hold certain factors constant in the flow of events and in this way allow for social learning.

The two faces of institutions – constraint and enablement – imply that both modes of institutional change – radical change during times of historical crisis and incremental change during times of normal history – are mixed blessings for institutional innovation. The 'advantage' of historical drama is that it offers the opportunity to replace old institutional constraints with new ones which are better or even optimally adapted to prevailing circumstances. However, the actors have to perform this act of large-scale social choice without the institutional enablement, which the broken-down institutional structure used to provide. Without institutional support, they suffer from confusion, behavioural uncertainty and insecurity as to what their preferences should be. Chances that they will be able to engineer an optimal collective choice process in this frame of mind seem rather low. Tellingly, the main concern during times of crisis is usually stability, not optimality. Almost any 'lock-in' is better than the fluidity of a 'non-locked-in' situation. Only when a new order stabilises, the emotional dust of the institutional disruption settles and society returns to normal history, can optimisation start again. Room for Pareto-improvements becomes identifiable, controlled experimentation with different institutional forms becomes feasible, etc.. The unspectacular process of incremental improvements sets in. However, this process of optimising depends on institutional inertia and institutional inertia, in turn, may prevent perfect adjustment. But this seems unavoidable. It may be the price of intelligent adjustment.

In short, there are costs and benefits attached to being locked-in to a given institutional structure – many constraints but also a lot of enable-ment – and there are costs and benefits attached to not being locked-in to any institutional structure – no constraints but also no enablement. Just comparing the costs of lock-in to the benefits of not being locked-in, as the Krasner model implicitly does, produces a lopsided picture of reality. It comes close to what Harold Demsetz called the 'Nirvana approach' (Demsetz, 1969): the real world is pitted against an unattainable ideal and then found deficient.

Notes

1 I thank Susanne Schmidt for helpful comments.
2 See, e.g., Luhmann (1962) on functional equivalence, and Ragin (1987) on causal complexity.
3 The following argument is based on Genschel (1997) and Lanzara (1998).

The Treaty of Amsterdam and the co-decision procedure

In June 1997 EU government leaders agreed to yet another round of EU treaty changes and approved the Treaty of Amsterdam. Even though the Treaty is considered by some as only a minor step toward further European integration, it contains once again a number of important institutional changes.[1] In particular, it alters the co-decision procedure, which was introduced by the Treaty of Maastricht (1992).[2]

The co-decision procedure intended to give the European Parliament (EP) a more important role in the EU legislative process. It provided for negotiations between the EP and the Council in case they approved different versions of a proposal. Crombez (1997a) concluded that the EP became a legislator equal in stature to the Council under co-decision. The EP (European Parliament 1992) claimed, however, that the procedure failed to provide for real co-decision 'since the Council [was] allowed to act unilaterally in the absence of an agreement' with the EP.

The EP's conclusions were echoed in the literature. Curtin (1993) found that 'the effective balance of power [was] indisputably weighed towards the Council.' Garrett (1996) and Tsebelis (1997) concluded that the co-decision procedure stripped the EP of the conditional agenda setting powers it enjoyed under the co-operation procedure. Steunenberg (1994) claimed that the co-decision procedure did not really increase the EP's powers.

The Treaty of Amsterdam alters the co-decision procedure to meet this type of criticism. In general, the institutional changes provided for in the Treaty seek to render EU decision-making more democratic and less complex. The reform of co-decision can be interpreted in that light. It emerged from negotiations that took place over the course of several years both among and within the EP, the Council and the Commission, and is essentially consistent with the EP's demands. In this chapter I show, however, that, rather than increasing the EP's power, the new procedure renders the Commission irrelevant, threatens to increase indecision (the

EU's inability to act) and may actually reduce the EP's power (its ability to obtain a policy that is close to its ideal policy).[3]

This chapter presents spatial models of co-decision in the EU. Alternative EU policies are represented by points in a policy space and policy-makers are assumed to have preferences over these points. The countries, Members of the European Parliament (MEPs) and Commissioners have complete and perfect information. The models yield equilibrium policies as functions of the countries', MEPs' and Commissioners' preferences, and the location of the status quo. I present unidimensional and multidimensional models of the old and new co-decision procedures, i.e., the procedure that was used before the Treaty of Amsterdam went into effect on 1 May, 1999, and the procedure that is being used today.[4]

In the next section I summarise the principal conclusions of the literature on spatial models of the EU institutions and legislative process.[5] The third section introduces the models analysed in this chapter. The fourth section studies the old co-decision procedure. It characterises equilibrium EU policies and sets of successful proposals under the old co-decision procedure, i.e., sets of policies the Commission can successfully propose. In the fifth section I analyse the new co-decision procedure. I characterise equilibrium EU policies and sets of successful joint texts, i.e., sets of policies the Council and EP Presidents can successfully propose. The sixth section presents the conclusions.

The conclusions of the models can be summarised as follows. I find that under the old co-decision procedure the Commission successfully proposes the policy it prefers most among the policies that satisfy the following two conditions: (1) the EP and a qualified majority in the Council prefer it to the status quo; and, (2) no policy is preferred to it by the EP and a qualified majority in the Council.[6] Furthermore, I show that the EP becomes a genuine co-legislator with the Council, and that the Commission has substantial agenda-setting powers under the old co-decision procedure.

By contrast, I conclude that the Commission's role is irrelevant under the new co-decision procedure. Under that procedure the EP and the Council, rather than the Commission, choose the EU policy by approving a joint text in the Conciliation Committee. The Commission plays no formal role in the committee, however, and its original proposal does not serve as the reversion policy. I also conclude that the changes to the co-decision procedure may weaken the EP's power. Furthermore, I show that the new co-decision procedure threatens to increase indecision in the EU.

Spatial models of the EU legislative process

In spatial models of political institutions and legislative procedures alternative policies are represented by points in a policy space. Each dimension of the policy space stands for a specific policy issue. The relevant political actors have preferences over alternative policies. Often, they are assumed to have Euclidean preferences. That is, each political actor has an ideal policy and prefers policies that are closer to, rather than farther away from, his ideal policy. Policy-making can then be thought of as choosing a point in the policy space.

Black (1958) presents an early spatial model. He shows that majority rule leads to an equilibrium outcome, if the political actors (1) have Euclidean preferences, (2) are deciding on a single issue and (3) can freely amend any proposals that are being made. The equilibrium outcome is the median voter's ideal policy. The median voter and all voters on her left (right) prefer the median voter's ideal policy to any policy right (left) of it. Under majority rule the median voter's ideal policy thus defeats any other policy in a pairwise comparison. If there are no restrictions on amendment rights, the median voter proposes her ideal policy and it becomes the equilibrium outcome.

If political actors consider multiple policy issues, however, majority rule yields equilibrium outcomes only under extreme circumstances. McKelvey (1976) shows that the use of majority rule in a multidimensional setting can lead to any outcome, except if a particular point in the policy space is the median in each direction. In this context the role of political institutions and procedures consists of providing stability, i.e., ensuring that an equilibrium outcome exists.

Spatial models analyse the impact of institutions and procedures on policy choices. They have been used extensively since the late 1970s to study the institutions of the United States government.[7] They examine, for example, the effects of proposal, amendment and veto rights on policy outcomes. Spatial models of the EU institutions and legislative procedures were introduced in the early 1990s. The models formulate conclusions in terms of equilibrium EU policies, and these policies depend on the preferences of the Commission, the Parliament and the countries and the location of the status quo.

Garrett (1992) offers an early spatial analysis of institutional change during the 1980s. In particular, he studies the introduction of qualified majority voting in the Council and the approval of the internal market programme, and finds that the new institutional arrangement reflects France and Germany's preferences, because their ideal policies are centrally located and because they have advantageous bargaining positions.

In another early model Tsebelis (1994) analyses the last steps of the co-operation procedure and finds that the EP has important powers, which he refers to as 'conditional agenda-setting' powers. According to him the EP can set the agenda under co-operation. This gives the EP considerable powers, because it is easier for the Council to accept an EP proposal than to amend it, provided that the Commission accepts it too. Accepting it requires a qualified majority whereas amending it requires unanimity. However, the EP cannot successfully propose any policy it wants: the proposal must satisfy a few conditions, whence comes the term 'conditional agenda-setting' powers. Tsebelis illustrates his claims with a discussion of legislation on car emission standards.

Tsebelis recognises and demonstrates the increasingly important legislative role of the Parliament, often considered to be weak and irrelevant. Nonetheless, his contribution suffers from a number of important problems. Moser (1996) identifies and addresses several of these problems. The principal shortcoming is that Tsebelis' analysis is limited to the last steps of co-operation. Under co-operation EP proposals are in fact amendments to proposals the Commission made in earlier steps of the procedure. Tsebelis disregards these earlier steps. If one incorporates them into his model, though, one comes to different conclusions. In particular, one finds that the Commission, rather than the EP, has agenda-setting powers.

The EP does make amendments, however, and many of them are accepted.[8] Tsebelis' claim that the EP has conditional agenda-setting powers under co-operation can be interpreted as being consistent with this observation. Tsebelis (1996) emphasises this in his reaction to Moser's critique. Nonetheless his claim does not follow from an extension of his model to the entire procedure. Under different assumptions, however, the Commission may accept EP amendments and the EP may have conditional agenda-setting powers. The Commission may indeed accept amendments, if it has incomplete information at the beginning of the procedure, for example, or if it does not behave as a unitary actor.[9]

Moser (1996) provides alternative explanations for the success of EP amendments. Changes in the countries' or Commissioners' preferences or in the perception of the status quo may give the EP opportunities successfully to amend the Commission proposal. The EP may propose policies the Commission could not successfully propose prior to the changes. Moser (1997a) elaborates on this explanation for the EP's powers and applies it to legislation on car emission standards and food sweeteners.

Steunenberg (1994) and Crombez (1996, 1997a) present comprehensive analyses of the EU's legislative procedures. Steunenberg analyses the consultation, co-operation and co-decision procedures. He concludes that the Commission dominates the legislative process, whereas the EP plays a minor role. It has no impact under consultation and only conditional veto powers under co-operation, where its veto can be overridden by a unanimous Council. Even under co-decision the EP merely has unconditional veto powers. However, Steunenberg ignores the Council and EP's opportunity under co-decision to amend Commission proposals in the Conciliation Committee.[10]

Crombez (1996) studies the consultation, co-operation and assent procedures. He finds that the Commission has considerable agenda-setting powers under all three procedures. Under consultation the Commission can successfully propose any policy a qualified majority in the Council prefers to the status quo. Its agenda-setting powers are somewhat smaller under the procedures introduced during the 1980s. Under co-operation a proposal cannot pass without being preferred to the status quo by the EP and a qualified majority in the Council, or else by all countries. Under assent the EP and all countries need to prefer the proposal.[11]

Crombez also concludes that the EP has no powers under consultation, but acquires veto powers under co-operation and assent. Under co-operation a unanimous Council can override its veto, but the EP is unlikely to have such extreme preferences that no country supports its veto. Crombez and Steunenberg both agree with Moser that the EP has no agenda-setting powers under co-operation.[12] Crombez also analyses the extent of indecision, i.e., the EU's inability to act, under the three procedures. He finds that there is considerable indecision under all three procedures, and that this indecision increases under the procedures introduced in the 1980s.

Crombez (1997a) analyses the co-decision procedure and finds that the EP becomes a genuine co-legislator with the Council under co-decision. Successful Commission proposals need the approval of both the EP and a qualified majority in the Council.[13] Moreover, the EP and a qualified majority in the Council can together amend Commission proposals in the Conciliation Committee.[14] The Commission retains considerable agenda-setting powers under co-decision, but these powers are smaller than under consultation and co-operation. The co-decision procedure reduces indecision in the EU as compared to the co-operation procedure, because the EP and the Council can amend Commission proposals. Hence, they may be able to move EU policy away from the status quo even if the Commission disagrees.

Garrett (1996), Garrett and Tsebelis (1996) and Tsebelis (1997) present alternative models of co-decision, and claim that the EP acquires unconditional veto powers, but loses the conditional agenda-setting powers it enjoys under co-operation to the Council, because the Council can revert to the Commission proposal if the Conciliation Committee fails to reach agreement. This argument suffers from a number of shortcomings. First, the EP does not have conditional agenda-setting powers under co-operation once the entire procedure is considered, as mentioned above. Second, the Council needs the EP's approval to revert to the Commission proposal under co-decision. Third, the EP and the Council together acquire agenda-setting powers under co-decision, since they can amend Commission proposals in the Conciliation Committee.

Schneider (1995a) recognises the EP's veto powers under co-decision as well as the agenda-setting powers it enjoys in the Conciliation Committee.

He also studies the negotiation processes at the constitutional level, which lead to institutional reforms, and concludes that the Commission and the EP have only limited powers in such negotiations. He points out that the EP's limited involvement at the constitutional level may restrict its legislative powers, as countries may use their powers at the constitutional level to curb the EP's influence. Schneider and Cederman (1994) note that countries may also use domestic politics to strengthen their bargaining positions.

Steunenberg (1998) analyses the co-decision procedure and its reform. He focuses on the last steps of the procedure and assumes that the EP has the sole power to make proposals in the Conciliation Committee. He estimates expected distances between EU policies and ideal policies, and finds that one can expect EU policies to be closer to the EP's ideal policy than to the Commission or any country's ideal policy. This conclusion, however, depends on the assumption that the EP makes the proposals. Steunenberg also expects EU policy to move even closer to the EP's ideal policy under the new co-decision procedure.

Some scholars use spatial models to study specific issues related to the EU legislative process. Steunenberg, Koboldt and Schmidtchen (1996) analyse the 'comitology' procedures, that is, the procedures governing the implementation of EU legislation. They find that the Commission and the Council play important roles in comitology, whereas the Parliament has no power. Steunenberg, Koboldt and Schmidtchen (1997) propose alternative comitology procedures that would increase the EP's involvement.

Crombez (1997b) endogenises the Commission's preferences by studying the Commission appointment process. He characterises sets of effective Commissions, i.e., Commissions that can be appointed and can successfully propose their own ideal policies, and concludes that the EP's increased role in Commission appointment and policy-making limits the sets of successful Commissions. Crombez (1998) provides a theoretical analysis of logrolling in the EU legislative process, and finds that it provides considerable opportunities for logrolling.

In short, there is a rapidly growing literature devoted to formal analysis of EU decision-making procedures. Spatial models are the dominant means of formalisation. The lack of consensus on which EU actors are powerful (and in what ways) highlights the need for extreme clarity about modelling assumptions and accuracy in representing important features of the institutional structure. It is also evident that informal, off-the-cuff assessments of how changes in the procedures alter the influence of the EP, the Council and the Commission are prone to error. Given the complexity of the EU legislative machinery, there is no substitute for rigor. In that spirit, the next sections present models of the old and the new co-decision procedures.

The models

I present spatial models of EU policy-making under the co-decision procedure. Alternative policies are represented by points in an n-dimensional policy space. Each dimension corresponds to a specific policy issue, such as the allowable non-cocoa fat level in chocolate or the length of daylight saving time. I assume that countries have Euclidean preferences over the EU policy $p(p^1, \ldots, p^n)$, with ideal policy $\hat{p}_k(\hat{p}_k^1, \ldots, \hat{p}_k^n)$ for country k. The MEPs and Commissioners are also assumed to have Euclidean preferences over EU policies.

I study the old co-decision procedure, as introduced by the Treaty of Maastricht, and the new co-decision procedure, as altered by the Treaty of Amsterdam. I present unidimensional as well as multidimensional models of both procedures. The unidimensional models study policy-making on a single policy issue. As the EU uses strict germaneness rules, proposals typically concern a specific issue, and only related amendments are considered. The multidimensional models apply to situations in which policy-makers consider multiple issues. [15]

The unidimensional models are simplified versions of the multidimensional models. In the unidimensional models the EP and the Commission are represented as unitary actors. When deciding on a single policy issue, a majority of MEPs prefers policies that are closer to, rather than farther away from, the median MEP's ideal policy on that issue. Since the EP uses majority rule and has no restrictions on amendments, it acts as a unitary actor with ideal policy equal to the median MEP's ideal policy. A similar argument holds for the Commission. The analysis of policy-making on a single issue can thus be simplified by focusing on the median Commissioner and the median MEP.[16]

The Council is not represented as a unitary actor because it uses qualified majority rule.[17] A qualified majority in the Council consists of sixty-two out of a total of eighty-seven votes. Nonetheless, the analysis of policy-making on dimension i can be simplified by focusing on the countries that are pivotal under the qualified majority rule. The country a^i that is pivotal for a move to the right on dimension i thus has an ideal policy to the left of the country with the median vote. In particular, country a^i is the country with the twenty-sixth vote (from the left). Country a^i and the countries to its right then have sixty-two votes, and the countries to its right do not constitute a qualified majority without country a^i. The country b^i that is pivotal for a move to the left is the country with the sixty-second vote.

The unidimensional models are shown in Figure 5.1. First, the Commission proposes a policy. The EP can then offer a joint text, which becomes EU policy if a qualified majority in the Council approves it.[18] The new co-decision procedure ends with this vote. The status quo then prevails if the joint text does not obtain the support of a qualified majority in the Council. Under the old co-decision procedure, however, the countries vote on the Commission proposal in the fourth stage, if no joint text is approved. If a qualified majority accepts the proposal and the EP approves it in the fifth stage, the proposal then becomes EU policy. Otherwise, the status quo prevails.[19]

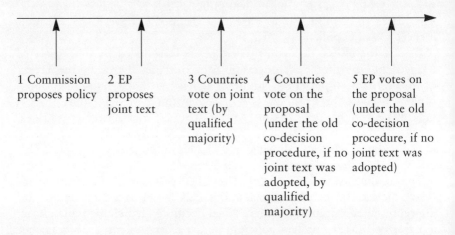

1 Commission proposes policy

2 EP proposes joint text

3 Countries vote on joint text (by qualified majority)

4 Countries vote on the proposal (under the old co-decision procedure, if no joint text was adopted, by qualified majority)

5 EP votes on the proposal (under the old co-decision procedure, if no joint text was adopted)

Figure 5.1 The co-decision procedure: one dimension

The multidimensional models of the procedures, shown in Figure 5.2, are similar to their unidimensional counterparts. The Commission and the EP are not considered as unitary actors, however. The relevant actors are thus the Commissioners, MEPs and countries. First, the Commission President proposes a policy.[20] Subsequently, the Commissioners vote on the proposal. If the proposal obtains the support of a simple majority of the Commissioners, it is sent to the EP and the Council. If the proposal fails to obtain the support of a majority of the Commissioners, a status quo proposal is sent to the EP and the Council.[21]

The MEPs and the countries, as represented in the Council, can together approve an amendment, referred to as a joint text.[22] In particular, the EP President can propose a joint text in the third stage. If the Council President approves the joint text in the fourth stage, it is subsequently voted on in the Council and the EP in the fifth and sixth stages. The joint text needs the support of a qualified majority in the Council and a majority of MEPs for adoption. The new co-decision procedure ends with the countries' and MEPs' votes on the joint text. The status quo then prevails, if no joint text is adopted. The old co-decision procedure consists of two more stages, however. In particular, the countries and MEPs vote on the original Commission proposal in the seventh and eighth stages of the old

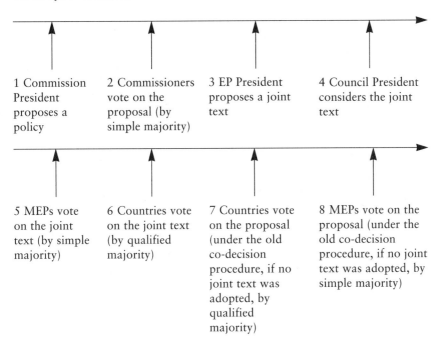

Figure 5.2 The co-decision procedure: multiple dimensions

co-decision procedure, if no joint text was adopted. The countries and MEPs compare the proposal to the status quo. To be adopted the proposal needs the support of a qualified majority in the Council and a majority of the MEPs. If no proposal is adopted, the status quo prevails.

The models incorporate complete and perfect information. The actors, i.e. the institutions, countries, MEPs and Commissioners, know each other's preferences, the location of the status quo, the impact of proposed policies, the sequential structure of the models and the actions taken in prior stages of the models.

An equilibrium consists of a strategy for each actor. Strategies tell the actors what actions to choose in the relevant stages of the procedure, given the actions taken in prior stages. The equilibrium concept is subgame perfect Nash. In a Nash equilibrium, no actor can achieve a higher utility by choosing another strategy, given the other actors' strategies. In a subgame perfect Nash equilibrium, actors can do no better than stick to their strategies in any stage of the procedure, even if an actor deviated from the equilibrium strategy in a prior stage.

The old co-decision procedure

In this section I present the unidimensional and multidimensional models of the old co-decision procedure. For each model I go through the different steps of the procedure. I determine sets of successful proposals and equilibrium policies, for any configuration of ideal policies and for any location of the status quo. I also discuss the institutions' powers and the extent of indecision.

The unidimensional model of old co-decision

Under the old co-decision procedure the Commission starts policy-making on dimension i by proposing a policy p^i, as shown in Figure 5.1. It wants the policy to be as close to its ideal policy as possible. This does not imply, however, that the Commission proposes its ideal policy. The Commission understands the roles the Council and the EP play in the next stages of the procedure and takes these into account when it makes its proposal.

In the fourth and fifth stages the countries and the EP vote on the Commission proposal. The proposal is adopted if the EP and a qualified majority in the Council approve it. They approve the Commission proposal if they prefer it to the status quo q^i. The set $P(q^i)$ of policies the EP approves in the fifth stage is thus the set of policies the EP prefers to the status quo. Similarly, the set $Q(q^i)$ of policies a qualified majority in the Council approves in the fourth stage, is the set of policies a qualified majority prefers to the status quo.

To illustrate policy-making on dimension i I use the configuration of ideal policies shown in Figure 5.3. Country a^i, the EP and the Commission, with ideal policies $\hat{p}^i_a$, $\hat{p}^i_p$ and $\hat{p}^i_c$ respectively, have ideal policies to the right of the status quo. For simplicity, the status quo q^i is assumed to be equal to zero. The EP has an ideal policy to the left of countries a^i and b^i that are pivotal under the qualified majority rule, whereas the Commission is located more to the right. In Figure 5.3 the EP, country a^i and thus a qualified majority prefer a move to the right. The set $P(q^i)$ of policies that the EP approves in the fifth stage is then the set of policies the EP prefers to the status quo. It contains all policies that are closer to the EP's ideal policy than is the status quo. Similarly, the set $Q(q^i)$ of policies that a qualified majority in the Council approves in the fourth stage is the set of policies country a^i prefers to the status quo.

A proposal that belongs to the sets $P(q^i)$ and $Q(q^i)$ does not necessarily reach the last two stages of the old co-decision procedure, however. In the second stage the EP can propose a joint text, and this joint text becomes EU policy if a qualified majority approves it in the third stage. Since the countries think ahead, they compare the joint text to the proposal in the third stage. The joint text is then adopted if a qualified majority prefers it to the proposal.

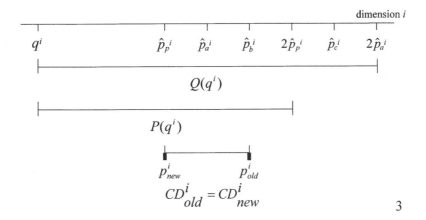

Figure 5.3 policy-making: one dimension

The EP can thus successfully propose a joint text in the second stage if there are policies a qualified majority prefers to the proposal. The EP uses this opportunity if it prefers such policies to the proposal. As a result, the proposal does not reach the last two stages of the procedure if there are policies that the EP and a qualified majority prefer to it.

The Commission realises that successful proposals need to be preferred to the status quo by the EP and a qualified majority in the Council. Moreover, it anticipates that proposals are amended if the EP and a qualified majority prefer another policy. In the first stage of co-decision the Commission proposes the policy it prefers most among the policies that will be approved and will not be amended. Proposition 1 presents the conclusions of the unidimensional model of the old co-decision procedure.

Proposition 1   Under the old co-decision procedure the set CD^i_{old} of
successful proposals on dimension i is the set of policies that satisfy
the following requirements: (1) they are preferred to the status quo by
the EP and a qualified majority, and (2) no policy is preferred to them
by the EP and a qualified majority. The Commission successfully
proposes the policy p^i_{old} that belongs to the set CD^i_{old} and is closest to
its ideal policy.

In Figure 5.3 the EP successfully proposes a joint text if the proposal is to the left of its ideal policy. The EP, country a^i and thus a qualified majority then prefer a policy to the right of the proposal. If the proposal is to the right of country b^i's ideal policy, the EP also successfully proposes a joint text. The EP, country b^i and thus a qualified majority then prefer a policy to the left of the proposal. If the proposal is between the ideal policies of the EP and country a^i, the EP cannot successfully propose a joint text. The EP prefers policies to the left of the proposal, whereas a qualified majority in the Council prefers policies to the right. If the proposal is between the ideal policies of countries a^i and b^i, the EP cannot successfully propose a joint text either, since the Council cannot agree on a policy change by a qualified majority. In Figure 5.3 the set CD^i_{old} of successful policies is thus the set of policies between the ideal policies of the EP and country b^i. The Commission successfully proposes country b's ideal policy, i.e., $p^i_{old} = \hat{p}^i_b$.

The multidimensional model of old co-decision

In the multidimensional model of the old co-decision procedure the Commission and the EP are not considered unitary actors. The Commission President makes the proposal and presents it to his fellow Commissioners. The EP President then proposes a joint text and she presents it to the Council President. In other aspects the multidimensional model is similar to the unidimensional model.

In the seventh and eighth stages the countries and MEPs vote on the Commission proposal. They compare it to the status quo. The set $P(q)$ of policies the EP approves in the eighth stage of the old co-decision procedure, as shown in Figure 5.2, is the set of policies a majority of MEPs prefer to the status quo. Similarly, the set $Q(q)$ of policies a qualified majority in the Council approves in the seventh stage is the set of policies a qualified majority prefers to the status quo.

Figure 5.4 shows the sets $P(q)$ and $Q(q)$ for a particular configuration of ideal policies in a two-dimensional policy space. In Figure 5.4 the two policies that the EU is addressing during the Commission's term are (1) market liberalisation (economic policy) and (2) cohesion (social policy). The ideal policies of the countries and MEPs were chosen for illustrative purposes, but they are intended to correspond to reality. The 'southern' countries (Spain, Greece, Ireland, Italy and Portugal) want to move far on cohesion, but want little change on market liberalisation. They have a total of thirty-one votes in the Council. The United Kingdom, with ten votes, wants a lot more liberalisation, but little change on cohesion. The 'core' countries (Belgium, Germany, France, Luxembourg, the Netherlands and Austria), as well as the 'northern' countries (Denmark, Finland and Sweden), have intermediate positions on both issues. They have thirty-six and ten votes respectively.

Figure 5.4 also presents the ideal policies of the two principal political groups in the EP. These groups are the conservative European People's Party (EPP) and the group of the Party of European Socialists (PES).[23] In Figure 5.4 I consider these two groups as unitary actors, as they tend to be cohesive in voting behaviour. In practice, for a policy to receive the support of a majority of MEPs, the approval of the two main political groups in the EP is needed. The set $P(q)$ is thus the set of policies that are preferred to the status quo by the EPP and PES groups. It is bounded by

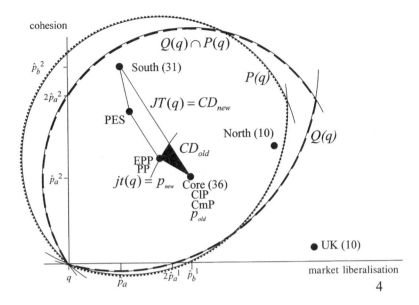

Figure 5.4 Policy-making: multiple dimensions

the dotted parts of the indifference curves of these groups through the status quo.

In the Council the core countries as well as the southern countries represent a blocking minority in Figure 5.4, i.e., without them no qualified majority can be formed. Together the core and southern countries form a qualified majority. The set $Q(q)$ is thus the set of policies that are preferred to the status quo by the core and southern countries. It is bounded by the dashed parts of the indifference curves of these countries through the status quo. As a result the set $P(q) \cap Q(q)$ of policies that are preferred to the status quo by a majority of MEPs and a qualified majority in the Council is the set of policies that are preferred to the status quo by the PES and EPP groups, the southern countries and the core countries. It is bounded by the indifference curves of these groups and countries through the status quo.

A proposal that belongs to the set $P(q) \cap Q(q)$ does not necessarily reach the last two stages of the old co-decision procedure, however. In the third stage the EP President can propose a joint text and this joint text becomes EU policy if the Council President, a majority of MEPs and a qualified majority approve it. Since the Council President, the MEPs and the countries think ahead, they compare the joint text to the proposal. The joint text is then adopted if the Council President, a majority of MEPs and a qualified majority prefer it to the proposal.

The EP President can thus successfully propose a joint text in the third stage if there are policies the Council President, a majority of MEPs and a qualified majority prefer to the proposal. The EP President uses this opportunity if she prefers such policies to the proposal. As a result, the proposal does not reach the last two stages of the procedure if there are policies that the EP and Council Presidents, a majority of MEPs and a qualified majority in the Council prefer to it.

Suppose that in Figure 5.4 the EP President (PP) belongs to the EPP group and that a core country is Council President (ClP). The set $JT(q)$ of proposals that get through the last six stages of the old co-decision procedure is then the trapezoid formed by the ideal policies of the PES and EPP groups and the core and southern countries. Suppose the Commission proposal belongs to the set $JT(q)$. The EP President then does not propose a joint text, because there is no policy the Council President, the southern and core countries and the PES and EPP groups prefer to the proposal. The proposal is approved by a majority of MEPs and a qualified majority in the Council, and becomes EU policy.

In the second stage the Commissioners vote on the proposal. Suppose a majority of MEPs and a qualified majority in the Council prefer it to the status quo. Suppose furthermore that there are no policies the EP and Council Presidents, a majority of MEPs and a qualified majority in the Council prefer to the proposal. If the Commissioners reject the proposal, a status quo proposal is sent to the Council and the EP. The EP President then successfully proposes the policy $jt(q)$ she prefers most among the policies that are preferred to the status quo by the Council President, a majority of MEPs and a qualified majority in the Council. The proposal thus moves on to the third stage if a majority of the Commissioners prefer it to the policy $jt(q)$. In Figure 5.4 the policy $jt(q)$ is equal to the EPP's ideal policy. If the Commission proposes the status quo, the EP President can successfully propose any joint text that belongs to the set $P(q) \cap Q(q)$. In particular, she successfully proposes her own ideal policy.

The Commission President realises what policies will be approved by a majority of the Commissioners and MEPs and a qualified majority in the Council. Moreover, he is aware of what policies will be amended in the Conciliation Committee. He takes this into account when he makes his proposal in the first stage of the procedure. Proposition 2 presents the conclusions of the multidimensional model of the old co-decision procedure.

Proposition 2   The set CD_{old} of successful proposals under the old co-decision procedure is the set of policies that satisfy the following requirements: (1) they are preferred to the status quo by a majority of MEPs and a qualified majority in the Council, (2) no policy is preferred to them by the EP and Council Presidents, a majority of

MEPs and a qualified majority in the Council, and (3) a majority of the Commissioners prefer them to the policy *jt*(q) the EP President proposes if the Commission sends her a status quo proposal. In the first stage the Commission President successfully proposes the policy p_{old} that belongs to the set CD_{old} and is closest to his ideal policy.

The first requirement ensures that the proposal receives final approval in the Council and the EP. The second requirement ensures that the proposal is not amended by the Council and the EP, whereas the third requirement states that the proposal needs to receive Commission approval.

Suppose that in Figure 5.4 all countries appoint Commissioners with ideal policies equal to their own, and that the ideal policy of the Commission President (CmP) is equal to the core countries' ideal policy. There are then seven Commissioners with ideal policies equal to the southern countries' ideal policy. Eight Commissioners have ideal policies equal to the core countries', three Commissioners concur with the northern countries' ideal policy, and two with the UK's. The set CD_{old} of successful proposals under the old co-decision procedure is then the shaded area. It is a subset of the set *JT(q)*. The policies in the northwestern part of the set *JT(q)* are not preferred to the policy *jt(q)* by a majority of the Commissioners: only the Commissioners of the southern countries prefer them. The policies in the set *JT(q)* southeast of the UK's indifference curve through the policy *jt(q)*, are preferred to that policy by a majority of the Commissioners and thus constitute the set CD_{old}. The Commission President then successfully proposes his own ideal policy as EU policy p_{old}. The Commissioners of the core and northern countries and the UK approve it, because they prefer it to the policy *jt(q)*. The EP President does not propose a joint text, because there is no policy the Council President prefers to the proposal. All countries, the EPP and PES groups, and thus a majority of MEPs, approve it because they prefer the proposal to the status quo.

Discussion of the old co-decision procedure
In this subsection I discuss the powers of the countries, the Commission and the EP, and the extent of indecision under the old co-decision procedure. A country's or institution's power, given a configuration of ideal policies and status quo, is defined as its ability to obtain a policy that is close to its ideal policy. It is measured by the distance between its ideal policy and the equilibrium policy, a smaller distance indicating more power. Indecision is defined as the EU's inability to act to alter the status quo. It is measured by the set of status quos that cannot be changed through equilibrium play of the procedure.

The Commission has considerable agenda setting powers under the old co-decision procedure. It can choose any policy that satisfies the

requirements summed up in Proposition 1. The EP becomes a genuine co-
legislator equal in stature to the Council. Both institutions need to
approve Commission proposals and they can amend them together in the
Conciliation Committee.

When setting policy on a single issue, the EU is unable to act in two
instances: (1) if no qualified majority in the Council agrees on a new
policy; and, (2) if the EP does not agree with a qualified majority in the
Council. When the EU is choosing policies on multiple issues, there are
two additional instances: (3) if no majority of MEPs agrees on a new
policy; and, (4) if neither a majority of the Commissioners nor the Council
and EP Presidents agree with a majority of MEPs and a qualified majority in the Council.

The new co-decision procedure

The unidimensional model of new co-decision
The new co-decision procedure looks like the old procedure without the
last two stages, as shown in Figure 5.1. The countries and the EP cannot
return to the Commission proposal if they fail to agree on a joint text. As
a result the countries compare the joint text to the status quo rather than
to the Commission proposal in the third stage of the procedure. The joint
text is adopted if a qualified majority prefers it to the status quo.

The EP can thus successfully propose a joint text in the second stage if
there are policies a qualified majority prefers to the status quo. The EP
uses this opportunity if it prefers such policies to the status quo. In particular, it proposes the policy it prefers most among the policies that belong
to the set $Q(q^i)$ of policies that are preferred to the status quo by a qualified majority. This policy is approved by a qualified majority in the
Council and becomes EU policy. The Commission proposal is irrelevant
under the new co-decision procedure, as it is no longer the reversion
policy if no joint text is approved. In Figure 5.3 the EP proposes its own
ideal policy as a joint text. This policy is adopted as a qualified majority
prefers it to the status quo.

In reality the EP does not necessarily get the chance to propose the
joint text. Countries could also get the opportunity to propose the joint
text. Moreover, the EP and the countries can propose amendments to
the joint text. In equilibrium the proposer of the joint text, whether it
be the EP or a country, thus proposes the policy it prefers most among
the policies that satisfy the following two requirements: (1) they are
preferred to the status quo by the EP and a qualified majority in the
Council, and (2) no policy is preferred to them by the EP and a qualified majority in the Council.

The proposal the Commission makes in the first stage of the procedure
has no formal impact on the subsequent stages of the procedure.

Proposition 3 presents the conclusions of the unidimensional model of the new co-decision procedure.

Proposition 3   Under the new co-decision procedure the set CD^i_{new} of
    successful joint texts on dimension i consists of the policies that
    satisfy the following two requirements: (1) they are preferred to the
    status quo by the EP and a qualified majority in the Council, and (2)
    no policy is preferred to them by the EP and a qualified majority in
    the Council. It is equal to the set CD^i_{old} of successful proposals under
    the old co-decision procedure. The proposer of the joint text, whether
    it be the EP or a country, successfully proposes the policy he prefers
    most among the policies that belong to the set CD^i_{new}. The
    Commission is irrelevant under the new co-decision procedure.

The multidimensional model of new co-decision
The multidimensional model of the new co-decision procedure is like the multidimensional model of the old co-decision procedure without the last two stages, as shown in Figure 5.2. As in the unidimensional model, no policy is adopted if the Council and the EP fail to agree on a joint text.

In the fifth and sixth stages the countries and MEPs vote on the joint text. They compare it to the status quo. The set $P(q)$ of joint texts the EP approves in the fifth stage is the set of policies a majority of MEPs prefer to the status quo. Similarly, the set $Q(q)$ of joint texts a qualified majority in the Council approves in the sixth stage is the set of policies a qualified majority prefers to the status quo. Figure 5.4 shows the sets $P(q)$ and $Q(q)$ for a particular configuration of ideal policies, as mentioned above.

In the fourth stage the Council President approves the joint text, if he prefers it to the status quo. The EP President can thus successfully propose a joint text in the third stage if there are policies the Council President, a majority of MEPs and a qualified majority prefer to the status quo. The EP President uses this opportunity if she prefers such policies to the status quo. In particular she proposes as a joint text the policy she prefers most among the policies the Council President, a majority of MEPs and a qualified majority prefer to the status quo. This joint text is approved by the Council President, a majority of MEPs and a qualified majority in the Council. As a result, it becomes EU policy. As in the unidimensional model, the Commission proposal is irrelevant because the countries and MEPs cannot turn back to it if they fail to agree to a joint text. In Figure 5.4 the EP President successfully proposes her ideal policy, which is equal to the EPP's ideal policy.

In reality the EP President does not necessarily get the chance to propose the joint text. The Council President could also get the opportunity to propose the joint text. Moreover, the EP and Council Presidents can propose amendments to the joint text. In equilibrium the proposer of the joint text, whether he be the EP or Council President, thus proposes the policy he prefers most among the policies that satisfy the following two requirements: (1) they are preferred to the status quo by the EP and Council Presidents, a majority of MEPs and a qualified majority in the Council, and (2) no policy is preferred to them by the EP and Council Presidents, a majority of MEPs and a qualified majority in the Council.

As in the unidimensional model, the proposal the Commission makes in the first stage has no formal impact on the subsequent stages of the procedure. Proposition 4 presents the conclusions of the multidimensional model of the new co-decision procedure.

Proposition 4   The set CD_{new} of successful joint texts under the new co-decision procedure consists of the policies that satisfy the following two requirements: (1) they are preferred to the status quo by the Council and EP Presidents, a majority of MEPs and a qualified majority in the Council, and (2) no policy is preferred to them by the Council and EP Presidents, a majority of MEPs and a qualified majority in the Council. The proposer of the joint text, whether he be the EP or Council President, successfully proposes the policy he prefers most among the policies that belong to the set CD_{new}. The Commission is irrelevant under the new co-decision procedure.

In Figure 5.4 the set CD_{new} is the trapezoid formed by the ideal policies of the southern and core countries and the PES and EPP. It is a superset of the set CD_{old}, because the approval of a majority of the Commissioners is not required.

Discussion of the new co-decision procedure
The Commission loses its agenda setting powers under the new co-decision procedure. In the absence of informational asymmetries and informal rules it becomes completely irrelevant. Under the old procedure the Commission could choose a policy that would not be amended in the Conciliation Committee and would receive final approval in the EP and the Council. The Commission cannot choose EU policy under the new procedure, because its proposal no longer provides a reversion policy in case the Conciliation Committee fails to agree to a joint text. If no joint text is approved, the status quo prevails. The Commission proposal is thus irrelevant during the negotiations in the Conciliation Committee.

Under the new procedure the Council and the EP have agenda setting powers, rather than the Commission. The proposer of a joint text can successfully propose any policy that satisfies the two requirements mentioned in Proposition 3. The first requirement ensures that the joint text receives final approval in the EP and the Council. The second requirement ensures that the joint text is not amended by the Council and the EP.

Whether the procedural changes do indeed lead to an increase in the EP's and countries' powers depends on the configuration of ideal policies and their bargaining powers within the Conciliation Committee. The countries and the EP gain power if the proposer of the joint text chooses a policy that is closer to their ideal policies than the policy the Commission would choose under the old procedure. Similarly, the EP and the countries gain power if they have much more bargaining power in the Conciliation Committee. The EP thus loses power if a country whose ideal policy is further from the EP's ideal policy than is the Commission's ideal policy proposes the joint text under the new procedure.

There is more indecision under the new than under the old procedure. When choosing policy on a single issue, the EU is unable to act in two instances, as under the old procedure: (1) if no qualified majority in the Council agrees on a new policy; and, (2) if the EP does not agree with a qualified majority in the Council. When the EU is considering multiple issues, there are two more instances: (3) if no majority of MEPs agrees; and, (4) if the Council and EP Presidents do not agree with a majority of MEPs and a qualified majority in the Council. The fourth requirement is stricter than under the old procedure, because the Council and EP Presidents have to agree to a change even if a majority of the Commissioners agrees. Moreover, indecision increases if the bargaining process in the Conciliation Committee is not well specified. The status quo prevails if the Committee does not reach agreement.

Conclusions

Under the old co-decision procedure a policy is successful if (1) the EP and a qualified majority in the Council prefer it to the status quo, and (2) no policy is preferred to it by the EP and a qualified majority in the Council. The Commission successfully proposes the policies it prefers most among the policies that satisfy these requirements.

Under the new co-decision procedure the Commission proposal is irrelevant. A joint text becomes EU policy if (1) the EP and a qualified majority in the Council prefer it to the status quo, and (2) no policy is preferred to it by the EP and a qualified majority in the Council. The equilibrium EU policy is not chosen by the Commission President, but, rather, is determined by the EP and Council and depends on their respective bargaining powers in the Conciliation Committee.

The changes to the co-decision procedure agreed to in Amsterdam thus reduce the Commission's powers. In fact, the Commission becomes irrelevant under the new co-decision procedure. Whether the EP's and the countries' powers increase depends on the bargaining within the Conciliation Committee and on their ideal policies. If they have little bargaining power and preferences similar to the Commission's, they lose power. Otherwise, they stand to gain power.

Rather than strengthening the EP's powers and reducing the Council's powers, as those responsible for the changes intended, they have thus reduced the Commission's powers. Moreover, they decrease the EP's powers, insofar as the EP can be considered to have preferences similar to the Commission's, as is often supposed, and to have little bargaining power compared to the Council. Indecision increases under the new procedure.

Even though some elements not included in the models introduced in this chapter – such as the Commission's expertise in a world characterised by imperfect information and informal rules – may somewhat soften the main conclusions, it seems fair to conclude that the drafters of the Amsterdam Treaty have taken powers away from appointed Commissioners. They might also have strengthened the powers of directly elected MEPs, but this is not an automatic consequence of their institutional tinkering. Indeed, the Amsterdam alterations might ultimately prove to bolster the position of national representatives in the Council. Hence, whether the democratic deficit will shrink or grow remains to be seen.

Notes

1   The Council, the EP and the Commission are the three principal institutions involved in the EU legislative process. The Council is an intergovernmental body. It consists of representatives of the member countries' national governments. It is the main legislative institution in the EU. The EP is directly elected. It co-legislates with the Council under some of the EU's legislative procedures. The Commission is the EU's executive. It is appointed by the Council and the EP. It proposes and implements EU legislation. Currently, the Council has 15 members, the EP 626, and the Commission 20. The five largest countries (Germany, Spain, France, Italy and the United Kingdom) have two Commissioners each, the other countries have one each. See Nugent (1994) for a more detailed description of the EU institutions.

2   The co-decision procedure is one of the three principal legislative procedures in the EU. The other two procedures are the consultation and co-operation procedures. Under consultation the Commission makes a proposal, which is then subject to a vote in the Council. Under co-operation the additional approval of the EP is needed. Under co-decision the Council and the EP can together amend Commission proposals. The consultation procedure accounts for about two thirds of EU legislation (154 opinions in 1997), the co-operation procedure for about 10 per cent (19 first readings in 1997) and the co-decision procedure for about 15 per cent (34 first readings in 1997).

3   I reach these conclusions based on the models I develop in this chapter. Even though these models capture the principal characteristics of the procedures, they simplify policy-making somewhat, as do all models. Informal rules and informational asymmetries that may exist, for example, are disregarded. As a

result, the conclusions do not reflect such rules and asymmetries. Nonetheless, the conclusions identify the principal consequences of the new procedure. Therefore, they can serve as a baseline for further research.

4 The unidimensional model of the old co-decision procedure was presented earlier by Crombez (1997a).

5 Aspinwall and Schneider (1998) provide an overview of other literatures on EU institutions.

6 A qualified majority in the Council consists of 62 out of a total of 87 votes. France, Germany, Italy and the United Kingdom have 10 votes each; Spain 8; Belgium, Greece, Portugal and the Netherlands 5 each; Austria and Sweden 4 each; Denmark, Finland and Ireland 3 each; and Luxembourg 2.

7 Krehbiel (1988) and Moser (1999) present excellent reviews of this literature.

8 See Westlake (1995) for data on the success of EP amendments.

9 A second important shortcoming concerns Tsebelis' treatment of Council amendments. The Council can unanimously amend an EP proposal. A successful proposal thus needs to be such that no policy is preferred to it by all countries. In Tsebelis' model, however, the Council compares its amendments to the status quo rather than to the EP proposal. As a result of this inaccurate specification of the procedure, Tsebelis mistakenly concludes that the EP's powers are a curvilinear function of the location of the status quo, i.e., that the EP has no powers if the status quo is close to or far away from the countries' ideal policies, but may have powers in intermediate cases.

10 Steunenberg also assumes, contrary to Crombez, that the Commission has veto powers. Whether the Commission does indeed have gatekeeping (and thus *ex ante* veto) powers remains a matter of debate among legal scholars. At issue is whether Council and EP's requests that the Commission make proposals are binding.

11 Crombez identifies an additional condition for proposals to be successful under all three procedures. As the Council can unanimously amend Commission proposals, there should be no policy that satisfies the other criteria for adoption and is preferred to the proposal by all countries. I ignore this additional requirement here, because the Commission is unlikely to have such extreme preferences that no country prefers its proposal.

12 That is, they agree that the EP has no agenda-setting powers under the assumptions mentioned above. These include that the countries and institutions have complete information, that their preferences and their perception of the status quo do not change during the legislative process and that the EP and the Commission behave as unitary actors.

13 More specifically, the EP can reject Commission proposals by a simple majority of its members. As Crombez does not consider abstentions, requiring a simple majority of members for rejection is equivalent to requiring a simple majority of votes for adoption. In reality, low attendance rates may, however, make it more difficult for the EP to reject Commission proposals and may thus reduce the EP's powers. Nonetheless, such reduction of powers is not inherent in co-decision.

14 Successful Commission proposals thus need to be preferred to the status quo by the EP and a qualified majority in the Council. Moreover, no policy should be preferred to them by the EP and a qualified majority in the Council.

15 Readers less familiar with formal models can skip the subsections on the multidimensional models, as the conclusions are similar to their unidimensional counterparts. I present the multidimensional models principally to show that equilibrium outcomes exist in multidimensional settings and that the conclusions of the unidimensional models can be extended to multidimensional settings.

16 In other words Black's median voter theorem applies (Black, 1958).

17 In some policy areas the Council uses unanimity rule.

18 I skip several steps of the co-decision procedure that precede the proposal of a joint text. These steps are irrelevant in perfect information models. In the presence of informational asymmetries, however, they might facilitate the exchange of information amongst political actors. As for the proposal of a joint text, this is not the exclusive right of the EP. Countries can propose joint texts as well. Nonetheless, the assumption that the EP proposes the joint text does not affect the conclusions, as will be clear below.

19 The following two paragraphs introduce the multidimensional models. They can be skipped by readers less familiar with formal models.

20 I assume that the Commission President makes a proposal within the Commission. This seems reasonable given the Commission President's prominent role in the Commission.

21 For simplicity I assume that Commissioners do not amend proposals made by the Commission President.

22 A joint text is worked out in the Conciliation Committee and then voted on in the Council and the EP. The Conciliation Committee consists of the members of the Council and an equal number of representatives of the EP. The Council and EP Presidents (or their representatives) take turns at chairing the Committee's meetings. Both Presidents also convene prior to the Committee's meetings to agree on a compromise. Therefore, it seems reasonable to assume that the Presidents present a joint text they agree on to the Council and the EP. In the model I assume that the EP President proposes the joint text. This assumption does not affect the conclusions. See Corbett et al. (1995) on the functioning of the Conciliation Committee.

23 Currently the EPP group consists of 224 members, whereas the PES group has 180 members in the 626 member EP.

Adrienne Héritier

Comment: 'The Treaty of Amsterdam and the co-decision procedure'

Using spatial models of EU co-decision procedures, Christoph Crombez studies the impact of the Amsterdam Treaty on the Commission's and the EP's decision-making powers. Assuming entirely correct and complete information he models the equilibrium policies – both unidimensionally and multidimensionally – as functions of the various countries' and MEPs' and Commissioners' preferences, as well as the location of the status quo. Power is defined – given an ideal policy and a specific status quo – as the ability to obtain a policy that is close to the institution's ideal policy. Crombez concludes that Commission proposals become irrelevant in the new co-decision procedures and that the Commission's powers are thereby reduced. The EP's powers, whose preferences, he argues, are often similar to the Commission's preferences, are likewise weakened rather than strengthened.

In the context of the spatial model approach, Christophe Crombez develops his argument very systematically and carefully. Against the background of its assumptions, the stringency and consistency with which he develops his thoughts is intriguing. He arrives at clear conclusions which can be subjected to empirical validation: e.g., 'The Commission becomes irrelevant under the co-decision procedure'. 'Indecision increases under the new procedure'.

The very strengths of the model, however, i.e., its parsimoniousness and logical stringency, also constitute its weakness. To what extent is it able to grasp the complex reality of European decision-making processes? In analysing the role of the Commission simply in terms of the co-decision rules of the Amsterdam Treaty, Crombez omits important areas of decision-making and decision phases where the Commission does, after all, have considerable powers of agenda-setting and indeed decision-making. Thus the Commission remains *the* important agenda-setter in defining the problems to be dealt with in the context of European policy-making in general, and in setting up working parties of experts and national representatives to hammer out solutions which are subsequently formed into legislative drafts. In areas such as competition policy the Commission can make a decision without even consulting the Council.

A further systematic weakness of this theoretical approach is that preferences are assumed to be fixed and known *ex ante*, and that the information is entirely correct and complete. This is, of course, simply not the case at many stages in several of the European decision-making processes. Frequently, the stakes of the actors involved are not quite clear and they do not know precisely what the implications of an issue are, particularly in complex policy-making areas. In other words: it only becomes clear in the course of negotiations and deliberations what the preferences of the parties involved are. Only in the course of these 'problem solving' negotiations do they gain information about what the implications of the issue may be. Thus, although the model presented by Crombez offers important insights in well-defined, specific areas and stages of European policy-making, in others it fails to do so. There is a price to pay for parsimoniousness and elegance.

A constrained Commission: informal practices of agenda-setting in the Council[1]

European legislation has been marked by complexity. A whole series of different procedures exists, which have been changed rather frequently. The polity has an unfamiliar structure, with the Commission having the right of initiative and the Council of Ministers being the main decision-making body, while the European Parliament (EP) is involved to varying degrees. European policy-making has proved to be a fruitful field for rational-choice analyses which have grappled with the institutional resources of the different actors in ever more sophisticated ways.

Thus, the weighing of votes of the member states in the Council has led to studies assessing the different importance of each one in terms of its possible decisiveness for coalitions under qualified majority voting (e.g., Hosli, 1996). The new co-operation procedure introduced by the Single European Act (SEA), and the co-decision procedure added with the Maastricht Treaty have given rise to several spatial analyses evaluating the relative power of the Commission, EP and Council under the different eventualities (Steunenberg, 1994; Tsebelis, 1994; Schneider, 1995a; Crombez, 1996; Moser, 1996). These and other works have undoubtedly advanced our understanding of European decision-making. However, in this chapter I argue that they also run the risk of blinding us to the realities of Community decision-making by concerning themselves only with the very basic formal decision rules or with more anecdotal evidence. What are lacking are in-depth empirical studies that test results obtained from formal modelling, and the willingness to adapt assumptions or to modify models in line with empirical findings. The lack of empirical testing is a common reproach to the rational-choice literature, and has been discussed at great length in the controversy surrounding the Green and Shapiro (1994) book (see Friedman, 1996b; Cox, 1999). It also has to be taken seriously in the analysis of European integration.

In this chapter I aim to bridge a gap that has increasingly marked the field of EU studies: despite the common institutionalist turn, historical and rational-choice institutionalist studies have not made much use of their respective results for their own research. In the following, I question a central claim of rational-choice institutionalist analyses of European decision-making by confronting it with the results of some qualitative studies from the historical institutionalist line of research. The powers of the European Commission as an agenda-setter, I argue, are overrated because of the failure to take account of the empirical realities of European decision-making beyond the basic formal rules. I will confront the argument of the Commission's agenda-setting powers with empirical findings from several policies. In these, the outcome was very different from what the rational-choice literature would predict. I present an alternative explanation of this unexpected outcome, focusing on informal rules of conduct in the Council, many of which are related to the Presidency. Informal rules have been as significant for European integration as for any political setting but they have received little attention outside of more descriptive case studies. The empty-chair crisis of the mid-1960s and the resulting Luxembourg compromise showed early on that formal rules explain only part of European integration. At the insistence of de Gaulle, the formal qualified-majority decision rule was replaced with unanimity. The well-known example of the Luxembourg compromise thus shows how an informal intergovernmentalist norm may replace a formal supranationalist one of Qualified Majority Voting.

My focus in this chapter will be a related one. I will explain the outcome of my cases with the impact of informal practices in the Council, which are mostly related to the Council presidency. In alternating six-monthly terms the member states take over important responsibilities for the management of the Council which are partly formalised and partly result from informal practice. The presidency complements and partly substitutes for the role of the Commission as an agenda-setter and broker of compromises, as I will show. As a result, the formal treaty rules have little predictive value for the actual behaviour of the Commission, as do rational-choice analyses which are exclusively based on these.

The formal agenda-setting powers of the Commission

Formally, the Commission enjoys the monopoly to direct legislative proposals to the Council and the EP (Beutler et al., 1993: 140). The latter two bodies may only request particular propositions, but legally the Commission need not respond. Once the Commission has made a proposal, the Council has to act unanimously if it wishes to enact alterations. It is because of this rule that the Commission's right of initiative is so important. Under Qualified Majority Voting, it may be easier for the Council to adopt a proposal than to alter it, giving agenda-setting powers to the Commission. Consequently, the Commission may effectively pick out of several possible coalitions in the Council the one which is closest to its own preferences.

While the Commission's agenda-setting power holds under conditions of Qualified Majority Voting, the relative power of the Commission, Council and EP depends on the underlying legislative procedure. Under the basic consultation procedure, the EP does not play a significant role, so that decision-making depends on the preferences of the Commission and the Council members. Under the co-operation procedure, which was introduced with the SEA and is therefore relevant for much of the Single Market initiative, the EP has the possibility of proposing changes in the second reading. If the Commission adopts these, the EP is a 'conditional agenda setter' (Tsebelis, 1994), since the Council can only accept these changes or alter the proposal unanimously.

Just as agenda-setting powers are central for rational-choice analyses in general (Cox, 1999: 153-7), the analysis of the Commission's agenda-setting powers can be said to be a core contribution of rational-choice institutionalism to European integration studies (Steunenberg, 1994: 648, 651, 663; Crombez, 1996: 199, 201, 204, 211, 213). Equally, the power of the EP, as we have just seen, is discussed with regard to its agenda-setting powers. A recent disagreement over its role is quite interesting for our discussion. The role of the EP is very different from that maintained by Tsebelis, writes Moser (1997b), if one takes into account an additional rule not mentioned in the original analysis: once the Council has adopted its common position, the Commission may no longer alter its proposal. The EP's influence as a conditional agenda-setter therefore actually depends on whether the Commission would like to change its proposal – because of changed preferences, superior knowledge or changed circumstances – but is not able to do so by itself without the EP suggesting the desired modifications.

This dispute demonstrates how results may differ once additional rules intervene. While it is a conflict about relevant formal rules, similar alterations could be expected from an institutionalist viewpoint that takes a broader conception of institutions encompassing informal rules and social norms.

It is interesting in this respect that the agenda-setting powers of the Commission have been better theorised than documented until now (Pollack, 1997: 124). Nonetheless, theorists have attached significant claims to findings based on formal modelling. Thus, Steunenberg (1994: 651) concludes from his formal analysis of this competence that 'the Council has limited power to affect the final outcome ... Given the agenda-setting power of the Commission the Council can hardly be called "the ultimate locus of Community decision-making"' (Wessels, 1991: 133). However, without empirical evidence it may be that the conclusions drawn from the Commission's formal powers are just as misleading as

Moser suggests is the case for the EP. Therefore it is important to analyse how the Commission uses this power in practice.

In the following, I will confront the claims of rational-choice analyses about agenda-setting with evidence of the Commission's behaviour in some examples of policy-making. Such an attempt at empirical testing immediately raises the question of generalisability. As I aim to show the limits of the agenda-setting argument I deliberately chose my cases with a view to the dependent variable, with the resulting methodological flaws (Geddes, 1990). This selection bias is not problematic for my purposes as I do not try to validate a hypothesis, but to argue that a certain general claim cannot be made. Even if I have stumbled on the only five cases out of all qualified-majority legislation where the Commission did not use its powers, it would be necessary for the proponents to come forward with some boundary rules to explain why these exceptions occurred.

However, it is unlikely that these cases are unique, even though they were not selected randomly. The generalisability of cases is difficult to prove. Examples of European policy-making, on the one hand, differ with regard to the underlying legislative procedures. In this respect it is relatively easy to determine the status of a case, as the composition of all EU legislation is known (König, 1997: 86). Being based on the co-operation and co-decision procedures, the following cases could thus be regarded as representative for the single market programme. However, cases differ significantly concerning the conflict they generate. For this, the generalisability is much more difficult to establish, as an in-depth knowledge of all cases would be necessary. The length of procedure and the number of alterations to a proposal (König, 1997: 86, 89) are not necessarily adequate proxies, since procedural conflict with the EP often postpones cases, and the lack of an officially altered proposal does not mean that there have not been many alterations – which the cases of posted workers and of electricity liberalisation will show.

Finally, a distinction should be drawn between negative and positive integration, or 'market-making' and 'market-shaping' (Scharpf, 1996). This distinction is important with respect to alternative venues of decision-making. Because of the Treaty's bias in favour of liberalising measures, the Council is under much more pressure where negative integration is at stake. Here, the Commission and private actors can use (directly binding) Treaty law to try to realise liberalisation via the courts (Schmidt, 2000).

Resigning agenda-setting powers

I will now turn to some empirical examples of the Commission's agenda-setting, and confront the predictions of rational-choice analyses with some empirical puzzles. Although the examples are based partly on the co-operation and partly on the co-decision procedure, the resulting differences need not concern us here. In all the cases the EP largely abstained from using its potential powers so that the examples are interesting foremost with a view to the Commission's possible exploitation of the qualified-majority decision rules for agenda-setting purposes.

The first two cases I discuss, the packaging-waste directive and the posting of workers, are examples of positive regulatory policies (measures of positive integration or market shaping). The other three examples, the liberalisation of electricity, postal and airport services, represent instances of negative integration or the lifting of market barriers.

Examples from positive integration

In his analysis of the *packaging-waste directive*, Golub (1996: 325) finds that 'the weakness of the Commission as an agenda-setter is striking.' Many of the Commission's original objectives did not even find their way into the first draft of the proposal because of the resistance of member states and lobby groups. In this case, Germany, the Netherlands and Denmark favoured strict environmental standards, while the Mediterranean countries and the UK aimed to dilute the Commission's proposal. Recycling and recovery rates, thresholds for landfill and burning were at issue here, with targets to be reached within five or ten years. The directive was initially subject to the co-operation and then to the co-decision procedure.

What should one expect on the basis of rational-choice analyses of agenda-setting powers in this case? Given the heterogeneity of member states' preferences the Commission might have been able, by using its agenda-setting powers, to make a proposal drawing in the high regulators Denmark, Germany and the Netherlands, if we follow the general assumption that the Commission prefers high environmental regulations as a means to enhance its own competencies and its legitimacy. Instead, however, a much weakened proposal was adopted as a common position and later as a directive against the wishes of Denmark, the Netherlands and Germany. After the original proposal had failed to gain sufficient support, the ensuing negotiations in the Council, guided by the presidencies, tended to be inclusive of the opposing member states' concerns. The Commission resigned its formal powers and backed the revision, which was a lowest common denominator one, so that no member state had to make special efforts to meet its demands (Golub, 1996: 326, 328). Those member states who could have supported the Commission in aiming for high European standards found themselves isolated.

Only drawing on secondary literature for this case, it should be mentioned that not all analyses share Golub's pessimistic interpretation but argue that some low-regulating countries had to improve as a result of the directive (Haverland, 1998: 196, 217). But it is not necessary here to determine the effect of the packaging-waste directive. It suffices that the

Commission missed its chance to use its agenda-setting powers to draw
the high-regulating countries into the compromise. As Figure 6.1 shows,
this would have necessitated drawing one country into the agreement to
break up the existing veto coalition. But no such attempts were made by
the Commission as the various detailed studies of this case show
(Haverland, 1998; Golub, 1996; Gehring, 1997). Rather, the Commission
took an approach of least resistance.

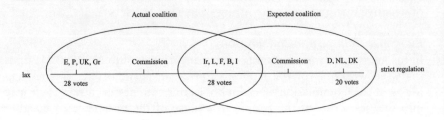

Blocking minority: 26

Figure 6.1 Preference distribution in the packaging waste case

The directive on the *posting of workers* is an example of a positive regulatory measure in the area of social policy.[2] The high-wage member states
like France, the Netherlands, Belgium, Denmark and particularly
Germany faced increasing problems in their construction industries with
workers being posted from member states with lower wage levels
(Portugal, Spain, Greece, Ireland, Italy and the UK). Because of the
freedom to provide services, subcontractors could send their workers
abroad, profiting from their lower national social standards and wages.

The Commission presented a first draft directive in 1991 under the co-
operation procedure which proposed extending a core of standards to all
posted workers staying longer than three months in another member
state. In 1993, a revised proposal was published which included amendments suggested by the EP in the meantime, most of all lowering the
threshold of being in another member state to one month. The directive
now fell under the co-decision procedure. In the Council, the governments
were divided: the UK and Portugal were firmly against a directive. The
other countries from which workers were being posted took a more
conciliatory stance. The high-wages countries, in contrast, wanted a directive, with the exception of Germany which was hesitant due to domestic
opposition from the liberal party and the employers' associations against
regulating this kind of regime competition.

In view of this deadlock at the European level, some member states like
France enacted domestic legislation to deal with the problem. In addition,

the Council presidencies tried to find a compromise. Because of the decline of its construction industry, the German presidency in the second half of 1994 made particular efforts. The Council met four times to discuss this question but too many issues remained open. The subsequent French presidency followed up with a new compromise position. But in addition to the 'hardliners' Britain and Portugal, Spain, Ireland and Italy as well as the Commission found the proposal too restrictive. Although the Commission soon signalled its willingness to be more forthcoming, no common position could be agreed upon. The same was true under the following Spanish presidency. Finally, the Italian presidency, building on these previous efforts, made a new proposal for a compromise after intense bilateral consultations with the relevant actors (Eichhorst, 1998a: 245). The contentious question of the threshold was now to be decided at the domestic level. The Commission supported this compromise and a qualified majority could be reached in the Council for the common position against Britain and Portugal. The EP accepted the negotiation outcome as well: judging the agreement in the Council as unstable (any modifications could have led to a new deadlock) and, like the Commission, the EP preferred a non-perfect to a non-existing solution.

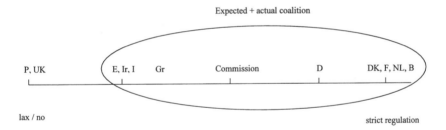

Figure 6.2 Preference distribution in the posted workers case

Thus, in contrast to the packaging directive, in this case the final compromise was one that came close to what one should have expected the Commission to aim for – achieving an agreement on a policy isolating the 'hardliners' Britain and Portugal. But the case study shows that it did not come about as expected. It was a result of intergovernmental bargaining in which the Commission had long lost its initiative to the presidencies.

Examples from negative integration
Liberalisation policies are interesting because of the more encompassing rights of the Commission. For these policies, there are alternative venues to achieve the desired results. The Commission and private actors can take cases to the Courts, and are therefore less dependent on the Council. Does

this stronger role mean that the Commission has a firmer grasp of its agenda-setting powers?

The liberalisation of European *electricity systems* is an interesting case to enquire into the relationship between the Commission and the Council in order to assess the relative weight of both institutions. Electricity liberalisation was very contentious, needing several years for a compromise to be negotiated. In questions of low political salience one should expect the Commission to play an important role. For instance, Garrett and Weingast (1993) have shown that ideas brought forward by the Commission may matter whenever there are multiple equilibria, determining which equilibrium will be chosen. When high political stakes are at issue, such as in electricity policy, in contrast, it should be much more difficult for the Commission to influence the course of a policy. Electricity can thus be seen as a 'least-likely' crucial case (Eckstein, 1975) for our purposes, with the exception that its independent powers for negative integration give the Commission additional leeway. With this caveat, should the Commission do well in the case of electricity, it could be expected to be generally in an influential position.

For European electricity policy the Commission introduced a liberalisation proposal to the Council and the EP in late 1991 under the co-operation procedure.[3] It followed an earlier directive that had achieved few changes (Argyris, 1993). Almost all member states opposed the way the Commission planned to open electricity networks, leading to an altered proposal in late 1993.

But the controversy remained. France especially saw its generally successful electricity system at risk. The long-term planning necessary for the nuclear power programme would be impossible under the Commission's plans. Other member states (Belgium, Spain, Italy, Greece, Ireland and later Portugal) were sceptical, but were not stable coalition partners since heterogeneous national systems meant that small modifications could easily soothe some opposition. But France could hardly be isolated in the Council, despite the formal decision rule of Qualified Majority Voting. Several member states were dependent on French electricity imports, Electricité de France (EdF) being the largest exporter of electricity. Moreover, electricity was an issue of high political salience for France, and in such circumstances the Council places significant importance on the building of a consensus. The electricity case demonstrates how this informal practice is institutionalised in the Council.

In view of the persistent deadlock after the modified Commission proposal in the Council, the Greek presidency in the first half of 1994 asked the member states for alternative proposals. In response, France submitted a proposal to the Council, called 'Single Buyer', which would leave the monopoly of EdF basically intact. Although the Commission and some member states (Britain, Germany and the Netherlands) had strong reservations, it was quickly accepted that a two-tiered policy had to be followed to meet French concerns. During the German presidency some aspects could be agreed on in a conclusion.

Conclusions of the Council are non-binding and do not have a formal legal standing. Nevertheless, they are of some importance and it is interesting to note that their usage has grown considerably over the course of the single market project.[4] Conclusions are a means for the presidency to document the progress achieved over its term in all those cases where legislation cannot be finalised. Conclusions are prepared by the presidency and have to be adopted unanimously. If the presidency fails to overcome all opposition, only 'conclusions of the presidency' can be published which do not have much impact for future negotiations. As presidencies have an incentive to be acclaimed as successful, it is in their interest to reach Council conclusions where a dossier cannot be finalised. For contentious issues such as the liberalisation of electricity this means that there will have been several unanimous conclusions, mapping out different items of the final compromise. This informal procedure backs the Council's tradition of decision-making by consensus, despite a formal majority rule.

Until their conclusion, the negotiations showed the dominance of the alternating presidencies over the Commission. The latter tried in vain to achieve significant alterations of the French proposal. This was despite the fact that the Commission had already (in 1991) initiated infringement procedures at the European Court against the import and export monopolies for electricity in several member states, so that the Council had been under some pressure to act (Schmidt, 2000). France was next with the presidency and managed to establish the single buyer as an equivalent option to the Commission's proposal. The following Spanish and Italian presidencies further developed compromises, increasingly helped by Franco-German efforts, who were using their special relationship to overcome the particular problems electricity liberalisation posed for both countries.

The common position that was finally agreed in the Council in June 1996 – now under the co-decision procedure – rested on a previous Franco-German compromise. It was adopted unanimously and also received the backing of the Commission. The Commission had not altered its proposal since the one time at the beginning, although negotiations soon left this proposal behind.

The electricity case shows how in a matter of high political and distributional salience the alternating presidencies may broker an agreement. The Commission altered its proposal once but afterwards each presidency tried to find a compromise. Several unanimous conclusions documented the success of the different member states' terms and ensured that the Council decided by consensus on this important topic. Although the

Commission was originally opposed, the French proposal was included in the negotiations. This was despite the fact that the Commission was well-posed to realise liberalisation by using competition law and the market freedoms.

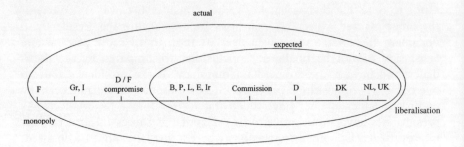

Figure 6.3 Preference distribution in the electricity case

In times of controversy and high distributional concerns, the role of the governments, notably the presidencies, seems generally heightened *vis-a-vis* the Commission. The governments were the actors searching actively for a compromise, and the Commission accepted it. Several presidencies altered the Commission's proposal, weakening its role as an agenda-setter considerably. This does not mean, however, that the EU is an intergovernmental enterprise. Rather, the electricity case shows how the supranational legal framework, and the Commission's right to enforce it by calling upon the Court, provides incentives for change. As such France had no reason to alter its electricity system in view of widely recognised efficiency and broad public support. But membership in the EU made it necessary (Schmidt, 2000). In sum, some of the liberalisation measures which the Commission had supported could be achieved, but the new European policy is one offering multiple options, which were notably forwarded by the French government.

The liberalisation of *postal services* (see Schmidt, 1998: 274–86) is an interesting example because the Commission planned to use its agenda-setting powers in the way described by rationalists but was openly forced to step back. The Commission initially wanted to enact the liberalisation of postal services itself, using its competition law powers. It dropped this plan because of the significant opposition of the member states. Instead of a Commission directive (Art. 90.3), the Commission directed a proposal to the Council. In addition, guidelines were planned on the application of competition law to postal services. With express carriers and other private actors interested in liberalisation, this meant that the Commission gained some possibilities of its own and was not reliant on the Council to achieve a degree of liberalisation. In order not to interfere with the decision-making of the Council, the Commission promised to hold back the publication of these guidelines for a year until the end of 1996 and was thus very conciliatory even before detailed negotiations started.

In its proposal for a directive – to be adopted under the co-decision procedure – the Commission suggested liberalising mail above 350g or five-times the tariff of a standard letter. Starting in 2001, direct mail and incoming international letters were to be liberalised. Of this proposal, the planned liberalisation of direct mail was particularly contentious, this being one of the few growth areas in an otherwise stagnant sector. France was the main opponent, supported by Belgium, Luxembourg, Greece, Austria and Portugal, so that a veto coalition existed. The Netherlands, United Kingdom and Germany, on the other hand, wanted more liberalisation. These countries, as well as some others, had already liberalised direct mail, making the French position a scarcely tenable one. The veto coalition as such was of little use given that the Commission would liberalise via competition law should the Council not agree on a directive.

In this situation, the Franco-German friendship was used to reach a compromise. Direct mail should be liberalised only from 350g onwards and further liberalisation steps should be stalled until 2003. However, the member states pushing for liberalisation, the Netherlands and the Scandinavian countries, did not back this compromise. All depended therefore on the Commission's decision to back the new compromise or its original proposal. At the Council meeting at the end of November 1996, it used its agenda-setting powers and sided with the more liberal member states.[5] By backing down, the Commission would probably have damaged its role as a neutral agenda-setter.

The deadlock led to a difficult situation, given that the Commission had announced its intention to liberalise via competition law. As such, the Council (short of unanimity) could not prevent liberalisation. However, the French postal minister had threatened with a *vrai conflit politique* should the Commission try to shape European postal policy without the consent of the Council.[6] The problem was solved at the next summit in Dublin where President Chirac pushed through an extraordinary meeting of the Postal Ministers Council before the end of 1996. In view of the support of the European Council for a political compromise, the Commission again ceded its agenda-setting powers and backed the Franco-German compromise, which could be adopted against the Netherlands, Sweden and Finland.[7]

A final example is the liberalisation of monopolies for *airport services* (ground-handling). Also here it is clear that the Commission can be more adequately described as launching an idea, which is subsequently transformed until it is acceptable in the Council, than as setting the agenda by using its formal powers strategically. The ground-handling monopolies at

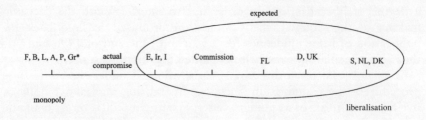

* veto coalition is not tenable
because of competition law

Figure 6.4 Preference distribution in the postal services case

several European airports attracted increasing criticism by airlines in the early 1990s. With the advent of competition in air transport, airlines wanted to avoid high monopoly prices and wished to have better opportunities for self-handling as a means of strengthening their corporate identity. Many complaints based on European competition law were handed to the responsible Directorate General IV (DG IV), which examined the situation in several member states, including Germany, Spain, Ireland, Greece and Italy. DG IV originally planned to liberalise with a Commission directive based on Article 90.3 as it had for postal liberalisation; but it backed down in view of opposition (Schmidt, 1998).

The Commission therefore chose to make a proposal for a directive to the Council on the basis of Art. 84 (which involves the EP under the co-operation procedure), while continuing to examine the monopolies of several member states under competition law. I have argued elsewhere that this facilitated the adoption of the directive in the Council given that the Commission had systematically broken the resistance of several member states in advance (Schmidt, 2000). In view of the institutionally strong position of the Commission which was not dependent on the Council to pursue liberalisation (being endowed with competition law instruments), it is surprising to see how little the Commission used its agenda-setting powers in this situation.

The Commission proposed opening airports with two million travellers or 50,000 tons of freight per annum to third-party handlers, which were to be chosen in a transparent, non-discriminatory process.[8] The self-handling for airlines was to be principally allowed for several services. The directive would enter into force within two years, but derogations were possible for airports with capacity constraints. Germany in particular opposed this proposal in the Council due to the resistance of its domestic airports, especially Frankfurt. Also the EP was critical and demanded to set restrictive limits for liberalisation at 4.5 million passengers or 150,000 tons of freight. Without the support of the Commission, however, the EP had no hope of realising this goal.[9]

In the Council, the Spanish presidency forwarded a compromise, responding to German demands in particular. The threshold was set at 3 million passengers and 75,000 tons of freight. In addition, Germany successfully bargained for the option to have two possible derogations for two years. In 2001, the threshold for third-party handling will be lowered to 2 million passengers. For airports with 1 million passengers self-handling was liberalised only outside the airport-hall. The Commission backed this compromise in the Council, ceding its agenda-setting powers. Despite these concessions, the compromise was adopted as a common position against the votes of Germany and Austria, at the end of 1995.[10] The directive was finally passed in October 1996.[11]

Much more than the positive-regulatory directives, ground-handling is a case demonstrating the conciliatory stance of the Commission. Here, it had an alternative venue for action because of its competition law powers, so that it did not have to follow the 'better something than nothing' logic employed especially in packaging waste. It therefore would have had the possibility of pushing a proposal through the Council that was initially not congruent with the preferences of a qualified majority of member states, as it is likely that some member states would have favoured far-reaching liberalisation to a situation of legal uncertainty governed by the Commission's case-specific interpretation of competition law. How much support did the Commission have for its original proposal?

Originally, a majority of member states was broadly in favour but Germany and Austria were strongly opposed. Among the supporters (Spain, Belgium, Italy, United Kingdom, Denmark, Sweden, Finland, Luxembourg, the Netherlands and France) some wanted specific alterations, like the Netherlands and France, who were in favour of a simplified and immediately binding liberalisation. Italy, in contrast, was willing to back Germany if no threshold was imposed on self-handling.[12] In a later Council meeting, Germany had much more support: Denmark, Greece, Italy, Luxembourg and Portugal backed its call for a threshold of 5 million passengers. Only Belgium, Spain, France, Ireland, Finland, Sweden and the UK defended the original Commission proposal. Together with the liberal Netherlands and the restrictive Austria, this meant that forty-eight votes were in favour and thirty-nine votes were against the Commission's proposal.[13]

In view of this situation, the Spanish presidency was asked to work towards a compromise. At the meeting in December, France bargained on the side of Germany in order to gain some privileges for the phasing out of duopolies, a problem for Orly airport. Along with the concessions achieved by Germany, the common position was then adopted.

The changing member states' support makes it difficult to judge the extent of the Commission's conciliation in this case. After all, Germany and Austria still voted against the final compromise so that, similar to the posted workers case, it could be seen that as much was achieved as possible, if not pushed mostly by the Commission but by the presidencies. However, another interpretation is more likely: after the presidency had succeeded in constructing a compromise that received the backing of a consensus in the Council, Germany and Austria took the liberty of voting against it given that the Commission did not pursue its agenda-setting rights. This allowed Germany and Austria to demonstrate their tough negotiating stance to domestic veto groups. That Germany got a very positive outcome is indicated by the positive reception of the deal by Frankfurt airport, whose interests were the ones pushed hardest by the German transport minister.[14]

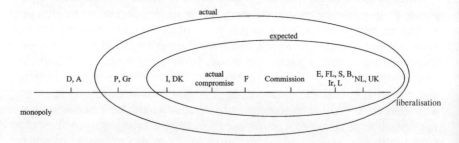

Figure 6.5 Preference distribution in the airport services case

The examples presented show several different cases. Packaging waste and ground-handling are two cases where the Commission did not use its agenda-setting powers; instead efforts were made to draw all laggards into the compromise. Postal services is the only example where the Commission threatened to use its agenda-setting powers but backed down after intervention from the European Council. Posted workers and electricity, finally, are examples of elaborate compromises which were entirely shaped by the Council and its alternating presidencies. In the former case this even led to the outcome one would expect under agenda-setting, albeit without the Commission having a significant impact.

Bridging the gap between modelling and empirical research

How can we account for the Commission failing to use its agenda-setting powers? From the perspective of institutionalist case studies, models of the Commission's agenda-setting powers seem to have too slight an empirical base. Building solely on the formal decision rules as they are laid down in the Treaty, these models leave out the host of informal rules

Role of Commission/ Presidency	Co-operation procedure	Co-decision procedure
Resigning agenda-setting powers	—airport services— ———————— packaging waste ————————	
Resignation after threat	———————— postal services ————————	
Expected outcome but shaped by presidencies not the Commission	———————— posted workers ————————	
Elaborate outcome shaped by Presidency	———————— electricity ————————	

Figure 6.6 Summary of cases

which institutionalists not exclusively rooted in the rational-choice paradigm generally include in their analyses (Scharpf, 1997: 38; Mayntz, 1998). The cases have shown that the formal decision rules are not the only guideline to decision-making in the Council. Rather, informal rules intervene – most of all related to the Council presidency – and complement or modify the implications of the formal ones. In the following, I will first expand on the importance of informal rules for decision-making in the EU. I will then turn to the implications of my findings for rational-choice analyses.

Joint responsibilities – the Commission and the Presidency, formal and informal rules
At the national level, it is broadly recognised that policy-making cannot be adequately analysed without recourse to informal rules (Wewer, 1991: 11). An example of informally-set but institutionalised behaviour were the working groups of the Christian Democratic-Liberal coalition in Germany, which informally replaced much of the formally necessary co-ordination between the different ministries (Manow, 1996: 102). Informal rules also complement formal ones at the international level (Lipson, 1991).

Informal rules offer some advantages over formal ones. They are more flexible and more easily changed which makes them better adapted to complex problems in a rapidly changing environment. This particularly concerns cases where the future distribution of benefits is difficult to assess. Because of their lower profile, informal agreements escape public controversies, and therefore allow compromises which could not be entered into openly (Lipson, 1991). The reduced public accountability is likely to play a particular role in EU decision-making.

At the national level, member states differ as to their degree of formalisation. Germany has a highly formalised polity which contrasts with Britain's low degree of formalisation (Kastning, 1991: 72). Informal arrangements may also get formalised. In the EU, the European Council is an example. It started informally in the 1970s and was formally integrated into the Treaty's framework only after it had grown in importance for the handling of difficult issues and the adoption of new priorities. But although degrees of formalisation differ, informal rules always play a role. In inter-organisational as well as in intra-organisational exchanges, informal practices complement and partly transform formal rules. Attempts to formalise informal rules generally lead to the emergence of new informal practices. Neither the abundance nor the relative lack of detailed rules thus seem to prevent informal practices (Dreier, 1994: 169, 175). Organisational theory provides some clues to this dynamic and to the question why informal rules are being adhered to. In long-term interactions, informal relations grow wherever exchanges are mutually profitable for the participants (Coleman, 1995). Compared to the formally prescribed relations, informal exchanges rely on more direct rewards: while formal exchanges only need to be viable overall, informal exchanges only arise if they are directly viable (Coleman, 1995: 129).

Considering the phlethora of informal rules, their absence is striking when turning to rationalist analyses of European decision-making. Considering the complexity of European decision-making procedures, such a neglect is understandable. But the results of rational-choice institutionalism may have to be modified, once informal norms are taken into account, and the case studies presented are evidence of this.

In particular, the cases have pointed to the importance of the presidency of the Council as an informal broker of compromise that has received relatively little attention in research so far. Not having the same formal status as the Commission's right of initiative and the different legislative procedures, the role of the presidency in EU decision-making is often forgotten. It is based on Art. 146 of the Treaty of Rome which contains the principal decision that the member states take turns in chairing the meetings of the Council, rather than giving the mandate to an independent secretariat. While not being important at the very beginning, the presidency gained relevance as an institution in the late 1960s and 1970s, when it made up for the weaker role of the Commission in the aftermath of the Luxembourg compromise (Wallace, 1985: 3). The rules of procedure of the Council, formally published only in 1979, set out the responsibilities of the presidency in greater detail, in particular with regard to the management of the Council (Westlake, 1995). The presidency schedules and convenes the meetings of the Council and its subgroups, sets the agenda, signs the minutes and the acts adopted. Originally, it was only the presidency that could call a vote in the Council but this was changed to speed up decision-making. Every member state, supported by an absolute majority, may now call a vote (Westlake, 1995: 80). The presidency is a contact point for third parties, which includes relations with the EP as well as with international organisations and trading partners. Since 1989, each presidency presents its programme to the EP (and also to the Council) at the beginning of its term and is accountable for the progress achieved at the end.

The European Political Co-operation, started in 1975, has relied heavily on the presidency, strengthening its role in turn. The institutionalisation of the second and the third pillar, the Common Foreign and Security Policy (CFSP) and Justice and Home Affairs (JHA), outside of the Community-framework emphasised this increased importance, and reflects the generally positive evaluation of the presidency through the member states (Wallace, 1985: 9).

How do member states approach the office of the presidency? For the member state concerned, the presidency is both the chance to further specific issues high on the domestic agenda and to take over a supranational office with all the possibilities this offers to improve its domestic, European and international standing. Evaluations of different presidencies abound even though it is clearly difficult to judge the success or failure of a presidency given the multiplicity of issues under negotiation, the very short, six-monthly term, and the significant degree of luck involved (for instance with regard to sudden international crises). The following citation, taken from a discussion of the British presidency in 1992, conveys an image of the pitfalls of this office:

> When every allowance is made for the UK's relative bad luck and its specific successes in terms of both personalities and policies, this must, one fears, be assessed as a presidency which singularly failed to provide the EC with the leadership that it needed in a period of considerable difficulty, which exposed the Community to quite unnecessary and unacceptable strains and which, as a result, left the EC weaker and the UK more vulnerable and isolated than either had been when the six-month period began. (Ludlow, 1994: 249)

For the member states it is thus important to present some breakthroughs at the end of their term as these will be remembered positively. It is also in this respect that each presidency presents a programme of priorities. And it is with this background that each member state when holding the presidency will not simply follow those issues high on the domestic agenda – as open partiality is highly disrespected – but has the incentive to achieve progress and possibly some success with ongoing

Community business. This brings the presidency very close to the mandate of the Commission as the formal broker of compromises, significantly modifying the latter's role. The cases presented show that the Commission determines the content of policies less than its formal responsibilities would lead us to expect. In addition, the presidency also has the right to determine the agenda of Council meetings. Thus, it is not sufficient for the Commission to use its right of initiative, the presidency actually has to put the items on the agenda of the meeting. As Kerremans (1996: 229) points out, this allowed the UK and Denmark to use their presidencies in 1992–93 to slow down the speed of integration.

At times, the Franco-German relationship also plays a considerable role as a broker of compromises in the Council, and is another example of an informal practice of intergovernmental decision-making modifying the formal institutional set-up of the EU (Webber, 1999). The relevance of compromise positions forwarded by the presidency increased much in the 1990s, making the European decision-making process even more opaque. Instead of negotiating published Commission proposals, the Council increasingly works on the basis of compromise positions drawn up by the presidency.[15] The cases I discussed are therefore unlikely to be exceptional. Compared to the Commission, the presidency seems to have some advantages for brokering an agreement. Among these, in particular, the 'confessionals' have to be noted in which the presidency questions each member state in confidence about its position and bottom line in the negotiations (Westlake, 1995: 115; Hayes-Renshaw and Wallace, 1997: 146). This privileged information makes the presidency much better placed than the Commission to draw up an acceptable compromise. The role of the presidency in achieving compromise in the Council is not fully captured by the formal rules. As governments agree that consensus should be sought in issues of high political salience, they trust themselves more than the Commission, which has to be suspected of favouring integration over domestic concerns.

The cases have shown that it is only in theory that the Commission's agenda-setting powers allow it to influence the Council's decision-making to an extent where the latter is no longer the decisive player. The image that emerges is not one of a Commission that lets the member states be trapped in their incapacity to alter a proposal unanimously. Rather the Commission forwards proposals which are subsequently modified by the Council presidencies. When, finally, at least a qualified majority of member states agree to the compromise, the Commission is most likely to go along. It seems to be much more acting under the rationale that 'something is better than nothing' than maximising its institutional power to influence policies.

Possible implications for agenda-setting models
Empirical examples match rational-choice models only imperfectly. Partly the Commission has additional powers in negative integration, partly the cases exhibit the expected results, albeit not because of the role of the Commission but of the presidency. This latter point, in particular, is related to a central ambiguity of rational-choice research: the conflict over whether models should provide for solid microfoundations (Esser, 1993; Coleman, 1990), or whether an instrumentalist view should be pursued, which aims at predicting the outcome (Green and Shapiro, 1994: 31; Friedman, 1996a: 12–14). It suffices here to take note of this disagreement. An instrumentalist view is at least contentious (Hovi, 1998), and in this sense it may be critically noted if a case – like the one of posted workers – shows the predicted results, but because of very different reasons.

What are the implications of my findings for the modelling of agenda-setting powers? Undoubtedly models could be adopted to take informal rules into account, – but this would then lead to the post-hoc fallacy criticised by Green and Shapiro (1994) as Simon Hug points out. The controversy over this book showed, however, that the standards advocated by Green and Shapiro are unrealistic (Friedman, 1996a). Also those critical of their work agree that more realistic models are necessary and that to achieve these, ad hoc assumptions cannot be avoided and some parameters need changes (Ordeshook, 1996: 180, 184; Fiorina, 1996: 92). In this respect, an adaptation to include informal rules would seem a possible option.

In his comments on this chapter, Simon Hug has pointed to another possibility, which may well have its advantages from a rational-choice perspective. He suggests relaxing assumptions to account for information asymmetries, for repeated games and for the principal–agent relationship between the member states and the Commission (instead of assuming common knowledge, one-shot decision-making and the separation of legislation from the appointment process of the Commission). Indeed, such a relaxation may be necessary to even start to bridge the gap between qualitative empirical research and formal models. Given that models are based on quite unrealistic assumptions, empirical tests are ultimately impossible since they cannot replicate these unrealistic assumptions.[16] It seems obvious that for more realistic models, these preconditions for a feedback from empirical analyses are needed.

A related critique has been advanced by Lane and Mattila (1998). They take the recently published data on decision-making in the Council and find a substantial proportion of unanimous decision-making of 75 per cent to 81 per cent in 1994–96. On this basis, they question the Commission's agenda-setting power, which they see mostly based on *a priori* spatial modelling assigning specific preferences to the different actors that have no empirical foundation (p. 342). Unanimous voting, which is so common in the EU, in contrast, is not considered in these analyses because it seems unlikely under the assumptions of spatial modelling (p. 330).

Conclusion

In this chapter I have aimed to confront a central tenet of rational-choice analysis – the Commission's agenda-setting powers – with case studies rooted in the historical institutionalist tradition. I have argued that formal analyses of EU legislation overstate the Commission's influence as an agenda-setter. Although the Commission has the institutional possibility of picking the proposal that is closest to its own preferences and still receives a qualified majority vote in the Council, in practice the Council and its alternating presidencies determine much of the shape of policies to come.

With regard to rational-choice analyses of agenda-setting this means that the postulated power of the Commission can only serve as a starting point. Instead of taking the formally available institutional power as given, the difference between the model and the empirically observable behaviour is a useful research question. Rational-choice analyses have to proceed by establishing the boundary rules under which the Commission uses its formal powers. They could come up with more realistic explanations once informal rules are included or the assumptions are modified so that informal practices of behaviour are taken into account alongside formal rules. Considering the institutional self-interest of the Commission, alongside its institutional competences, its cautious conduct is not surprising. First, compared to the governments, the Commission will often be the actor most interested in European legislation. Every so often legislation needs to be passed for the Commission to acquire new competences at the European level. The principal–agent relationship Hug alludes to (in his comment on this chapter), is not only restricted to the appointment process. Being in a comparatively weak bargaining position, one should expect the Commission to be most conciliatory to heighten the chances of agreement.

In liberalisation policies, the Commission is less dependent on the Council. It is therefore not surprising that it was for postal policy that the Commission threatened to use its agenda-setting powers. But in view of the long-term co-operation and the general dependence on the Council, the Commission backed down once the European Council had emphasised the political salience of the issue. This brings me to the second point to be taken into account. Being involved in long-term co-operation with the Council, the Commission has a fundamental interest in good working relations. Resentment by governments of unreasonable behaviour on the part of the Commission would harm its long-term prospects of achieving backing for its proposals.

Fundamentally, it is due to the behaviour of the Council that informal rules of restraint play such a role for the Commission. By giving up its agenda-setting powers, the Commission worsens the position of a minority of member states which would have been able to realise their interests with the help of the Commission (e.g., the packaging waste directive and postal liberalisation). Since governments do not have fixed positions on an issue at the start but change during negotiations (for instance in ground-handling), side with other member states (especially France and Germany) and value decision-making by consensus in the Council generally more than their chances to get a better deal on an issue by isolating other member states, the Commission can only rarely use agenda-setting strategically. Despite the formal preponderance of majority voting and the different weights of member states as analysed by power indexes, consensus-seeking is an informal norm of considerable significance in the Council. This becomes apparent in the following quote: 'As nature abhors a vacuum, so the Council abhors a majority if unanimity is possible' (Westlake, 1995: 111). The electricity case especially has demonstrated how the seeking of consensus is institutionalised in periodic unanimous conclusions documenting the success of the presidencies and ensuring that no governments are being isolated.

Several instances of the broadening of majority votes have been accompanied by agreements in the European Council on how to safeguard veto possibilities in extraordinary cases through the Luxembourg and Ioaninna compromises (Westlake, 1995). This shows that majority voting in the Council is only accepted by the member states if it is modified by informal norms to reduce the risk of being isolated on issues of high political salience. The attempts of the presidencies to seek compromises and the periodic approval of conclusions demonstrates how the informal emphasis on consensus also permeates day-to-day decision-making. Given that the Council operates only imperfectly according to the formal decision rules, it is not surprising that the Commission can only rarely capitalise on its formal institutional powers. In order to determine under which conditions the Commission or the Presidency is more likely to be important it would be necessary to analyse cases that vary in this respect. This question therefore cannot be answered in the context of the present chapter.

Further research is also needed comparing successful agenda-setting with failed cases to establish the relevance of formal and informal rules in greater detail. In so doing, care should be taken to include examples of politically contentious and less contentious cases. Finally, it also needs to be emphasised that the need to transgress borders is not a one-way street. Case studies often fail to note the specifics of the decision-making process under discussion, as analysed by rationalists. This concerns even less descriptive, analytical papers. For instance, in their analysis of the packaging directive neither Golub (1996) nor Gehring (1997) mention the fact that the Commission gave up its agenda-setting powers to back the compromise position in the Council.

Notes

1 I would like to thank Werner Eichhorst, Jon Golub, Markus Haverland, Marc Smyrl and the editors of this book for their comments. Most of all, I would like to thank my discussant, Simon Hug, for providing such excellent comments. I am also grateful to Klara Vanek for research assistance.
2 I am following here the work of Werner Eichhorst (1998a; b).
3 COM(91) 548 fin, 21 February 1992.
4 Interview Council Secretariat General, 16 June 1995.
5 *Handelsblatt*, 6 November 1996; *Le Monde*, 7 November 1996; *Financial Times*, 26 November 1996.
6 *Le Monde*, 27 September 1996 – Interview with François Fillon.
7 *Financial Times*, 16 December 1996; *Handelsblatt*, 20/21 December 1996.
8 Proposal for a Council Directive on access to the groundhandling market at Community airports (presented by the Commission). Com(94) 590 final, 13 December 1994.
9 The recommendations of the EP which the Commission included related to the social situation of labour.
10 *Frankfurter Allgemeine*, 8 December 1995, 9 December 1995; *Financial Times*, 8 December 1995. Common Position (EC) No 21/96 adopted by the Council on 28 March 1996 with a view to adopting Council Directive 96/_/EC on access to the ground-handling market at Community airports. OJ C 134/19, 6 May 1996.
11 Council Directive 96/67/EC of 15 October 1996 on access to the ground-handling market at Community airports. OJ L 272/ 10, 25 October 1996.
12 *Aviation Europe*, 11 May 1995.
13 *Aviation Europe*, 21 September 1995.
14 *Frankfurter Allgemeine*, 9 December 1995.
15 Hayes-Renshaw and Wallace (1997: 146). Many examples can be found in House of Commons (1995: xxivf.).
16 Thomas König pointed this out in personal communication.

Simon Hug

Comment: 'A constrained Commission'

One of the central advantages – or drawbacks, depending on the perspective adopted – of formal models, is the considerable preciseness of their predictions. Adopting a series of assumptions, mathematical tools derive predictions in a manner that Binmore (1994: 86) likens to an autopilot. This preciseness in the predictions makes formal models an easy target for empirical challenges,[1] but at the same time allows theoretical progress to be easily achieved. Faulty assumptions can be changed and the autopilot will do the dirty work for us again.

Both the preciseness of predictions and the possibility of changing assumptions in formal models are at the centre of my comments on Susanne Schmidt's chapter on the 'constrained Commission.' Based on a careful analysis of five decision-making processes in the European Union (EU), she argues that the postulated 'powers of the European Commission as an agenda-setter ... are overrated'. She finds that in two cases of positive and three cases of negative integration, the Commission has not exploited its privilege as the agenda-setter. She demonstrates this by showing that in some cases the Commission has backed down from its original proposal, and that in others the final outcome failed to reflect its preferences.

I start my comments by briefly reviewing the models that Susanne Schmidt criticises. Based on this review I briefly discuss what the careful case studies in her chapter demonstrate and what they mean for the theoretical models under attack. I then go on to discuss some possible ways in which existing models of EU decision-making might be changed to account for the informal rules that seem, in Susanne Schmidt's reading of the cases, to play an important role.

The models

Before evaluating Susanne Schmidt's claims in a larger context it is useful to return briefly to the models and modellers that are under scrutiny.

Various scholars have attempted to demonstrate how the different deci-sion rules employed in the EU affect policy outcomes. Relying on simple spatial models, these authors have shown that depending on the rules used, the policy outcome may be quite different. For instance Steunenberg (1994) notes that policy outcomes depend on preferences and institutions. Under the consultation procedure, he writes, 'in most cases, the Commission can act as an agenda setter' (1994: 65). Similarly, for the co-operation procedure he concludes that '[p]arliament may limit, at least in some cases, the agenda setting power of the Commission' (Steunenberg, 1994: 654). He then goes on to note that very similar outcomes are to be expected for the co-decision procedure. Steunenberg's findings largely echo Tsebelis' (1994) main argument that under certain circumstances the European parliament may obtain 'agenda-setting power.'[2] Obviously, it obtains these agenda-setting powers at the disadvantage of the Commission. In a very similar vein, Crombez (1996: 209) notes that '[i]n general, the equilibrium policies depend on the configuration of ideal poli-cies and on the location of the status quo relative to the ideal policies.'

This brief and partial review of the models criticised by Susanne Schmidt suggests three points: (1) the Commission's agenda-setting is not absolute; (2) even if the Commission has absolute agenda-setting power, this does not imply that it will be able to impose its will under all circum-stances; (3) whether the Commission has agenda-setting power and whether this will find reflection in the final policies adopted depends on the preferences and the decision rules employed.

Models under 'friendly fire'

The five cases discussed by Susanne Schmidt suggest at least two things. First, according to her description of the decision-making processes, the Commission failed to take advantage of its agenda-setting power, at least at some stages of the process, in each of her five cases. Second, her analy-ses of the policy outcomes suggest that these are systematically at odds with the predictions that one might obtain from the theoretical models under attack.

By establishing these two points for the five cases under consideration, Susanne Schmidt provides an important empirical assessment of models on EU decision-making rules. Her first point provides an empirically grounded critique of the assumption that under most decision rules the Commission enjoys agenda-setting power. Her second point suggests that not only this basic assumption is faulty, but it also leads theoretical models to make faulty predictions.

These two points are powerful; however, they should not be seen, in my opinion, as frontal attacks on formal models on EU decision-making, but much more as 'friendly fire'. Such 'friendly fire' necessarily leads to some casualties, but if well taken by scholars engaged in proposing formal models of EU decision-making they might strengthen theoretically grounded research.

An easy, but not recommended, escape route for scholars employing formal models would be to rely on questioning the selection of the cases discussed by Susanne Schmidt. This escape route is problematic, since the models criticised all yield deterministic predictions. More precisely, the conditions under which the Commission can choose policies as close as possible to its ideal-point are necessary conditions. Testing such conditions is far from a trivial matter, and selecting on the dependent variable, as Susanne Schmidt does, is appropriate in some cases (e.g., Dion, 1998). Hence, the appropriate route to take is to explore problems for formal models that Susanne Schmidt's analysis suggests.

Changing assumptions

Given the selection of cases, however, it would be at least as erroneous to propose new models exclusively focusing on reproducing the patterns observed by Susanne Schmidt. At that point her selection of cases becomes an impediment. The conclusion she draws from her five cases can under no reasonable circumstances be generalised to all decision-making processes in the EU. Selecting on the dependent variable, by definition, excludes this possibility.

Consequently, the question of what assumptions in the formal models should be changed in order to account for these 'anomalies' arises. Susanne Schmidt argues that informal rules giving the presidencies additional power shift the balance of power away from the Commission. Consequently, formal models should account for these informal rules giving the presidency these additional powers.

Models relying on informal rules are, however, a tricky matter. On the one hand formal models in general should focus on the decision environment that the relevant actors face (e.g., Binmore, 1994: 96). This would speak in favour of models taking these informal rules seriously. On the other hand, these informal rules might also correspond to equilibrium behaviour in a more adequate model. This would require changed models from which informal rules would emerge endogenously.[3] Such an avenue would also reflect the recent turn in institutionalist research employing formal tools, which envisions institutions (including informal rules) as equilibrium behaviour.

Following along this latter path we would start with Susanne Schmidt's empirically derived finding that the Commission, despite its considerable formal powers, rescinds in some cases its 'agenda-setting powers'. Why would such a powerful actor do this? Informal rules as such seem to me of little explanatory value. A more interesting starting point appears in the formal models under scrutiny. Probably no one would challenge the argument that all of them rely on very simplistic assumptions. I will focus on three central ones. First, all models assume that all aspects of the game are common knowledge. All actors involved know all aspects of the game, the preferences of all actors, etc.. Second, decision-making is assumed to be a one-shot affair. What has happened in previous decision-making processes has no impact on the current decision. Finally, models of decision rules are isolated from the appointment process of the Commission.[4]

All these assumptions are central to the main conclusions of models of EU decision-making. Changing any of them is likely to affect the conclusions and might probably account for the emergence of the informal rules that Susanne Schmidt finds in her analysis. First, it is very likely that Council and Commission are in a situation of asymmetric information. Probably the Commission has some private information, and so does the Council and its presidency. The latter's private information might well provide a rationale for the Commission testing the waters with particular proposals which, sometimes, it withdraws and changes considerably. Second, together with the private information of the Commission, the iterated nature of EU decision-making might provide a second rationale for informal rules giving some leverage to the Council's presidency. Finally, by neglecting the appointment process, most existing models of EU decision-making obfuscate the principal–agent relationship between the Council (and increasingly the EP) and the Commission.

Conclusion

Susanne Schmidt's analysis of five decision-making processes in the EU is a very valuable contribution and should be taken up by scholars employing formal models as a challenge. She argues in favour of paying closer attention to the informal rules that appear to be prevalent in EU decision-making. While I do not dispute this argument, I suggest that formal modellers should consider more closely the underlying causes of the emergence of these informal rules. I find that in the present context directly modelling these informal rules would be of little theoretical and empirical interest.[5] More fruitful would be future research efforts attempting to build upon existing models and relaxing crucial assumptions. I have highlighted the crucial nature of three assumptions, namely the common knowledge assumption, the one-shot nature of the strategic interaction and the obfuscation of the principal–agent relationship. Work along all these lines, I argue, would increase our understanding of decision-making in the EU and, in addition, might provide explanations for the emergence of the informal rules that Susanne Schmidt so adequately documents.

Notes

1 Green and Shapiro (1994) illustrate this point rather clearly for some areas, while Cox (1999) convincingly challenges their simplistic view of theoretical progress.
2 It is interesting to note that as one of the proponents of the school Susanne Schmidt criticises, Tsebelis (1994) actually argues that in practice both the EP and Council have the possibility to initiate legislation.
3 Binmore (e.g., 1994: 96) provides some rather scathing remarks on employing manifestly erroneous models and superimposing informal rules. A recent example along these lines is Scharpf (1997).
4 Crombez' (1997b) model is an exception in this regard.
5 In fact such an endeavor would run into one of the main critiques of formal modelling that Green and Shapiro (1994) advance in their book, namely *ad hoc* assumptions.

Top Commission officials on capitalism: an institutionalist understanding of preferences

With few exceptions, new institutionalist theoretical approaches to European Union (EU) politics have tended to conceive of European Commission actors – like other supranational actors – as agents of deeper integration (Pierson, 1996; Schneider, 1997; Steunenberg, 1996; Tsebelis, 1994, 1996; Tsebelis and Kreppel, 1998). The assumption is that institutional self-interest induces Commission actors to promote further integration. This is in line with the prevailing paradigm of utility maximisation in the study of bureaucracies. Bureaucrats seek to maximise budgets, bureaucratic discretion or status and work conditions (for an EU application see Pollack, 1997). To what extent, though, will such goals dominate those who work in, or lead, bureaucracies? New formal institutionalist analyses, in particular, are reluctant to relax the assumption of the Commission as a unitary and pro-integration actor. They argue that there is little theoretical mileage to be gained from endogenising the preferences of Commission actors. But this reluctance contrasts with recent contributions to the new-institutionalist literature, which seek to unpack the notion of a monolithic bureaucracy and specify the conditions under which bureaucrats actually defend institutional interests (for EU applications see Cram, 1997a; Peters, 1992).

The argument that Commission officials reflect the institutional interests of the Commission hinges on the Commission being a bounded institution capable of instilling within its employees a uniform set of norms. But is the Commission sufficiently insulated from the outside world to prevail upon its employees to be willing advocates of its interest? Relaxing that assumption invites one not only to consider carefully how the institutional rules of the Commission may affect officials, but also to examine how rules outside the Commission may shape their political preferences. My central contention is that, to understand officials' basic orientations to European governance, one should combine insights from sociological institutionalism, which emphasises socialisation, with instrumental-rational institutionalism, which gives priority to the maximisation of utility (see Aspinwall and Schneider in Chapter 1).

This chapter presents an important slice of this agenda. It examines how senior Commission officials conceive of relations between market and state in Europe.[1] Rarely have the economic values of Commission actors been examined systematically. And yet, the completion of the internal market and the start of economic and monetary union (EMU) – processes of market deepening – have raised fundamental questions concerning the relationship between state and market, individual and society in Europe. These have been subject to a deeply politicised struggle among national government leaders, parties in the national and European parliaments, social movements, interest groups and opinion leaders (Hooghe and Marks, 1999). I argue that these questions are also contested in the Commission. What form of capitalism, then, do top Commission officials support?

The first section charts divergence on regulating capitalism in Europe among top Commission officials. In the following section I discuss how different strands of new-institutionalist theorising may help to formulate hypotheses concerning sources of variation in their preferences. I then test the hypotheses against data collected between July 1995 and May 1997 from extensive interviews with 140 senior Commission officials – director-generals, deputy director-generals, directors and senior advisors – and mailed questionnaires from 106 of these 140 people.

Contention on European capitalism

Political actors in the EU have different projects for regulating capitalism in Europe (Crouch and Streeck, 1997b; Hooghe, 1998; Hooghe and Marks, 1999; Rhodes and Van Apeldoorn, 1997; Wilks, 1996). At one end of the ideological spectrum stands a neoliberal project, which seeks to insulate the European-wide market from political interference by combining European market integration with minimal European regulation. This project attracts those who want minimal political interference in economic decision-making, market-liberals seeking selective European and national regulation of market forces, and, in part, nationalists intent on sustaining state sovereignty. Opposing them is a loose coalition supporting European regulated capitalism. This project attempts to increase EU capacity for regulation to achieve something akin to a European-wide social market economy. It attracts social christian democrats and market-oriented social democrats. They concede that markets rather than governments should allocate investment, but they also insist that markets work more efficiently if the state helps to provide collective goods including transport infrastructure, workforce skills and co-operative industrial relations. The coalitions behind these projects are neither fixed nor monolithic. Yet each project has a crystal-clear bottom line:

neoliberals seek to constrain European authoritative decision-making; proponents of European regulated capitalism want to deepen it.

How do Commission officials stand in relation to these projects? Table 7.1 shows responses on three questions. The first one summarises key components of a model of European regulated capitalism, which entails extensive welfare services, social dialogue between both sides of industry, redistributive regional policy and industrial policy. The item is a virtually literal translation of Jacques Delors' concept of organised space, which has become the linchpin of the project for European regulated capitalism (Delors, 1992; Ross, 1995). Item two indicates support for cohesion policy, which finances the provision of collective goods and some redistribution; cohesion policy now absorbs 35 per cent of the EU budget.

The third question distinguishes proponents of European regulated capitalism – the new left – from the traditional left. A defining feature of regulated capitalism is its friendliness to markets and opposition to state ownership or control. Contrary to the traditional left, proponents of European regulated capitalism are less inclined to oppose capital owners. The third question, which probes top officials' preferences towards corporate interests ('big business'), indicates that only a small minority is worried about the influence of big business.

Table 7.1 European regulated capitalism (% of respondents, n=105)

Item	Yes	Yes, but	Neutral	No, but	No	Mean*
1 Europe has developed a unique model of society and the Commission should help to preserve it: extensive social services, civilised industrial relations, negotiated transfers among groups to sustain solidarity, and steer economic activity for the general welfare.	42.5	38.7	4.7	9.4	4.7	3.21
2 No united Europe without a mature European cohesion policy.	46.7	31.4	1.9	18.1	1.9	3.24
3 Europe is too much influenced by big business.	5.7	22.6	0.9	56.6	14.2	2.20

Note: * Values range between 1 (no) and 4 (yes), with 2.5 as neutral value. In the questionnaire, I deliberately omitted a neutral choice and as a result only a very small number of respondents insisted on neutrality or abstained. Here, they are allocated a value of 2.5.

Table 7.1 demonstrates that the Commission is a bastion of European regulated capitalism, borne out by a high mean value on the dependent variable, though there is a substantial dissenting minority. But then support for some form of European regulated capitalism is relatively high throughout Europe with both elites and the public.[2] So the real issue is not the level of support, but how one explains variation in support. In this chapter, I examine why some officials are keener on advocating European regulated capitalism than others.

Preference formation: socialisation or utility?

Top officials work in a multifaceted institutional environment, of which the Commission is a central, but far from the only, setting. An analysis of top officials' motivations requires a systematic understanding of the interplay between various institutional settings and individual top officials. I conceptualise this interplay along two theoretical tracks. One line of theorising explores the extent to which preferences result from socialisation. The second track examines to what extent preferences constitute a function of their utility to *a priori* material goals.

The standard argument is that socialisation is a gradual, slow process by which individuals, through countless experiences, internalise particularly over time (Rohrschneider, 1994, 1996; Verba, 1965). For example, one may hypothesise that top officials who have worked in the Commission for many years are more likely to have internalised the Commission's institutional interest in maximising competencies and budgetary resources. Other socialisation theorists have specified how critical junctures in people's lives may define preferences. For example, one may hypothesise that the preferences of people who participated once in an election campaign as candidate or party militant are marked for life by that short, but intense, politicisation. More generally, I will argue that, in forming their preferences on European capitalism, Commission officials may be influenced by experiences in four institutional settings: the work place in the Commission, previous work experiences in state institutions, party-political linkages and in the capitalist system of their home country.

Some theorists of socialisation utilise a definition of socialisation that encompasses all but the most utilitarian experiences. I propose to limit socialisation to those instances in which individuals change their preferences for social reasons that cannot be attributed to direct material incentives or coercion (for a similar definition, see Jeffrey Checkel in Chapter 2 of this book).[3]

The basic premise of the utility logic is that institutions have transparent calculable consequences for the ability of individuals to achieve their goals. Actors are rational, in that they want to maximise their individual life chances. Individuals are expected to bring their preferences in line with the institutional opportunities that are available to them. The principal–agent model captures a prevailing structure of opportunities. It specifies how principals – actors who create an agent to perform certain functions on their behalf – can constrain agency discretion (Bawn, 1995;

Pollack, 1997; Ringquist, 1995; Wood and Waterman, 1993). For example, one may expect top officials who owe their appointment to their national government to be more reluctant to embrace European regulated capitalism for fear of snubbing their career masters. Conversely, one may anticipate that officials appointed by Commission president Jacques Delors, the most outspoken advocate of European regulated capitalism, are much more favourable. All in all, I discuss how top officials may adjust their preferences in response to the influence of national govern-ments or Commission presidents on their career chances.

Some scholars of utility maximisation limit their notion of rationality to the maximisation of economic self-interest. I propose to expand this notion slightly to include material goals that influence individual life chances; an important facet for top officials concerns goals related to career advancement. Under those definitional conditions, it becomes possible to separate utility-driven processes from socialisation processes.[4]

In what follows, I examine the circumstances under which socialisation and a utility logic shape top officials' preferences on regulating European capitalism. The two logics imply fundamentally different understandings of institutions and of the people within (Aspinwall and Schneider in Chapter 1; Checkel in Chapter 2; March and Olsen, 1989; Nørgaard, 1996; Searing, 1991, 1994; Yee, 1997). Socialisation works best when institutions resemble sets of relatively dense, integrated, uniform norms that bring individuals to act in ways that are appropriate within that context. Roles and preferences of individuals are largely built into these institutions. Individuals are social beings – *homines sociologici* – who live their lives to a large extent in the shadow of effective social norms and values. Utility maximisation suggests that institutions constitute primarily a strategic terrain within which optimising behaviour takes place. Individual preferences adjust to changing institutional constraints. Individuals are self-interested beings – *homines economici* – who consciously calculate the costs and benefits of their actions and prefer-ences. The question is not whether top officials live either in utilitarian cocoons or in sociological cages, but rather to understand the interplay between socialisation and utility maximisation and to specify the condi-tions under which the balance between the two varies (Searing, 1991, 1994).

Socialisation

State or Commission socialisation   The first set of hypotheses elaborates the argument that top Commission officials are first and foremost profes-sionals. From a socialisation perspective, norms and practices in their current or prior professional environment may shape their preferences. But a sophisticated socialisation argument should make the extent to which top officials have internalised their institution's interests conditional upon type and length of work experience.

- *Commission career*: The first hypothesis relates length of service in the Commission to support for European regulated capitalism. The European Commission should have an institutional interest in supporting European regulated capitalism, because these economic and social policies would increase supranationalism. Socialisation leads one to hypothesise that the longer officials have worked in the Commission, the more likely they are to have internalised the Commission's preference for European regulated capitalism. I use *Commission Career*, that is, the number of years served in the Commission until the interview, as indicator.[5]
- *State career*: The second hypothesis associates length of career in national administrations with Commission officials' preferences. The corollary of the supranational self-interest argument is that national administrations should be reluctant to support European regulated capitalism because of its threat to national sovereignty. And this reluctance should be reflected in the preferences of former national civil servants all the more firmly if they spent a considerable proportion of their career in national institutions. *State Career* is the number of years served in state service, usually as national civil servants, prior to joining the Commission.

Functional socialisation   Many EU public policy studies draw attention to institutional variation in the immediate, circumscribed policy world within which officials perform daily. Laura Cram has characterised the European Commission as a multi-organisation (Cram, 1994, 1997a). Others have identified different DG cultures or styles (Abélès, Bellier and McDonald, 1993; Cini, 1996; McGowan and Wilks, 1995). A socialisation argument links length of service in particular functional policy tasks to support for European regulated capitalism. Policy areas have policy legacies, which provide officials with moral templates for evaluating initiatives (Hall, 1993; Skogstad, 1998). Commission officials are most likely to internalise a particular moral template when they stay in one DG for a long time, or when they have spent much of their career in DGs with comparable templates. One may hypothesise that the longer senior Commission officials have worked in units dealing with social and redistributional issues, the more they support European regulated capitalism. For the variable *ERC DG* I calculate years spent in DGs dealing with European regulated capitalism.[6]

Party socialisation   Top Commission officials are not merely professional employees. They are also key political participants in the EU arena.

In conjunction with their Commissioner, they propose and negotiate legislation to Council and the EP, which often necessitates transparently ideological choices. As elite members, they should have higher than political awareness, participate more frequently in political events and organisations and have more crystallised political preferences (Putnam, 1973). Furthermore, ideological preferences and more precisely partisanship can be important selection criteria for top administrators in the Commission (Ross, 1995). So ideology and partisanship are part and parcel of top Commission officials' daily life. The primary institutional settings that come in sight, then, for ideological socialisation are political parties, which have been key articulators of different policies for regulating capitalism.

Recent party research demonstrates that party positions on European integration are to a large extent a function of parties' position on the left/right cleavage (Marks and Wilson, forthcoming; Ray, 1997). Essentially, it is argued that leftwing parties have become more pro-European as the EU has become a more propitious arena for social democratic goals. With the goal of an internal market achieved, parties on the economic right have become reluctant for fear that further integration would strengthen the EU's capacity to re-regulate market forces. Christian democratic parties used to be strong supporters, but they have become less enthusiastic as economic and social conservativism has grown in their ranks. These substantive findings can be combined with political-psychology research, which has shown that partisan attitudes tend to crystallise during the formative years of young adulthood and then remain fairly stable or strengthen with age (Converse, 1976; Sears and Valentino, 1997; Weisberg, 1998). The implication is that, when parties reposition themselves over time, older partisans tend to hold on to the parties' prior positions, while younger partisans reflect newer positions. This generational effect leads to the hypothesis that Commission officials who identify with a particular party family will reflect their party's preferences to European regulated capitalism at the time of their socialisation. So older socialists should show qualified support for European regulated capitalism and their younger colleagues stronger support; older christian democrats strong and younger party fellows weak support; older and younger liberals reluctant support; conservatives deepening scepticism. *Party Identification* consists of a set of dummies for the main party families and, in addition, interaction terms consisting of a generation dummy with socialist and christian democratic families. I derive raw data from the interviews, in which I asked Commission officials which party or ideological current they most identify with.[7]

Territorial-institutional socialisation   Individuals in Europe only acquire European citizenship through national citizenship. This applies no less to

top Commission officials. This basic reality is reflected in most conceptu-
alisations of EU politics, which consistently take pains to demonstrate
how national differences shape European politics. Theories differ though
on the predominance of national difference and on the logic through
which it works. Liberal intergovernmentalism gives near-exclusive
explanatory power to national difference and it focuses mainly on divergent national interests – a utility argument (Moravcsik, 1993). Other
approaches influenced by comparative politics perceive the EU as 'a deli-
cate balancing act' between territorial and functional or ideological claims
(Sbragia, 1993). Approaches influenced by new institutionalism, like the
partisan model (Hix, 1999; Hooghe, 1998; Hooghe and Marks, 1999) or
the new governance model (Héritier, 1996; Hix, 1998; Richardson,
1996), alert us to different institutional legacies and identities as sources
of variation in preferences – a socialisation or learning argument.

Capitalism in Europe has evolved differently across Europe. David
Soskice (1999) distinguishes between co-ordinated and liberal market
economies. Michel Albert (1993) contrasts Rhenish and Atlantic or
Anglo-Saxon capitalism. Colin Crouch and Wolfgang Streeck (1997) pit
institutional against neoliberal capitalism. Stephen Wilks (1996) analyses
continental/social democratic and neo-American models. Martin Rhodes
and Bastiaan Van Apeldoorn (1997) compare the Anglo-Saxon market-
oriented with two network-oriented versions, the German social market
model and the Latin state interventionist model. Each type is characterised
by distinct institutional arrangements, and they mould preferences and
behaviour of firms, labour and state elites. One would expect Commission
officials' preferences about European capitalism to be influenced by political-economic institutions and practices in their country of birth. One
hypothesis builds on the theoretical notion that individuals draw lessons
that may lead them to alter predispositions. Socialisation, in other words,
is not a passive process. Actors from extensively co-ordinated economies
may conclude that European regulated capitalism would undermine
national practices.

European regulated capitalism is unlikely ever to replicate the post-war
social contract of Europe's most advanced societies. Moreover, substitut-
ing European for national regulatory efforts may erode the capacity of
national regimes to impose political control on market forces (Streeck,
1996). This reasoning leads one to hypothesise that officials from systems
of national regulated capitalism are less likely to support European regulated capitalism. For the variable *Capitalism* I use a four-category ranking
reflecting a decreasing degree of non-market co-ordination in the
economy (Kitschelt, Lange, Marks and Stephens, 1999; Soskice, 1999; for
southern Europe: Esping-Andersen, 1999; Rhodes and Van Apeldoorn,
1997). The four categories consist of the national co-ordinated market
economy (CME) (value 4: Scandinavian countries), sectoral CME (3:

Germany, Austria and Benelux), partial CME (2; France, Italy, Spain, Greece and Portugal), and liberal ME (1: Ireland and the UK).

Material utility
If Commission officials were autonomous decision makers with full control over their career chances, they would probably defend preferences that are the sediment of socialisation and learning. In reality, other actors have power to influence top officials' career chances. To the extent that top officials are concerned with maximising professional utility, their dependence on others for professional success may induce them to adjust their preferences accordingly. Two types of actors are in a position to influence the calculations of top officials, through their role in decision-making and, more directly, their input in recruitment: national governments and the college of Commissioners.

Political control over career advancement   Formal recruitment rules ensure that the political Commission is well placed to select officials on the basis of their preferences *if it so wishes*. Former Commission president Jacques Delors had a strong interest in influencing the ideological make-up of his top bureaucracy. During his ten years of office (1985–94), Mr. Delors was the driving force behind an action plan for European regulated capitalism. According to George Ross' authoritative study, 'Delors, with Pascal's [Lamy, Delors' chef de cabinet] advice, had very carefully replaced a considerable number of high Commission officials, directors general and division heads, in critical areas.' (Ross, 1995: 67) One may therefore hypothesise that top officials appointed under Delors should be more supportive of European regulated capitalism than earlier or later appointments. The variable *Delors* is a dummy, which takes on a value of one for officials appointed under the Delors presidencies.

Positional power   Recruitment practices are one channel to constrain agents' behaviour and preferences; *ex ante* rule design is another (McCubbins and Page, 1987; for an EU application see Franchino, 1999; Pollack, 1997). Officials with extensive regulatory responsibilities or large funds need routine access to regulatory autonomy and financial clout to maximise positional power, and these resources are at the core of European regulated capitalism. Officials with limited regulatory responsibilities, on the other hand, may find access to information, mediation skills, or credibility more valuable resources, and these do not depend on European regulated capitalism. So one may hypothesise that officials with regulatory autonomy or financial resources have greater incentives to support European regulated capitalism. To assess the extent to which Commission officials regulate autonomously from member state control,

I use a composite index *Power DG* of formal and reputational measures of Commission power.[8]

National economic interest   Whether the EU promotes European regulated capitalism or trade, liberalisation influences costs and benefits for individual member states. Liberal intergovernmentalism links national economic utility to the political-economic preferences of Commission officials. It argues that national governments seek to maximise national (economic) gains from European integration and that Commission officials should be perceived as their national governments' agents. The fact that national governments play an informal role in top recruitment for the Commission and have formal powers in policy-making should be a constant reminder to top officials of the significance of different national interests. On the basis of this, one would expect Commission officials to support European regulated capitalism to the extent that their country benefits. So one may hypothesise that officials from countries with transparent net gains from European market regulation and redistribution should favour European regulated capitalism. As an indicator for national economic interest, I use *Cohesion Transfer,* a measure for EU structural intervention in the 1994–99 programming period as a percentage of GDP in 1994 prices.

- *Dependent variable: preferences on European capitalism.* I combine the first two items in Table 7.1 in an additive index of *European Regulated Capitalism*. Item one summarises the most comprehensive formulation of European regulated capitalism to date, Jacques Delors' concept of 'organised space'. His conception was based on the social market economy in Germany, Benelux and to some extent Denmark, and in contradistinction to the Anglo-Saxon liberal market economy. It probes whether European institutions should help bring about a social market economy. The second item taps into Commission officials' support for the flagship policy of European regulated capitalism, EU cohesion policy. Values range between 1 (unconditional opposition) and 4 (unconditional support), with a mean of 3.22 and a median of 3.5.[9] Table 7.2 contains descriptive statistics for all variables in the analysis and Table 7.3 contains the results of the multivariate linear regression analysis.[10]

Explaining preferences on European capitalism

Ideology and territorial difference are the prime sources of variation in top Commission officials' preferences on European capitalism. Four factors in the multivariate regression account for 38.5 per cent of the variance (Adj. R^2 = 0.35, Model 2, Table 7.3). By far the strongest bivariate

Table 7.2 Descriptive statistics

	N	Mean	Median	Std. Dev.	Mini- mum	Maxi- mum	Description
European regulated capitalism	105	3.22	3.50	.67	1.00	4.00	index of items 1 and 2
Commission career	105	17.96	21.00	10.70	1	38	number of years in Commission
State career	105	6.01	3.00	7.21	0	28	number of years in state service
ErcDG	105	4.84	.00	7.86	0	33	number of years in DGs for european regulated capitalism
Soc.	105	.24	.00	.43	0	1	1: socialist
Christ.	105	.11	.00	.32	0	1	1: christian democrat
Con.	105	.057	.00	.23	0	1	1: conservative
Lib.	105	.17	.00	.38	0	1	1: liberal or centrist
Young Soc.	105	.12	.00	.33	0	1	1: socialist born 1940 or after
Young Christ.	105	.06	.00	.25	0	1	1: christian democrat born 1940 or after
Young Lib.	105	.11	.00	.32	0	1	1: liberal born 1940 or after
Capitalism	105	2.26	2.00	.91	1	4	index (Kitschelt et al., 1999)
Cohesion transfer	105	.64	.2500	1.03	0.11	3.98	EU structural funds as %GDP by country
Delors recruit	105	.50	1.00	.50	0	1	1: recruited during 1986–1994
PowerDG	105	4.60	5.00	2.05	1	9	index: extent of power/ purse (Page, 1997)
Erc Utility	105	.35	.00	.48	0	1	1: currently in DG for european regulated capitalism

association is with Party Identification (R^2 = 0.23), overshadowing all others in the multivariate analysis.[11] Two of the three remaining factors tap into territorial difference: State Career and Cohesion Transfer. The fourth factor, PowerDG, suggests that top officials' preferences on European capitalism are also somewhat influenced by functional characteristics of their job in the Commission.

Partisanship is alive and well in the top layers of the Commission bureaucracy. More generally, external influences weigh more heavily than internal Commission factors. There appears little space for experiences or calculations on-the-job to shape top officials' preferences on European governance. The European Commission is a porously bounded institution; other institutional environments – party and country – matter more. The remainder of this chapter examines key results for each hypothesis.

Partisanship
Party identification is the single most powerful predictor of where officials stand on European regulated capitalism. In the simple regression, the coef-

Table 7.3 Explaining preferences on European regulated capitalism

	Correlation	Simple regression	Model 1	Model 2	Model 3	Model 4
Commission Career	.205**	.042**	.00088 (.009)		.051 [.0032] (.009)	
State Career	−.352***	.124***	−.0256** (.011)	−.0298*** (.008)	−.0258** (.010)	−.0287*** (.008)
ERC DG	.235**	.055**	.00072 (.008)			
Party Identification		.226***				
Socialists	1.42	.011	−.0610 (.189)		−.0873 (.189)	
Christian democrats	.045	.002	.484* (.275)	.442* (.255)	.480* (.273)	.520** (.254)
Conservatives	−.388***	.150***	−1.110*** (.251)	−1.054*** (.233)	−1.133*** (.250)	−1.090*** (.233)
Liberals	−.079	.006	−.0863 (.170)		−.0293 (.169)	
Young Soc.	.183*	.034*	.163 (.252)		.172 (.250)	
Young Christ.	−.105	.011	−.922*** (.350)	−.916*** (.332)	−.907*** (.347)	−.962*** (.331)
Political system: Capitalism	−.108	.012	−.0684 (.072)		−.0664 (.071)	
Cohesion Transfer	.187*	.035*	.167*** (.063)	.191*** (.054)	.158** (.063)	.160*** (.055)
Delors Recruit	.159	.026	.0242 (.118)		.02607 (.117)	
Power DG	.164*	.027*	.0473 (.031)	.0660** (.026)	.03336 (.033)	
ERC Utility	.193**	.037**			.197 (.142)	.294** (.113)
R²			.410	.385	.417	.387
Adj. R²			.325	.347	.333	.350
N			N=105	N=105	N=105	N=105

Notes: Multivariate linear regression (constant included in equation, pairwise deletion of missing values); unstandardised coefficients (B); standard errors are between brackets; * significant at 0.10 level; ** significant at 0.05 level; *** significant at 0.01 level (two-tailed).

ficient of determination (R^2) equals 0.23 and this rises to 0.31 among the subgroup of partisans. Top officials reflect to a large extent their party's preferences to European regulated capitalism, but they do so with a generational twist. Changes in party positions over the last decades are most strongly absorbed by younger people. I take as baseline for the party dummies the non-partisans, that is, officials who have not disclosed their ideological predisposition. So the party dummies reflect, in standardised form, the difference between the means for these party families and the means for non-partisans; the interaction terms reflect the difference between the means of young and old socialists, and young and old christian democrats respectively.

The expectation was to discern a generational effect for christian democrats and for socialists, as these party families have shifted position most significantly over past decades. The results for christian democrats strongly confirm the hypothesis: the christian democrat dummy is positive and significant, and the young christian democrat dummy is negative and highly significant. So the pre-war generation (born before 1940), socialised in party thinking in the 1950s and 1960s, consists of hard core supporters for European regulated capitalism. European regulated capitalism seems a logical choice for those who internalised the values of social personalism, the social and political theory developed by Mounier and Maritain, which permeated European christian democracy in the first post-war decades (Hanley, 1994; Van Kersbergen, 1997, 1999). Jacques Delors, a socialist but also a practising catholic of the older generation, relied explicitly on personalist principles in his elaboration of European 'organised space'. However, with religion rapidly losing salience in Europe, christian democratic parties are increasingly emphasising social and economic conservatism and this sits uncomfortably with European regulated capitalism. In the Commission, younger christian democratic officials reflect this repositioning of recent years. The data are less clear-cut about the hypothesis that socialists have shifted from lukewarm to very strong support. Nevertheless, of all top officials, young socialists are very strong supporters of European regulated capitalism (3.55 out of 4) and second only to older christian democrats (3.80 out of 4). But this socialist effect withers away when controlling for other powerful influences. The findings for conservatives and liberals are in line with expectations. Conservative officials are highly unlikely to support European regulated capitalism. The dummy is strongly negative. A combination of nationalism and economic conservatism has generally predisposed conservative parties to be reluctant supporters of greater European regulation and redistribution, and these partisan officials espouse this stance. Liberal and centrist officials do not have consistent party cues to rely on and this is reflected in the insignificance of the liberal dummy.

The strong showing of party identification challenges theories of European integration that have downplayed the impact of encompassing ideological frameworks and party-programmatic appeals. For officials with close party allegiance, partisanship is the primary prism through which they evaluate EU issues.

Commission versus state socialisation

Partisanship does not exhaust variation among top officials. Career socialisation is the second strongest predictor of their stance on European capitalism, albeit at a respectable distance from party identification. Former national officials are far less outspoken in their support for European regulated capitalism than former professors, business people or professionals. The negative association with a state career is strong for partisans and non-partisans alike. State institutions seem effective in socialising individuals into EU-sceptical preferences. Commission sociali- sation, on the other hand, is significant in the simple regression, but it fizzles out when controlling for other factors. The main reason is that Commission socialisation is only significantly associated with European regulated capitalism for non-partisans. In other words, the two forms of career socialisation play out very differently among the forty-four non- partisan officials and their sixty-one partisan colleagues. For the majority of European Commission officials then, current association with the European Commission leaves a far weaker imprint than a prior job in the state sector. The Commission's capacity to instil its institutional self-inter- est in its employees is limited.

Territorial diversity: national interest versus national institutional learning

The liberal intergovernmental hypothesis that officials' positions on European regulated capitalism reflect material interests of their country finds support. Officials from countries reaping net financial benefits from EU structural policy are more inclined to favour further EU regulation and redistribution. Though the association with Cohesion Transfer is modest in the bivariate analysis, it is reinforced in the multivariate analysis. The reason is that Cohesion Transfer picks up consistently higher support among officials from the greatest beneficiaries of EU structural policy (Greece, Ireland, Spain and Portugal). While average support outside these countries is 3.17 out of 4, it is 3.56 for officials from those four countries.

The association with capitalism, the indicator for measuring the impact of divergent capitalist institutional arrangements, is negative but it falls short of significance ($r = -0.108$) and it drops out completely in the multi- variate analysis. The main reason for the non-significance of the relationship lies with non-linearity. The inverse linear relationship between the extent of co-ordination in the economy and support for European regulated capitalism is powerful when limited to the three types of co-ordinated market economies (r = –0.410), but it does not work at all for liberal market economies. This finding strongly suggests that there is a fundamental rift in Europe between the Anglo-Saxon system and various types of continental capitalism, each of these evolving around specific forms of non-market co-ordination. This conclusion is of course not new. It is consistent with Soskice's theory of varieties of capitalism and it is increasingly recognised among policy-makers.

Territorial difference matters, but the impact of Cohesion Transfer and capitalism is strongly mediated by partisanship. First of all, though it is true that 'northern' officials are on the whole less supportive of European regulated capitalism than are their colleagues from Spain, Greece, Ireland and Portugal, their positions are strongly coloured by partisanship. Northern socialists (3.31) are more in favour than northern christian democrats (3.25), who are in turn considerably more supportive than liberals (3.00) and conservatives (2.20). Non-partisans are in the middle of the pack (3.27). Similarly, southern socialists (3.87) are more enthusiastic than southern christian democrats (3.50), who are more in favour than conservatives (2.00), though not more than liberals (4.00); again, non-partisans sport median values (3.50).[12] So though European regulated capitalism can count on a constant bonus in cohesion countries, national interest as expressed by Cohesion Transfer does not alter the slope of the relationship between partisanship and support for regulated capitalism.

Partisanship also filters through the influence of type of capitalism. Socialist officials from liberal market economies are more in favour of European regulated capitalism (3.37) than are their conservative (2.25) or liberal (3.09) colleagues from co-ordinated economies. In three of the four types of capitalism, socialists are more supportive than christian democrats, who in turn are more supportive than liberals and conservatives.

Delors factor
The Commission may shape the outlook of top officials through targeted ideological recruitment. However, the Delors effect is not very strong. The main reason is that the overall results mask major differences between partisans and non-partisans. For partisans the association is strongly positive (r = 0.310, p = .015), but it is non-significant and negative among non-partisans (r = –0.152, p = 0.324). The Delors effect works only for partisans, and even then mainly for some categories of partisans. However, whether by design or by luck, Delors was able to improve on partisanship for precisely those partisans who would otherwise have leaned to sceptical positions. Hence, when recruited under Delors, old socialists (3.56 against 3.06), young christian democrats (3.50 against

2.56) and liberals (4.00 against 2.68 for old liberals; 3.35 against 2.92 for young liberals) are far more supportive than their partisan allegiance would otherwise have predicted. Only for conservative partisans is there no Delors effect (2.00 for Delors recruits against 2.25 for non-Delors recruits). These findings suggest that Jacques Delors and his team were effective in screening the bulk of partisan appointments to top positions, but far less effective – or attentive – to the recruitment of non-partisans.

On the job: position and function

There is some support for the power-positional interest hypothesis, which predicts that the more regulatory or financial autonomy officials have, the more they want to expand European-wide regulatory competencies. However, the association is significant only among non-partisans ($r = 0.290$, $p = 0.05$); it is virtually non-existent among partisans ($r = 0.074$). To put it clearly, other factors being equal, non-partisan officials with extensive regulatory powers in competition policy are more likely to favour European regulated capitalism than weak European regulators in education and training. There is no evidence that socialisation is at work rather than instrumental response to given incentives. Long-serving officials in autonomous DGs are not more supportive than are newly appointed officials. The defining feature is where one works in the Commission, not since when. These results sit uncomfortably with scholarly work emphasising socialisation on the job in the Commission.

The weakness of socialisation in the Commission is reinforced when we look at functional socialisation. Though the variable ERC DG is significant in the simple regression ($R^2 = 0.55$), it drops out when controlling for other variables. The hypothesis that officials may acquire positive attitudes to European regulated capitalism by working on issues of social regulation and redistribution finds support among non-partisans only ($r = 0.339$, $p = 0.024$). Here too, the variable drops out when controlling for other influences. These results qualify a popular argument, among scholars and Commission officials alike, that DGs nurture certain ideological cultures or missions.

To test further the relative power of utility versus socialisation, I create a dummy variable *ERC Utility*, which allocates a value of one to current employees in ERC-friendly services. If functional utility rather than socialisation motivates officials, current policy-makers in areas central to European regulated capitalism should be more inclined to support European regulated capitalism than those who have moved on to other jobs. Concretely, officials in regional policy should have professional reasons for supporting European regulated capitalism: to ensure resources for policy-making, to enhance the status of their policy field and administration and to increase their chances for promotion. Models 3 and 4 (Table 7.3) present the multivariate results of the ERC utility model.

Though the simple regression result ($R^2 = 0.04$) is lower than that for the ERC socialisation variable, ERC utility gains power in the multivariate analysis to the extent that it replaces PowerDG. The overall model is marginally better than our original model.

The results from the PowerDG and the ERC Utility variables enable us to single out more precisely the subset of officials for whom positional interests appear to shape preferences. Support for regulated capitalism appears significantly higher for officials who work in those ERC-related services that have medium or high regulatory/financial autonomy. The high-autonomy services are the big services DG VI (agriculture), DG XVI (regional policy), and DG V (social policy) (average = 3.40); the medium-autonomous services deal with development, culture, environment and fisheries (average = 3.48). Officials in non-ERC services with high regulatory autonomy (essentially industry and competition, but not external trade) are significantly more reluctant to support European regulated capitalism (2.95). There is no consistent pattern for officials in other categories. It seems, then, that relatively high regulatory autonomy is a prerequisite for top officials to allow for material professional incentives to colour preferences on regulating capitalism. Officials with considerable autonomy are in favour of regulated capitalism when they pursue careers in ERC-related services and critical when they are in charge of non-ERC related tasks.

Conclusion

New institutionalism promises to overcome the traditional debate – and impasse – between neofunctionalism/multilevel governance and liberal intergovernmentalism in the study of European integration (Pollack, 1996; Tsebelis and Kreppel, 1998). Yet the main challenge for adherents of new institutionalism is to avoid replacing an EU-confined sterile debate with a new one between sociological, historical or rational choice institutionalism. This chapter deliberately borrows from all strands of new institutionalism to examine how various settings of rules may shape the way individuals think and act. I conceptualise this interplay between institutions and individuals along two theoretical tracks. One line of theorising explores the extent to which preferences result from socialisation in particular institutional settings. The second track examines to what extent preferences constitute a function of their utility to *a priori* material goals within a given institutional environment. It is true that each of these logics draws primarily from a particular strand of new institutionalism. Yet the question that guides my study is not to discover whether individuals are deeply socialised beings or utilitarian agents, but rather to understand the interplay between socialisation and utility maximisation and to specify the conditions under which the balance between the two varies.

I use this to shed light on how top officials in the Commission – director-generals, deputy director-generals, directors and senior advisors – perceive relations between the market and the state in Europe. The point of departure is that these top officials work in a multifaceted institutional environment, of which the Commission is a central, but far from the only, setting. The comparative advantage of an institutionalist analysis is that it provides key analytical concepts to examine systematically the relative impact of institutional settings. So I explore how institutional constraints inside the Commission – the work environment – and outside the Commission – country and party – affect the way top officials think about regulating capitalism in Europe. Whether these impacts are transmitted through socialisation or utility maximisation then becomes a secondary question.

Political parties constitute by far the most formative setting for top officials' preferences on the regulation of capitalism in Europe. Officials reflect their party's positions to European regulated capitalism, with left wing parties generally more in favour than right wing parties. More precisely, they reflect their party's preferences to European regulated capitalism at the time of their socialisation. So older christian democrats show strong support and younger party fellows weak support; older socialists show more qualified support than do their younger colleagues and conservatives demonstrate deepening scepticism. The strong impact of party identification is consistent with a growing EU literature, rooted mainly in comparative politics, which emphasises the role of ideology and partisanship in shaping contention in EU politics.

However, as liberal intergovernmentalists have emphasised, national territory matters too. It plays a role both in the guise of national socialisation and of national economic interest, though both take second place to partisanship. The strongest territorial influence is prior socialisation in national state institutions: former national civil servants are more reluctant to support European regulated capitalism. National economic interest plays a role for individuals from countries that draw net redistributive benefits from the EU: they are the strongest supporters of European regulated capitalism.

So top officials' preferences on regulating European capitalism are to a large extent formed outside the Commission. They bring preferences to their job that are the residue of external experiences, most strongly the position of their preferred party, but also state socialisation, national interest (but only those from cohesion countries) and to some extent type of capitalism (form of capitalism they grew up with). For partisans at least, ideological and territorial influences are not antithetical. Does work in the Commission then have no effect at all on top officials' preferences? Those who lack a strong party identification are somewhat more responsive to institutional incentives from the inside. The longer they have

served in the Commission, the more likely they will support the organisation's self-interest in promoting European regulated capitalism. However,
non-partisans do not escape the profound impact of external experiences
either: former state officials are less likely, and officials from cohesion
countries more likely, to support European regulated capitalism.

Neither the Commission nor particular administrative services within it
appear effective transmission belts for values on the market and state in
Europe. However, the Commission environment makes some difference in
an instrumental sense. There is a tendency for officials to defend preferences that correspond well with their professional interests. All other
things being equal, officials dealing with policies central to positive
market regulation or redistribution are more likely to support European
regulated capitalism – provided that they have significant regulatory or
financial autonomy. These officials can expect to draw immediate professional benefit from more European regulated capitalism: it would ensure
key resources for policy-making, enhance the status of their policy field
and administration and increase their chances for promotion. Finding
conclusive proof for this logical inference is near impossible. But there is
no supporting evidence for the alternative hypothesis – that top officials
favour European regulated capitalism because they have internalised
certain values through their work.

In shaping its top employees' preferences on regulating capitalism in
Europe, the Commission is no match for external bodies – parties, state
administrations or national governments. It is neither an effective socialising agent nor does it offer a particularly influential structure of material
incentives. Fifty years after its creation, the Commission is still porously
bounded.

Notes

1 This project depended on the generous co-operation of 140 senior
   Commission officials. The Catholic University of Brussels provided hospital-
   ity during interviewing and the Robert Schuman Centre (EUI, Florence) gave
   me the opportunity to work on the project as Jean Monnet Fellow (1996-97).
   This chapter is part of a larger project supported by the Department of
   Political Science (University of Toronto) and the Canadian Social Science and
   Humanities Research Council (grant SSHRC Research No. 72005976, Fund
   No. 410185). I am grateful to Simon Hug, Gary Marks, Neil Nevitte, Gerald
   Schneider and all participants of the conference on 'The Rules of Integration:
   The New Institutionalist Turn in European Integration Studies' (organisers:
   Gerald Schneider and Mark Aspinwall), University of Konstanz, 8–10
   October 1998, for helpful comments.
      This chapter is part of a book project on top Commission officials' orien-
   tations to basic questions of EU governance (Hooghe forthcoming).
2 In an elite survey conducted by Eurobarometer in the Spring of 1996, elected

politicians, high-level civil servants, business and labour leaders, media and cultural leaders were asked to evaluate whether policy areas should be decided at national/regional or European level. A value of 1 refers to exclusively national/regional competence and a value of 10 for exclusively European competence. This is an indirect way to assess the potential for European regulated capitalism, which prescribes partnership between European, national and regional governments in flanking policies to EMU. Mean scores for such flanking policies range between 7.6 and 4.3. Top leaders want primary EU competence for environmental policies (7.6), scientific and technological research (6.7), employment policy (6.0) and social policy (5.4). They support secondary EU competence for regional development (4.6), health insurance (4.5) and education policy (4.3). (European Commission, 1996. *Top Decision Makers Survey: Summary Report*. Brussels: Directorate-General X.) To my knowledge, comparable data for the general public do not exist. Eurobarometer regularly presents respondents with a list of policy areas, but merely asks them whether they want these policies to be decided at national or European level. Such either/or reasoning is not conducive to assessing support for European regulated capitalism which champions multilevel policy-making. Nevertheless, a 1996 survey shows that for an absolute majority of respondents the following policy areas central to European regulated capitalism should be decided at European level: science and technology research (70 per cent), protection of environment (65 per cent), regional support (63 per cent) and the fight against unemployment (53 per cent). There is minority support for European-level policy-making for health and social welfare (34 per cent), education (37 per cent), and workers' rights *vis-a-vis* employers (53 per cent). (European Commission, 1997. *Eurobarometer. N.46*. Brussels: Directorate-General X. The fieldwork was conducted in October–November 1996. The results on these questions have been fairly stable.)

3   A critical issue in the socialisation literature, which bears on my topic indirectly, concerns the micro-processes of socialisation. Through what processes are norms and values transmitted? Four processes, which range from the self-conscious to the subconscious, have been identified. On one side of the continuum stands persuasion, or social learning, whereby individuals are convinced through self-conscious cognition that particular norms and causal understandings are correct and ought to guide their own behaviour. Second, there is social influence which refers to the process whereby an individual's desire to maintain or increase social status or prestige induces her to conform to group norms. The group concerned rewards an actor's behaviour with back-patting and status markers or punishes it with opprobrium and status devaluation (Johnston, 1998). Some scholars are reluctant to consider social influence or pressure as a genuine socialisation process because it does not necessarily require that an individual change her preferences. Social influence is 'public conformity without private acceptance' (Johnston, 1998). A third process is social mimicking, whereby an individual 'inherits' or copies norms and behaviour without putting much conscious thought in it (Johnston, 1998). Finally, attitude crystallisation refers to a largely subconscious process whereby individuals extend deeply held, stable beliefs or preferences to new attitude objects (Converse, 1964; Sears and Valentino, 1997).

4   At the heart of utility theory *stricto sensu* is a definition of rationality that emphasises the maximisation of economic self-interest (Yee, 1997). However, many new institutionalists, including several rational choice scholars (Levi, 1997; North, 1990; Ostrom, 1991; Weingast, 1995), use less restrictive notions of rationality, which, at the extreme, entail the maximisation of a range of values: economic self-interest, economic group interest, non-economic interests and ideas or norms. This is also the line taken by most rational choice contributors to this volume. The cost of conceiving rationality in purely procedural terms is that it is impossible to specify a set of unique expectations that can be tested. That is why I define rationality in more restrictive terms as the individual maximisation of life chances. But this is broader than economic self-interest in that it includes career advancement, while it excludes social goals.

It is important to point out that this definitional approach to the concepts of socialisation and utility maximisation constitutes only one of several possible strategies to search for complementarity between sociological and rational choice institutionalism. The approach taken in this paper seeks to delineate *a priori* the *substantive scope* of each mechanism for preference formation. Another strategy would be to examine the *division of labour* between sociological and rational choice institutionalism. While specifying the institutional rules under which socialisation may take place is particularly important to understand the formation of individual preferences, a logic of utility maximisation draws our attention to the rules that constrain the extent to which individuals pursue and/ or realise *given* preferences. So the former endogenises preferences; the latter accepts them as exogenous. Whatever strategy one takes, at one point, definitional choices have to be made to be able to operationalise these concepts effectively.

5   Unless otherwise indicated, data were collected during the interviews. Data information can be obtained from the author.

6   I use a narrow definition of services for European regulated capitalism: social regulation (social policy, culture, environment, vocational training and education, consumer services) and redistribution (agriculture, third-world development, fisheries, regional policy).

7   Self-reporting is a powerful indicator of the subjective importance of ideological belief systems, as it registers whether interviewees themselves choose to give weight to partisanship. About 42 per cent refused to disclose their preference or insisted that their personal ideological beliefs are irrelevant for their job. I use this information in two ways. First, I consider non-partisans as the base category against which I compare various groups of partisans. But this assumes that non-partisans are simply partisans for whom information on their ideological position is lacking; partisans and non-partisans are inherently similar. I then relax this assumption to examine whether the causal logic underlying the structuring of preferences of partisans may differ from the one driving non-partisan officials. Technically, I do this by reporting results from separate analyses for partisans (N = 61) and non-partisans (N = 44), where these differ significantly.

8   This indicator combined data collected by Edward Page and evidence from the interviews (Page, 1997). Page measures two types of secondary legislative

activity by the Commission: regulations, directives and decisions that require Council approval and those that do not. As there are no official statistics on legislative output per DG, Page and his collaborator White used keywords (author; form; year; subject) to scan the Justis CD-Rom for legislation over the period 1980–94 (over 30,000 pieces), and allocated output to the DG considered to be the most plausible author. I did a manual recount for 1980-94 for some policy areas, and arrived at a comparable breakdown. (Source: European Commission. N.d. *Directory of EU legislation in Force until Dec 1994.*) Amendments to Page's data pertain to DGs created since 1994. For the reputational indicator, I use a question posed to the top officials in which they name the three or four most powerful DGs or services in the Commission. DGs with a high reputation (mentioned by 50 per cent or more) obtain a value of two, those with medium reputation (mentioned by 5–49 per cent) a value of one and the remainder zero. I then add scores for the four indicators to create PowerDG. Values range between one and eight.

9   The standard deviation is 0.677. The distribution is heavily skewed to European regulated capitalism (skewness = –0.767) and steeper than a normal distribution (kurtosis = 0.342). 4 per cent of officials are radical market-liberals, another 4 per cent moderate market-liberals, as against 51 per cent radical and 24 per cent moderate European regulated capitalists; the remaining 17 per cent balance these principles quite evenly.

10 Strictly speaking, it is a bit of a stretch to use multivariate linear regression for this analysis. The dependent variable is not continuous but has instead ten discrete categories, and though its categories can be ranked from low to high (ordered), it is debatable whether distances between adjacent categories are accurately known. (Is a value of 1.5 exactly equidistant from 1 (no) and 2 (no, but)? Is 2 (no,but) equidistant from 1 (no) as it is from 3 (yes, but)?) Technical textbooks argue that under those circumstances the more prudent statistical models are ordered probit or logit models. A major downside of these models, however, is that the coefficients are notoriously difficult to interpret because they are not – as in linear regression – estimates of unit change effects of X on the observed Y dependent variable but instead on a hypothetical Y^* dependent variable (see Long, 1997). A rerun of the analysis with ordered logit generated very similar results, with exactly the same variables shouldering the explanatory weight, suggesting that distortion due to the use of linear regression is very small indeed. But the logit coefficients are difficult to interpret. That is why I reproduce here the more easily understandable coefficients of the linear regression model.

11 A General Linear Model (GLM) analysis, with party as fixed factor, confirms that party identification (eta-squared = 0.23) dwarfs other factors (State career: eta-squared = 0.06; Cohesion Transfer: eta-squared = 0.07; Power DG: eta-squared = 0.025).

12 The small number stretches the reliability of these averages to the limit, with only four socialists, three christian democrats, one conservative, two liberals and five non-partisans.

Gerald Schneider

Comment: 'Top Commission officials on capitalism'

During the 1980s and 1990s, the study of regional integration has greatly neglected cultural and ideological factors. The only group that consistently explored their relative importance were political sociologists who employed survey data to report changes in the European spirit. Most studies, especially the ones of the intergovernmentalist vintage, however, were interest-oriented while the institutionalists only reluctantly adopted the constructivist conviction that norms and ideas are important 'institutions' that form and affect human behaviour. Liesbet Hooghe's study belongs to the recent and theoretically diverse set of papers that explore the role of ideology and thus culture within specific institutions of the EU, showing that national origin is far less important than one would initially suspect.[1] On the contrary, the careful empirical examination convincingly demonstrates that the top mandarins within the European Commission are largely thinking along partisan lines.

This result is puzzling for two reasons. First, an intergovernmentalist observer would immediately expect that the Franco-German version of tamed capitalism would find its main supporters in countries with a corporatist or interventionist culture. Second, the results also contradict the widespread assumption that bureaucrats would largely reflect the interests of those institutions which appointed them and which might offer the key for the future professional career.

In this comment, I will first discuss why I think that the Hooghe result mirrors to a considerable extent the institutional interests of the Commission rather than deeply entrenched beliefs. My (admittedly relatively orthodox) sketch of a rationalist causal mechanism of preference formation within the European Commission will lead into a discussion of the role that beliefs and culture play in European integration.

The puzzle that Commission officials largely think in ideological dimensions quickly dissolves if we think in institutional terms. If we follow the standard rational choice explanation of bureaucracies pioneered by Niskanen (1971), it becomes obvious that bureaucrats like most individuals try to increase their own power. In the context of the EU, power largely means policy. The main way in which a directorate, a commissioner or a high-ranking civil servant can maximise their influence at the moment is by pushing for market liberalisation and reregulation at the European level simultaneously. The European Commission has been a champion of both causes for a long time, while the EP is mainly interested in gaining power through increasing its own legislative capacity. Since positive integration has gained importance after the more or less successful completion of the Internal Market, the institutional wish for a regulated Europe does not come as a surprise. In the public choice perception of Eurocrats, regulation and deregulation are thus not completely opposed goods, but rather serve as perfect substitutes in the mandarins' minds. In sum, Hooghe's chapter partly reflects the old saying that the EU 'stand where they sit'. Studying belief systems without taking the institutional framework into account remains reductionist. From a rationalist perspective, the ideal research strategy would thus consist of a study that examines the impact of culture on political decision-making and clearly distinguishes between beliefs and interests.

This should not, however, mean that beliefs are unimportant or that the study of European integration should only focus its attention on interests and revealed preferences. Rationalists have, to their own detriment, largely neglected culture and ideas as their natural underpinning. This is unfortunate because these factors were always considered to be important in the process of European integration, even if they were not attributed to be at the origin of the whole process (Schneider, 1998). Second, ignoring culture is completely unnecessary since some tools allow us to study the relationship between beliefs, rules and preferences in a rigorous fashion.

Let me sketch the rationalist conceptualisation of these terms briefly. First, while ideas and beliefs can be conceived of as 'conditional probabilities' in the sense of Bayes, culture is just the aggregate of ideas. Recent extensions of the so-called Condorcet Jury Theorem[2] allow us to study this aggregation process. The new results demonstrate that the relationship between ideas (beliefs), interests and institutions is much more complicated than previously thought (Schneider, 1998). While the social choice literature, also largely initiated by Condorcet, unambiguously shows the limitations of majority voting in the aggregation of individual preferences, studies on the Jury Theorem, conversely, demonstrate the limitations of unanimity voting in reaching truth (Austen-Smith and Banks, 1996; Feddersen and Pesendorfer, 1998). If we can trust the game-theoretic work on Condorcet's second contribution to social choice theory, it becomes obvious that interests and beliefs are occasionally at loggerheads.

For the study of European integration, these new results provide a possibility to study the interplay between interests and beliefs. In particular, we can examine how different ideas about the future course of integration come about and how voting procedures and the hierarchy of particular groups influence the aggregation of these convictions. The results also enable us to perceive the notion of political and administrative culture in a more meaningful way – namely as aggregated beliefs and belief systems.

This gives me, finally, the opportunity to tap these results into the chapter by Liesbet Hooghe and the non-rationalist research programme in integration studies more clearly. My main recommendation would be to separate beliefs and interests more clearly. In the current version, no clear distinction between these competing terms is made. Further, the chapter could also profit from a discussion of the aggregation of beliefs and whether the hierarchical structure and institutional interests shape the basic conviction of the Euro-mandarins to some extent.

Notes

1 This is not the place to offer a complete overview of the interrelationship between cultural factors and European integration. Some of the more prominent empirically guided studies that come up with similar results are, however, Beyers and Dierickx (1997, 1998) for the working groups of the Council of Ministers and Kreppel and Tsebelis (1999) for the EP.

2 The Condorcet Jury Theorem states that the ability of a group in discovering the truth is larger than the corresponding ability of an individual. This implies that juries would have a lower probability of error than individual judges. Some recent game-theoretic extensions question this optimistic conclusion (Austen-Smith and Banks, 1996).

Moving beyond outworn debates: a new institutionalist research agenda

Proponents of scientific paradigms often resemble the leaders of major powers in world politics and believe in the everlastingness of their influence, simply forgetting that progress often follows a Darwinian logic and that the established wisdom of today might be the belittled aberration of tomorrow. The illusion of infinite dominance becomes especially acute if one reaches the top and no contender is in sight. This is, to exaggerate mildly, the position that neoinstitutionalism has reached in EU politics. Obviously, the growing influence of this newcomer on the theoretical scene has a lot to do with the weakness, if not degeneration, of the earlier paradigmatic approaches, neofunctionalism and intergovernmentalism. Although these two approaches were influential in structuring the debate on regional integration until the early 1990s, most observers now agree that the over-simplifying debate between the exponents of these two theories is over (e.g., Schmidt, 1996).

A further and more important reason for the rise of neoinstitutionalism within European studies is the success that the approach has had in other fields. The EU with its myriad of complicated and ever-changing procedures seemed to be an ideal testing ground for rule-based reasoning. This trend has changed the field dramatically. Almost no one believes now that regional integration is a *sui generis* phenomenon that requires its own analytical concepts. On the contrary, the most advanced methods developed in political science are now used to study the collaborative network that the EU has helped to create. Neoinstitutionalist research has played the central role in the professionalisation of EU politics, and it does not seem inconceivable that the sub-field will become an exporter of new analytical tools rather than the passive importer it has been for decades.

It goes without saying that the growing institutionalist consensus in EU politics has not escaped criticism. We thus still observe frequent attempts to cast the integration debate as a conflict between intergovernmentalism and neofunctionalism (e.g., Moravcsik, 1998). However, none of these challenges has left serious damage or endangered the acceptability of the general and widely shared premise that European integration cannot be properly understood without due reference to the formal and informal rules that govern the political interactions within the EU.

Nevertheless, as certain dangers loom ahead, there is no need for self-congratulatory complacency. To begin with, one liability of neoinstitutionalism will be its sheer diversity and lack of common understanding of what the research programme is about. The present volume shows that this disturbing cacophony might, however, only be a temporary problem. Despite the possibly lingering ontological disagreements, some common ground exists at least for those scholars who take questions of research design seriously and believe that standard social scientific methods can be used to explain European integration. We are thus confident that the epistemological convergence reported in this book will continue.

Neoinstitutionalism will, in the long run, face more serious challenges. This conclusion explores a number of puzzles and fallacies that hamper the debate and delay the intellectual progress of the field. In this concluding chapter, we want to discuss some of these emerging issues in more detail and offer a research agenda for the future. We will do so after a review of the main theoretical insights that the contributions to this book offer.

Common achievements

Only some years ago a common statement of successful job candidates was the enthusiastic remark that 'institutions matter'. The usual reaction to this truism is, half a decade later, heartfelt yawning. Indeed, the institutionalist revolution has led to a proliferation of studies that move far beyond the general insight that rules are important in all sorts of decision-making processes. The new institutionalist vintage looks past this obvious point and offers detailed causal mechanisms to explain how formal and informal rules affect the behaviour of human agents. The catchphrase 'institutions matter' is thus too imprecise to describe this diverse set of findings which begins to revolutionise the way we think about political interactions.

The implications of institutionalist thinking for our understanding of EU politics are profound. We now know that the constitutional changes brought about by several treaty reforms have changed the power balance within the EU in often under-estimated ways. The most recent example is the Treaty of Amsterdam which has once again altered the legislative power game between the Council of Ministers, the EP and the Commission. This volume shows how new analytical tools can be fruitfully used to understand such momentous changes. It was institutionalist scholarship which first brought attention to the central role that the European Commission plays in these interactions (Steunenberg, 1994).

More questionable was the conjecture that the EP already possessed considerable agenda setting power through the Single European Act (Tsebelis, 1994; Moser, 1996). Most scholars agree, however, that the subsequent reforms and especially the Treaty of Amsterdam weakened the Commission and strengthened the EP. Although the ramifications of these studies are quite precise, they have not yet inspired the reform discussions. It is, however, conceivable that institutionalist research will guide the selection of rules in the future since it allows us to assess precisely the consequences of different wordings in the constitutional base.

Institutionalist analysis, especially in its guise as 'discourse' analysis, also helps us to understand why national culture impedes or advances certain developments at the European level. We now know from this research tradition how deeply entrenched cultural practices influence the ways in which actors behave at the European level. One important manifestation of this is the surprising revelation in Hooghe's research in this book (Chapter 7) that the dominant influences upon European Commission staff precede their appointment to the Commission. National party politics and territorial provenance have an enduring influence on conceptions of appropriate modes of capitalism in Europe.

Checkel (Chapter 2) offers a more general view of how European integration has 'socialisation and identity-shaping effects on national agents'. Taking a social constructivist approach, he enumerates several mechanisms by which social learning and normative diffusion occur at the European and national levels. These chapters are part of a broader trend beginning to highlight the importance of values, beliefs, norms and identity in European integration – their formation, propagation and ultimate causal influence upon subsequent behaviour.

We also increasingly understand how the vertical interactions between member states and EU institutions function. Bulmer and Burch (Chapter 4) explore this realm, suggesting that feedback processes ensure a reciprocal impact between the member states, whose responses to 'Europeanisation' are deeply influenced by national tradition, and the European level, which is in turn (obviously) influenced by these same member states. The literature on two-level games has also been influential in this area, displaying not least the causal mechanism behind Isaac Goldberg's saying that 'Diplomacy is to do and say the nastiest things in the nicest way.' The formal literature on two-level games allows us to see the conditions under which government leaders can use a reference to a domestic ratification procedure as a credible threat to bolster their demands at the European level (Putnam, 1988; Schneider and Cederman, 1994). Several studies qualify Schelling's (1960) hypothesis that the weak (or domestically constrained) government is a powerful negotiator at the international level. Yet, under conditions of incomplete information, not all allusions to constraining domestic ratification procedures are successful, while other factors such as the distribution of preferences also affect the credibility of a ratification threat (Iida, 1993; Mo, 1994, 1995; Milner, 1997).

Neoinstitutionalist analysis in political science is intellectually closely affiliated with other disciplines, not least constitutional economics and public choice. One common goal of all these fields is to find a social contract that all members of a certain group can accept. This is exactly the fundamental question that guides the treaty reform and enlargement negotiations of the EU. At these intergovernmental conferences (IGCs), governments are largely concerned about future power constellations in central policy fields when they negotiate over new rules. Bräuninger et al. use this assumption in Chapter 3 and explore how changing rules affect the power distribution within the EU.

We now know from this and related studies that the evolutionary mechanism underlying these negotiations is not a mystical (and never properly defined) force like the spill over effects that early neofunctionalists propagated. It seems rather that the main impetus that pushes the constitutional development of the EU forward comes from the bargaining processes among governments and, to some extent at least, supranational actors. This observation has obviously already been made by some intergovernmentalists such as Scharpf (1988) and Moravcsik (1991, 1998). Neoinstitutionalists move, however, beyond the thick diplomatic history which first generation intergovernmentalists offer to account for the influence of member states on EU decision-making. As this book demonstrates, rule-based reasoning allows us to derive parsimonious models which can subsequently be tested empirically. Hence, Gresham's law that theory drives out description and casual generalisations in the long run also holds true for the still fragile field of EU politics.

Neoinstitutionalism in political science also has close intellectual contacts with historical analysis and sociology. Political scientists are increasingly examining the role of temporal processes in politics, elucidating mechanisms under which positive reinforcement occurs (see especially, Pierson, 1999). Persistent behaviour or ingrained and shared cognitive patterns are thought to be the result of any number of factors which may be reinforced over time, including individual cost/benefit calculations, elite control and legitimacy. These factors may lead to consistent behaviour, which means that at any given moment in time certain outcomes are more likely than others. Yet problems emerge in this line of thinking too, for most concede that over-deterministic temporal theories are mistaken: exogenous or endogenous forces can induce change, throwing behaviour on to a new path. If this occurs, we have difficulty sorting out (and this becomes an important empirical question) how much importance the original path had in the first place.

Another area in which institutionalist research becomes increasingly important is the system of delegation that structures the relationship between member states and EU institutions. It has become clear that comitology is itself a bargaining process (Franchino, 2000) and not so much a deliberative process, as some observers would have us believe (e.g., Joerges and Neyer, 1997a and b). The research community is also making headway in understanding how specific institutions within the EU function. The inner working of the EP and the European Commission are no longer the black boxes they seemed to be in the 1990s. We now understand that sanctioning mechanisms rather than socialisation seem to influence the behaviour of individual members of the EP (Bailer and Schneider, 2000) or that the world views of civil servants in the Commission largely follow ideological cleavages rather than inner-bureaucratic interests (Hooghe, 1998).

Although all these results are impressive, they are still not sufficient to give us an adequate picture of how crucial decisions are made in the EU. To our knowledge, no convincing institutionalist research exists for instance on the question of how the EU makes its foreign aid or trade policy. Systematic knowledge on regulatory policy-making in general is only starting to emerge. The lack of progress is partly a consequence of the trend to focus first on legislation and interstate bargaining. The research gap is, however, also a consequence of some larger issues which have not yet been resolved convincingly in the debate between the competing institutionalisms. We discuss these questions below.

Remaining misunderstandings

The three branches of institutionalist research on the EU have the full potential to establish the kind of dialogue that will be essential for the further theoretical development of the field. One necessary precondition is that neoinstitutionalists avoid being drawn into the polemical fights that hamper the interactions between the competing paradigms in International Relations (IR). Serious misperceptions, however, all too often hamper this necessary discourse. It seems to us rather unfortunate that the resort to populist battle-cries are still a frequently used means to close the ranks and to defend 'citations cartels' or other vested interests. We briefly want to discuss the error in some of these remaining fallacies and misunderstandings.

The 'This is positivism' fallacy
One of the usual objections against rationalist reasoning is the reproach that it is based on a purely positivist understanding of science. This reproach – often made against the use of any sort of quantitative technique – is not only wrong, but also not up-to-date. Most assessments of the state of the art in the philosophy of science now agree that rationalist

reasoning is based on newer tendencies such as 'scientific realism'. This approach especially shares with rationalist institutionalists the interest in forms of explanation that are based on models. Ironically, this analytical focus renders the orientation of institutionalist research rather anti-positivist (but not anti-scientist) since 'realists see their position *as more rather than less rigorous* than positivism' (Lane, 1996: 378, emphasis in the original): 'Where positivism judged research on statistical significance. . ., realism demands scientific significance, a deeper search into actual political processes and the development of explanations that satisfy an audience of peers, laypersons and officials, all of whom demand real answers' (ibid.).

In sum, we believe that trying to label another approach as 'positivist' (or 'post-positivist' for that matter) is as mistaken as still differentiating between quantitative and qualitative research strategies. In our view, science is a universalistic enterprise in which we are only able to distinguish 'good' from 'bad' and 'true' from 'false'. Any research strategy that leads us closer to the truth has to be welcomed. All of these techniques necessarily involve a blending of quantitative and qualitative aspects. Hence, any qualitative assessment of whether or not a factor has an influence on another variable is inherently quantitative. The reverse is true as well: quantitative assessment of causal influence that shows statistical significance is inherently an influence that can and should be made qualitatively too. In other words, the 'quantitative' aspects cannot and should not be separated from the more 'qualitative' concerns. Investigation of given effects must be made using a variety of techniques. A further dichotomy that should finally be dismissed is the separation of 'understanding' from 'explanation', a differentiation that is often wrongly attributed to Max Weber. In fact, the German sociologist rather integrated the two categories that neo-Kantian philosophers had earlier introduced.

The 'Selection bias' fallacy

Rationalists also often deride research by sociological institutionalists, claiming that the cases are badly chosen. A very frequent and often cogent point is that the implications of some studies cannot be trusted because the variation on the variables is limited and restricted to some interval or category on the dependent variable (Geddes, 1991). This argument can be made against the 'impossibility theorem' nourished by those early intergovernmentalists who believed that the integration process would never encroach into 'high politics' (Hoffmann, 1966). A similar selection bias bedevils the teleological optimism that guided the writings of some early neofunctionalists. However, as convincingly argued by Hug in this volume (Comment on Chapter 6), the deterministic predictions that rational choice theorists (or adherents of competing camps) make can easily be refuted by one single case study. Since rational choice models often entail point predictions, even a minor mismatch between the anticipated and the observed outcome is sufficient to undermine a theory in a devastating manner.

However, one case that illustrates this is the lament by Scharpf (1988) that the EU has permanently moved into a 'joint decision trap' where the *nay* of one single member state is sufficient to block the organisation permanently. As the development of the EU has demonstrated, the organisation has not yet reached this nadir although institutional self-blockade can never be excluded as a possible option in a predominantly intergovernmental setting. It should also be noted in this context that some recent institutionalist research (Colomer, 1999) also suggests that the unanimity rule which is often only used to demonstrate the power of the most conservative member state (Scharpf, 1988, Schneider and Cederman, 1994) entails subtleties that reach beyond the metaphor of the 'joint decision trap' or other forms of institutional self-blockade that intergovernmentalists propagate.

Thus, the generalism of rational choice and the particularism of historical institutionalism need not be problematic. Methodological pluralism is to be welcomed, for we can often learn a great deal more about a given puzzle by taking at least two shots at it: one involving formal modelling, the other involving detailed descriptive research. The result is not pandemonium, it is a clearer understanding of cause and effect – if all scholars are careful in their research execution. Variables should be identified and defined, the relationships between them carefully explained and these relationships should be tested as rigorously and honestly as possible.

The 'Endogenous preference change' fallacy

In IR, the debate between the competing institutionalisms is largely driven by the attitude of these approaches towards the phenomenon of 'endogenous preference change'. This dispute is not new, as the Latin saying 'De Gustibus Non Est Disputandum' indicates. The dispute over whether or not rationalism is able to deal with the effects of socialisation or learning on preference structures is, however, superfluous at best. This is first of all the case because most rationalists simply do not want to deal with changing tastes. Their primary goal is to explain how changing budget constraints or institutional arrangements influence the behaviour of individuals. They keep preferences constant in their models because some of the variables in any sensible model have to remain stable to explain the variation in the other parameters. If one wants to deal with changing tastes instead of changing context, one needs to fix the latter. This requires, however, that one has a sound idea about the mechanisms which lead to preference change. The only theoretical framework we know that comes close to that is Becker's (1996) expected utility model that explains how individuals change their taste. It should also be noted that non-Bayesian learning has been frequently studied throughout the 1990s, especially in evolutionary game theory. There is thus hope that endogenous preference change can be studied in a rigorous fashion in the future (see also Steunenberg's comment on Chapter 2 in this book).

This issue has some resemblance to the selection bias fallacy discussed above: we have a methodological pluralism in the field today. Historical and sociological institutionalists are preoccupied with change and persistence over time, and they try to account for these; rational choice institutionalists take a cross-sectional approach: why do actors make certain choices at certain times? Rational choice analysis is not ahistorical, but it needs to be repeated over and over again to provide a temporal picture. These are not incompatible methodologies but to avoid the 'anything goes' mentality, research should be conducted in accordance with scientifically-valid and commonly-accepted principles, as suggested above.

The 'Unrealistic assumption' fallacy

One easy but not very convincing criticism of a different approach is simply to state that it is based on unrealistic assumptions. Interestingly, both rationalists and constructivists use this 'argument' when they talk about the models of the competing camp. We often hear the complaint that to use a Habermasian logic of social communication is unrealistic because the underlying model is normative and not positive. The classic Simonian reproach towards rational choice reasoning is that it exaggerates the mental capacities of the individuals whose actions it models. The classic defense is the position advocated by Friedman (1953) that the realism of the underlying assumptions do not matter and that a model shall only be judged on the validity of the predictions that it generates. We believe, in line with Hovi, that neither position is tenable and that a middle position that limits the number of 'unrealistic' assumptions is desirable: 'The question is, therefore, not whether any particular statement in a model is true or false, but if the full model can in any way be of help to understand the subject at hand, *despite* it being grounded on unrealistic assumptions' (Hovi, 1998, italics in original). In Hovi's view, any model has to be based on some simplifying assumption in order to be tractable.

One example that we frequently encounter in the modelling of European decision-making processes is the assumption of complete information. Although we are of course all certain that political actors do not know the future, this assumption has helped us to understand the basic prerequisites of agenda setting in the EU. If we move to the more realistic case of incomplete information, we will be able to discover the extent to which strategic considerations are able to alter the basic political equilibria. It is still important to begin with a model that describes the general structure.

A further issue is that the assumptions built in to rational choice modelling, such as the role of identity and beliefs, which are unpacked and examined by sociological and sometimes historical institutionalists, do not usually lend themselves to easy modelling. Yet it remains an important (even if rationalists claim *preliminary*) objective to bring these assumptions into the open, explain what is meant by them and how they might influence behaviour, and show how they are related to other variables, before attempting to model them formally. Ultimately, what is gained by this preliminary exercise is a better understanding of the subject.

Common problems

Neoinstitutionalism will most likely continue to remain influential if the dialogue between the different branches of neoinstitutionalist research on the EU is led in a meaningful way. We believe that this book shows how such a discourse can be organised. Obviously, not all disagreements can or should be solved since debates are the essence of scientific progress. The dialogue between the different branches of neoinstitutionalist reasoning can move forward if it avoids the fallacies sketched out above, among others. To make substantive progress, however, also requires that some of the more serious issues are addressed in the future. These problems are common to the different approaches.

The biggest danger of institutionalist reasoning is that it over-stretches (like a hegemonic power) the role that institutions play in human action. Hence, not all relevant questions in political analysis have to refer to the rules that guide the process under scrutiny. In other words we firmly believe that institutions matter, but that they do not matter all the time and to the same extent. Such situations include personal discussions and other forms of social communication which are not purely guided by the interests of the participants. Some formal modellers have used so-called 'cheap talk' models to analyse situations in which the costs of communication are negligible (Morrow, 1994). Such models can be used powerfully to distinguish between situations in which words are able to influence human actions from others where the social exchange only amounts to a perhaps nice, but inconsequential, chit-chat. The technical term for this latter outcome is accordingly described as a 'babbling equilibrium'.

Although such 'cheap talk' models and other attempts to formalise persuasion are an interesting starting point, they do not yet cover the emergence of ideas. Constructivists are right in pointing out that rationalists have not paid sufficient attention to commonly shared beliefs. This has largely to do with the fact that most research has focused on the question of collective choice or interest aggregation and not on ways in which a group changes its beliefs about a certain social outcome. We believe that many political processes including voting are not only based on the interests of the participants, but also on their competing ideas about how the world is structured and how it should work. The political science literature should take this issue seriously and start to think about belief aggregation in applied context. As indicated by one of us (Gerald Schneider) in this volume, the literature on the so-called Condorcet Jury Theorem opens up interesting avenues of research.

Another area in which institutionalist reasoning has to remain largely silent within the near future at least are the questions typically dealt with by political sociology. It remains a legitimate and necessary endeavour to explore what kind of attributes influence a person's attitudes and actions. In European studies, we have recently witnessed a surge of interest-based explanations of popular attitudes towards the integration process. Especially Gabel (1998a, b) shows in an evaluation of competing models that the socioeconomic background of the *Eurobarometer* is key in this regard. A powerful challenge to this interpretation is offered by Sánchez-Cuenca (2000). He shows that the dissatisfaction with the national government seems to be important in turning respondents into supranationalists. These major studies do not deal with institutional aspects. Hug and Sciarini (2000) show, however, that such a focus can be fruitfully employed to study European attitudes. Moreover, sociological institutionalists and others with a constructivist world view are assembling a tool kit which will eventually enable us to understand much more about the relationship between beliefs and integration than we do now.

The shortcomings of institutionalist research are, in our view, largely a consequence of the promiscuous ways in which the competing schools employ the term 'institutions' to describe any sort of contextual variables that affect human behaviour. The easy way out of this dilemma is to state clearly that one strives to disentangle the relative weight of institutional factors on a certain social process while controlling for other relevant influences. Another possible, but less desirable, course is to give up the aspiration that some sort of unifying institutionalist approach will emerge in the near future. The consequence would be that researchers properly divide the approach into the schools that advocate different explanatory factors and label the theoretical models accordingly. There is, for instance, quite a difference between a transaction cost approach to political organisation and an evolutionary explanation. Both might be labelled institutionalists, but it remains doubtful whether the general term carries any specific importance. We think that it is unnecessary to drop the term institutionalism from the research agenda as long as the scholars engaging into this paradigm refer to a common understanding of scientific procedures.

Table 8.1 Possible future research practice in institutionalist studies on the European Union

Questions	Rational choice	Historical	Sociological
What kind of institutions matter?	Widening of focus to informal rules and cultural practices	Role of culture, sequencing, and time	Organisational and national; professional and epistemic: role of cognitive patterns on institutionalisation
Relationship between institutions and strategies	Strategic use of institutions	Process of assimilating institutional norms into strategies over time	Cross-cutting influence of national and non-national norms
What causes institutions to arise and change?	Institution creation as a bargaining process	Role of actor choice, agency initiative. Internal and external forces	Role of external and internal pressures or shocks
Role of intentionality	Extension to models with limitedly rational actors	How intentionality is modified by institutional history	Process of organisational adaptation to external forces. Concept of 'bounded intentionality'
Role of history	Modelling specific 'historical' influences	Internalising effect over long term	Effect of cross-cutting sociological influences. Assimilation of norms into beliefs, identity, etc.

Source: Adapted from Aspinwall/Schneider (forthcoming).

With these thoughts in mind, we offer a set a guiding questions that could serve to channel future research in this area. First, what kind of institutions matter in the context of European integration and how do they affect behaviour by agents at all levels of decision-making? Second, under what circumstances do certain institutions arise, and how much can we attribute in this emergence to intentional behaviour and the passage of time? Third, how are institutions altered or maintained, and how do EU institutions affect institutions at other levels and vice versa? Fourth, how do EU institutions impact on decision-making? Table 8.1 elaborates this research framework and suggests possible lines of inquiry generated from the foregoing discussions and extant research on institutions.

References

Abélès, M., I. Bellier, M. McDonald (1993), 'Approche anthropologique de la Commission européenne', Brussels, Report for the European Commission (unpublished).

Adler, E. (1997), 'Seizing the Middle Ground: Constructivism in World Politics', *European Journal of International Relations*, 3, 319–63.

Adler, E. and M. Barnett (1996), 'Governing Anarchy: A Research Agenda for the Study of Security Communities', *Ethics & International Affairs*, 10, 63–98.

Albert, M. (1993), *Capitalism against Capitalism*, London, Whurr Publishers.

Almond, G. A. (1990), *Discipline Divided: Schools and Sects in Political Science*, Newbury Park, Sage.

Alter, K. (1998), 'Who are the "Masters of the Treaty"? European Governments and the European Court of Justice', *International Organization*, 52, 121–47.

Anderson, J. (1995), 'The State of the (European) Union: From the Single Market to Maastricht, from Singular Events to General Theories', *World Politics*, 47, 441–65.

Argyris, N. (1993), 'Regulatory Reform in the Electricity Sector: An Analysis of the Commission's Internal Market Proposals', *Oxford Review of Economic Policy*, 9, 31–43.

Armstrong, K. (1998), 'Conceptualising the European Union: The Contribution of New Institutionalism', *Academy of European Law Online*, http://www.law.harvard.edu/programs/jeanmonnet/seminar.

Armstrong, K. and S. Bulmer (1998), *The Governance of the Single European Market*, Manchester, Manchester University Press.

Arthur, W. B. (1994), *Increasing Returns and Path Dependence in the Economy*, Ann Arbor, University of Michigan Press.

Aspinwall, M. (1995), 'International Integration or Internal Politics? Anatomy of a Single Market Measure', *Journal of Common Market Studies*, 33, 475–99.

—— 1998), 'Collective Attraction: The New Political Game in Brussels', in J. Greenwood and M. Aspinwall (eds), *Collective Action in the European Union: Interests and the New Politics of Associability*, London, Routledge, 196–213.

—— (1999), 'Planes, Trains, and Automobiles: Transport Governance in the European Union', in B. Kohler-Koch and R. Eising (eds) *The Transformation of Governance in the European Union*, London, Routledge.

Aspinwall, M. and G. Schneider (1998), 'Same menu, separate tables: the

Institutionalist Turn in Political Science and the Study of European Integration', Working Paper, University of Konstanz.

—— (forthcoming), 'Same Menu, Separate Tables: The Institutionalist Turn in Political Science and the Study of European Integration', *European Journal of Political Research*.

Austen-Smith, D. and J. S. Banks (1996), 'Information Aggregation, Rationality and the Condorcet Jury Theorem', *American Political Science Review*, 90, 34–45.

Bailer, S. and G. Schneider (2000) 'The Word Policy of the European Parliament: Informal Rules and the Enlargement Debate in the European Parliament', in B. Steunenberg and J. Thomassen (eds), *The European Parliament On the Move: Towards Parliamentary Democracy in Europe*, Lanham, MD., Rowman and Littlefield.

Baker, D. and D. Seawright (eds) (1998), *Britain For and Against Europe: British Politics and the Question of European Integration*, Oxford, Clarendon Press.

Barber, L. (1998) 'A Punctured Image', *Financial Times*, 15 June.

Barry, B. (1989), *Theories of Justice: A Treatise on Social Justice*, London, Harvester Wheatsheaf.

Bawn, K. (1995), 'Political Control versus Expertise: Congressional Choices about Administrative Procedures', *American Political Science Review*, 89, 62–73.

Becker, G. S. (1996), *Accounting for Taste*, Cambridge, MA, Harvard University Press.

Bednar, J., J. Ferejohn and G. Garrett (1996), 'The Politics of European Federalism', *International Review of Law and Economics*, 16, 279–94.

Bender, B. (1991), 'Governmental Processes: Whitehall, Central Government and 1992', *Public Policy and Administration*, 6:1, 13–20.

Berg, S. and J.-E. Lane (1999), 'Measurements of Voting Power: Individual and Collective Properties with Applications to the EU', in M. Holler and G. Owen (eds), *Power Indices and Coalition Formation*, Dordrecht, Kluwer.

Berger, P. and T. Luckmann (1967), *The Social Construction of Reality: A Treatise in the Sociology of Knowledge*, Harmondsworth, Penguin.

Beutler, B., R. Bieber, J. Pipkorn and J. Streil (1993), 'Die Europäische Union'. *Rechtsordnung und Politik*, Baden-Baden, Nomos.

Beyers, J. (1998), 'Where does Supranationalism Come from? The Ideas Floating through the Working Groups of the Council of the European Union'. Paper presented at the Third Pan-European Conference on International Relations, Vienna.

Beyers, J. and G. Dierickx (1997), 'Nationality and European Negotiations: The Working Groups of the Council of Ministers', *European Journal of International Relations*, 3, 435–71.

—— (1998), 'The Working Groups of the Council of the European Union: Supranational or Intergovernmental Negotiations?', *Journal of Common Market Studies*, 36, 289–317.

Binmore, K. G. (1994), *Playing Fair: Game Theory and the Social Contract*, Cambridge, The MIT Press.

Black, D. (1958), *The Theory of Committees and Elections*, London, Cambridge University Press.

Brams, S. and P. Affuso (1976), 'Power and Size: A New Paradox', *Theory and Decision*, 7, 29–56.

—— (1985), 'New Paradoxes of Voting Power on the EC Council of Ministers', *Electoral Studies*, 4, 135–9.

Bräuninger, T. (1996), *Die Modellierung von Entscheidungsverfahren internationaler Organisationen am Beispiel der Meeresbodenbehörde*, Mannheim, Zulassungsarbeit.

Bruce-Gardyne, J. (1986), *Ministers and Mandarins: Inside the Whitehall Village*, London, Sidgwick and Jackson.

Buchanan, J. M. and G. Tullock (1962), *The Calculus of Consent*, Ann Arbor, University of Michigan Press.

Buller, J. and M. Smith (1998), 'Civil Service Attitudes Towards the European Union', in D. Baker and D. Seawright (eds), *Britain For and Against Europe: British Politics and the Question of European Integration*, Oxford, Clarendon Press.

Bulmer, S. (1986), *The Domestic Structure of European Community Policy-Making in West Germany*, New York, Garland.

—— (1994), 'The New Governance of the European Union: A New Institutionalist Approach', *Journal of Public Policy*, 13, 351–80.

—— (1997), 'Shaping the Rules? The Constitutive Politics of the European Union and German Power', in P. Katzenstein (ed.), *Tamed Power: Germany in Europe*, Ithaca, NY, Cornell University Press.

Bulmer, S. and M. Burch (1998), 'Organising for Europe: Whitehall, the British State and European Union', *Public Administration*, 36, 601–28.

Bulmer, S., C. Jeffery and W. Paterson (1998), 'Deutschlands europäische Diplomatie – die Entwicklung des regionalen Milieus', in W. Weidenfeld (ed.), *Deutsche Europapolitik – Optionen wirksamer Interessenvertretung*, Bonn, Europa Union Verlag.

Burch, M. and I. Holliday (1996), *The British Cabinet System*, London, Prentice Hall/Harvester Wheatsheaf.

Burley, A.-M. and W. Mattli (1993), 'Europe Before the Court: A Political Theory of Legal Integration', *International Organization*, 47, 41–76.

Calvert, R. L. (1995), 'The Rational Choice Theory of Social Institutions: Cooperation, Coordination, and Communication', in J. S. Banks and E. A. Hanushek (eds) *Modern Political Economy*, New York, Cambridge University Press, 216–67.

Cameron, D. R. (1992), *The 1992 Initiative: Causes and Consequences*, in A. M. Sbragia (ed.), *Euro-Politics: Institutions and Policymaking in the 'New' European Community*, Washington, D.C., The Brookings Institution, 23–74.

Caporaso, J. (1998), 'Regional Integration Theory: Understanding Our Past and Anticipating Our Future', *Journal of European Public Policy*, 5, 1–16.

Checkel, J. T. (1997a), *Ideas and International Political Change: Soviet/Russian Behaviour and the End of the Cold War*, New Haven, Yale University Press.

—— (1997b), 'International Norms and Domestic Politics: Bridging the Rationalist-Constructivist Divide', *European Journal of International Relations*, 3, 473–95.

—— (1998), 'The Constructivist Turn in International Relations Theory (A Review Essay)', *World Politics*, 50, 324–48.

—— (1999a), 'International Institutions and Socialization'. Paper presented at the International Studies Association Annual Convention, Washington, DC.

—— (1999b), 'Norms, Institutions and National Identity in Contemporary Europe', *International Studies Quarterly*, 43, 84–114.

Christiansen, T. (1997), 'Reconstructing European Space: From Territorial Politics to Multilevel Governance', in K. E. Joergensen (ed.), *Reflective Approaches to European Governance*, London, Macmillan.

Christiansen, T., K. E. Joergensen and A. Wiener (eds) (1999) 'Constructivism in European Studies', special issue of *Journal of European Public Policy*, 6, 528–44.

Cini, M. (1996), *The European Commission: Leadership, Organization and Culture in the Commission*, Manchester, Manchester University Press.

Cohen, M. and L. Sproull (1996) 'Introduction', in M. Cohen and L. Sproull (eds), *Organizational Learning*, London, Sage, ix–xv.

Coleman, J. S. (1971), 'Control of Collectivities and the Power of a Collectivity to Act', in B. Lieberman (ed.), *Social Choice*, New York, Gordon and Breach, 269–99.

—— (1990), *Foundations of Social Theory*, Cambridge, Belknap Press.

—— (1995), 'Organizational structure and the emergence of informal norms', in P. Foss (ed.), *Economic Approaches to Organizations and Institutions. An Introduction*, Aldershot, Dartmouth.

Collier, R. and D. Collier (1991), *Shaping the Political Agenda: Critical Junctures, the Labor Movement, and Regime Dynamics in Latin America*, Princeton, Princeton University Press.

Colomer, J. M. (1999), 'Research Note: On the Geometry of Unanimity Rule', *Journal of Theoretical Politics*, 11, 543–53.

Converse, Philip E. (1964), 'The Nature of Belief Systems in Mass Publics', in David E. Apter (ed.), *Ideology and Discontent*, New York, Free Press of Glencoe.

—— (1976), *The Dynamics of Party Support*, Beverly Hills, Sage.

Conzelmann, T. (1998), '"Europeanization" of Regional Development Policies? Linking the Multi-Level Governance Approach with Theories of Policy Learning and Policy Change', *European Integration Online Papers 2*, http://eiop.or.at/eiop

Cook, S. and D. Yanow (1996), 'Culture and Organizational Learning', in M. Cohen and L. Sproull (eds), *Organizational Learning*, London, Sage, 430–59.

Corbett, R., F. Jacobs and M. Shackleton (1995), *The European Parliament*, London, Cartermill International Ltd.

Council of Europe (1993), 'Interim Report of the Committee of Experts on Multiple Nationality', Strasbourg: *Restricted* CJ-PL (93) 11.

—— (1994), 'Meeting Report: Committee of Experts on Multiple Nationality', Strasbourg: *Restricted* CJ-PL (94) 18.

Cox, G. W. (1999), 'The Empirical Content of Rational Choice Theory, A Reply to Green and Shapiro', *Journal of Theoretical Politics*, 11, 147–69.

Cram, L. (1994), 'The European Commission as a Multi-Organization: Social Policy and IT Policy in the EU', *Journal of European Public Policy*, 1, 195–217.

—— (1997a), *Policymaking in the European Union: Conceptual Lenses and the Integration Process*, London, Routledge.

—— (1997b), 'The European Commission and the "European Interest": Institutions, Interaction and Preference Formation in the EU Context'. Paper presented at the Fifth Biennial Conference of the European Community Studies Association.

Crombez, C. (1996), 'Legislative Procedures in the European Community', *British Journal of Political Science*, 26, 199–228.

—— (1997a), 'The Co-Decision Procedure in the European Union', *Legislative Studies Quarterly*, 22, 97–119.

—— (1997b), 'Policy Making and Commission Appointment in the European Union', *Aussenwirtschaft*, 52, 63–82. Also forthcoming in Moser, P., G. Schneider and G. Kirchgässner (eds), *Decision Rules in the European Union: A Rational Choice Perspective*, London, Macmillan.

—— (1998), 'Spatial Models of Logrolling in the European Union', Working Paper 9823, Katholieke Universiteit Leuven.

Crouch, C. (1993), *Industrial Relations and European State Traditions*, Oxford, Clarendon.

Crouch, C. and W. Streeck (eds) (1997a), *Political Economy of Modern Capitalism*, London, Sage.

—— (1997b), 'Institutional Capitalism: Diversity and Performance', in C. Crouch and W. Streeck (eds), *Political Economy of Modern Capitalism: Mapping Convergence and Diversity*, London, Sage.

Curtin, D. (1993), 'The Constitutional Structure of the Union: A Europe of Bits and Pieces', *Common Market Law Review*, 30, 17–69.

Delors, J. (1992), *Our Europe: The Community and National Development* (Translated from French) London, Verso.

Demsetz, H. (1969), 'Information and Efficiency: Another Viewpoint', *Journal of Law and Economics*, 12, 1–22.

Diez, T. (1999a), 'Speaking Europe: The Politics of Integration Discourse', in Christiansen, T., K. E. Joergensen and A. Wiener (eds) 'Constructivism in European Studies', special issue of *Journal of European Public Policy*, 6, 598–613.

Diez, T. (1999b), 'Riding the AM-track Through Europe. Or, the Pitfalls of a Rationalist Journey Through European Integration', unpublished paper, Copenhagen Peace Research Institute.

DiMaggio, P. J. and W. Powell (1991), 'Introduction', in W. Powell and P. J. DiMaggio (eds), *The New Institutionalism in Organizational Analysis*, Chicago, University of Chicago Press.

Dinan, D. (1994), *Ever Closer Union? An introduction to the European Community*, Houndsmills, Basingstoke, Macmillan.

Dion, D. (1998), 'Evidence and Inference in the Comparative Case Study', *Comparative Politics*, 30, 127–45.

Dobbin, F. (1994), 'Cultural Models of Organization: The Social Construction of Rational Organizing Principles', in D. Crane (ed.), *The Sociology of Culture: Emerging Theoretical Perspectives*, Cambridge, Blackwell.

Dogan, R. (1997), 'Comitology: Little Procedures with Big Implications', *West European Politics*, 20, 31–60.

Dreier, H. (1994), 'Informal Administrative Actions', in T. Ellwein, D. Grimm, J. Hesse and G. Schuppert (eds), *Jahrbuch zur Staats- und Verwaltungswissenschaft*, 7, Baden-Baden, Nomos.

Eckstein, H. (1975), 'Case Study and Theory in Political Science', in F. I. Greenstein and N. W. Polsby (eds), *Handbook of Political Science*, 7, Reading, MA, Addison-Wesley.

Economist (1998) 'The Brussels Lobbyist and the Struggle for Ear-Time', 15 August.

Eichhorst, W. (1998a), 'Europäische Sozialpolitik zwischen nationaler und supranationaler Regulierung: Die Entsendung von Arbeitsnehmern im Rahmen der Dienstleitungsfreiheit innerhalb der Europäischen Union', Dissertation, Universität Konstanz.

—— (1998b), 'European Social Policy between National and Supranational Regulation: Posted Workers in the Framework of Liberalized Services Provision', MPIfG-Discussion Paper 98/6.

Esping-Andersen, G. (1999), 'Politics without Class: Postindustrial cleavages in Europe and America', in H. Kitschelt, P. Lange, G. Marks and J. Stephens (eds), *Continuity and Change in Contemporary Capitalism*, Cambridge, Cambridge University Press.

Esser, H. (1993), *Soziologie. Allgemeine Grundlagen*, Frankfurt, New York, Campus.

European Parliament (1992), *Maastricht, the Treaty on European Union, Position of the European Parliament*. Luxembourg, Office for Official Publications of the European Communities.

Evans, P., D. Rueschemeyer and T. Skocpol (eds) (1985) *Bringing the State Back In*, Cambridge, Cambridge University Press.

Everling, U. (1997), 'Constitutional Problems of the European Union – A Lawyer's View', in D. Schmidtchen and R. Cooter (eds), *Constitutional Law and Economics of the European Union*, Cheltenham, Elgar.

Falkner, G. (1998), 'How Intergovernmental are Intergovernmental Conferences? Lessons from the Maastricht Social Agreement'. Paper presented at the European Consortium for Political Research 26th Joint Session, University of Warwick.

Favell, A. (1998), 'The Europeanization of Immigration Politics'. Paper presented at ARENA research seminar, Oslo.

Feddersen, T. and W. Pesendorfer (1998), 'Convicting the Innocent: The Inferiority of Unanimous Jury Verdicts', *American Political Science Review*, 92, 23–35.

Ferejohn, J. and D. Satz (1995), 'Unification, Universalism, and Rational Choice Theory', *Critical Review*, 9, 71–84.

Fierke, K. M. and A. Wiener (1999), 'Constructing Institutional Interests: EU and NATO Enlargement', in T. Christiansen, K. E. Joergensen and A. Wiener (eds) 'Constructivism in European Studies,' special issue of *Journal of European Public Policy*, 6, 721–42.

Finnemore, M. (1996a), *National Interests in International Society*, Ithaca, NY, Cornell University Press.

Finnemore, M. (1996b), 'Norms, Culture, and World Politics: Insights from Sociology's Institutionalism', *International Organization*, 50, 325–47.

Finnemore, M. and K. Sikkink (1998), 'International Norm Dynamics and Political Change', *International Organization*, 52, 887–917.

Fiorina, M. P. (1996), 'Rational Choice, Empirical Contributions, and the

Scientific Enterprise', in J. Friedman (ed.), *The Rational Choice Controversy: Economic Models of Politics Reconsidered*, New Haven, London, Yale University Press.

Fligstein, N. (1998), 'Institutional Entrepreneurs and Cultural Frames: The Case of the European Union's Single Market Program'. Paper presented at the Workshop on 'Ideas, Culture and Political Analysis', Center of International Studies, Princeton University.

Florini, A. (1996), 'The Evolution of International Norms', *International Studies Quarterly*, 40, 363–89.

Franchino, F. (1998), 'The Commission's Executive Discretion, Information and Policy Preferences'. Paper presented at the European Consortium for Political Research 26th Joint Session, University of Warwick.

—— (1999), 'The Determinants of Control of Commission's Executive Functions', *European integration online Papers* (EIoP), 3, 2, http:/eiop.or.at/eiop/texte/1999-002a.htm

—— (2000), 'Control of the Commission's executive functions: uncertainty, conflict, and decision rules', *European Union Politics*, vol. 1, no. 1, Feb, 63–92.

Frey, B. S. and R. Eichenberger (1997), 'FOCJ: Creating a Single European Market for Governments', in D. Schmidtchen and R. Cooter (eds), *Constitutional Law and Economics of the European Union*, Cheltenham, Edward Elgar.

Friedman, J. (1996a), 'Introduction: Economic Approaches to Politics', in J. Friedman (ed.), *The Rational Choice Controversy: Economic Models of Politics Reconsidered*, New Haven, London, Yale University Press.

—— (ed.) (1996b) *The Rational Choice Controversy: Economic Models of Politics Reconsidered*, New Haven, London, Yale University Press.

Friedman, M. (1953), 'The Methodology of Positive Economics', in M. Friedman (ed.), *Essays in Positive Economics*, Chicago, University of Chicago Press.

Gabel, M. J. (1998a) 'Public Support for European Integration: An Empirical Test of Five Theories', *The Journal of Politics*, 60, 333–54.

—— (1998b) *Interests and Integration: Market Liberalization, Public Opinion, and European Union*, Ann Arbor, The University of Michigan Press.

Gaddum, E. (1994), *Die deutsche Europapolitik in den 80er Jahren*, Paderborn, Verlag Ferdinand Schöningh.

Garrett, G. (1992), 'International Cooperation and Institutional Choice: The European Community Internal Market', *International Organization*, 46, 533–60.

—— (1996), 'From the Luxembourg Compromise to Codecision Making in the European Union', *Electoral Studies*, 14, 289–308.

Garrett, G. and B. Weingast (1993) 'Ideas, Interests and Institutions: Constructing the EC's Internal Market', in J. Goldstein and R. Keohane (eds), *Ideas and Foreign Policy: Beliefs, Institutions and Political Change*, Ithaca, NY, Cornell University Press.

Garrett, G. and G. Tsebelis (1996), 'An Institutional Critique of Inter-governmentalism', *International Organization*, 50, 269–99.

Garrett, G., R. D. Kelemen and H. Schulz (1998), 'The European Court of Justice, National Governments and Legal Integration in the European Union', *International Organization*, 52, 149–76.

Geddes, B. (1990), 'How the Cases You Choose Affect the Answers You Get: Selection Bias in Comparative Politics', *Political Analysis*, 2, 131–50.

Gehring, T. (1997), 'Governing in Nested Institutions: Environmental Policy in the European Union and the Case of Packaging Waste', *Journal of European Public Policy*, 4, 337–54.

Genschel, P. (1997), 'The Dynamics of Inertia: Institutional Persistence and Change in Telecommunications and Health Care', *Governance*, 10, 43–66.

Giddens, A. (1976), *New Rules of Sociological Method*, London, Hutchinson.

Giddens, A. (1984), *The Constitution of Society: Outline of the Theory of Structuration*, Cambridge, Polity Press.

Goetz, K. (1995), 'National Governance and European Integration: Intergovernmental Relations in Germany', *Journal of Common Market Studies*, 33, 91–116.

Goldstein, J. (1993), *Ideas, Interests and American Trade Policy*, Ithaca, NY, Cornell University Press.

Golub, J. (1996), 'State Power and Institutional Influence in European Integration: Lessons from the Packaging Waste Directive', *Journal of Common Market Studies*, 34, 313–40.

Goodman, L. A. and W. H. Kruskal (1954), 'Measures of Association for Cross-Classifications', *Journal of the American Statistical Association*, 49, 732–64.

Green, D. and I. Shapiro (1994), *Pathologies of Rational Choice Theory*, New Haven, CT, Yale University Press.

Greenwood, J. and M. Aspinwall (eds) (1998), *Collective Action in the European Union: Interests and the New Politics of Associability*, London, Routledge.

Grieco, J. (1995), 'The Maastricht Treaty, Economic and Monetary Union and the Neorealist Research Program', *Review of International Studies*, 21, 21–40.

—— (1996), 'State Interests and Institutional Rule Trajectories: A Neorealist Interpretation of the Maastricht Treaty and European Economic and Monetary Union', *Security Studies*, 5, 261–306.

Haas, E. (1958), *The Uniting of Europe: Political, Social, and Economic Forces, 1950–1957*, London, Stevens and Sons, Ltd.

Haas, E. (1964), *Beyond the Nation-State: Functionalism and International Organization*, Stanford, Stanford University Press.

Haas, P. (1990), *Saving the Mediterranean: The Politics of International Environmental Cooperation*, NY, Columbia University Press.

—— (ed.) (1992), 'Knowledge, Power and International Policy Coordination', *International Organization*, Special Issue.

Hall, P. (1986), *Governing the Economy: The Politics of State Intervention in Britain and France*, Cambridge, Polity Press.

—— (1992), 'The Movement from Keynesianism to Monetarism: Institutional Analysis and British Economic Policy in the 1970s', in S. Steinmo, K. Thelen and F. Longstreth (eds), *Structuring Politics: Historical Institutionalism in Comparative Analysis*, Cambridge, Cambridge University Press.

—— (1993), 'Policy Paradigms, Social Learning and the State: The Case of Economic Policymaking in Britain', *Comparative Politics*, 25, 275–96.

Hall, P. and R. Taylor (1996), 'Political Science and the Three New Institutionalisms,' *Political Studies*, 44, 936–57.

Hanf, K. and B. Soetendorp (1998), 'Small States and the Europeanization of

Public Policy', in K. Hanf and B. Soetendorp (eds), *Adapting to European Integration: Small States and the European Union*, Harlow, Addison, Wesley, Longman Limited.

Hanley, D. (ed.) (1994), *Christian Democracy in Europe: A Comparative Perspective*, London, Pinter.

Hattam, V. (1993), *Labor Visions and State Power: The Origins of Business Unionism in the United States*, Princeton, Princeton University Press.

Haverland, M. (1998), 'Convergence and Persistent Diversity. Policy Transformation and Regulatory Change in the European Union. The Case of Packaging Waste'. Dissertation, University of Utrecht.

Hayes-Renshaw, F. and H. Wallace (1997), *The Council of Ministers*, Houndmills, Macmillan.

Heclo, H. and A. Wildavsky (1974), *The Private Government of Public Money*, London, Macmillan.

Héritier, A. (1995), '"Leaders" and "Laggards" in European Clean Air Policy', in B. Unger and F. van Waarden (eds), *Convergence or Diversity? Internationalization and Economic Policy Response*, Aldershot, Avebury, 278–305.

—— (1996), 'The Accommodation of Diversity in European Policy Making and its Outcomes: Regulatory Policy as a Patchwork', *Journal of European Public Policy*, 3, 149–67.

Herman, R. (1996) 'Identity, Norms and National Security: The Soviet Foreign Policy Revolution and the End of the Cold War,' in P. Katzenstein (ed.), *The Culture of National Security: Norms and Identity in World Politics*, New York, Columbia University Press.

Hesse, J. J. and K. Goetz (1992), 'Early Administrative Adjustment to the European Communities: the Case of the Federal Republic of Germany', in E. Heyen (ed.), *Jahrbuch der Europäischen Verwaltungsgeschichte*, no. 4 (special issue on Early European Community Administration), Baden-Baden, Nomos Verlagsgesellschaft.

Hix, S. (1998), 'The Study of the European Union II: The "New Governance" Agenda and its Rival', *Journal of European Public Policy*, 5, 38–65.

—— (1999), 'Dimensions and Alignments in European Union Politics: Cognitive Constraints and Partisan Responses', *European Journal of Political Research*, 35, 69–106.

Hix, S. and C. Lord (1997), *Political Parties in the European Union*, London, Macmillan.

Hoffmann, Stanley (1966), 'Obstinate or Obsolete? The Fate of the Nation-State and the Case of Western Europe', *Daedalus* 85, 862–915.

Holm, U. (1997), 'The French Garden is No Longer What it Used to Be', in K. E. Joergensen (ed.), *Reflective Approaches to European Governance*, London, Macmillan.

Hooghe, L. (1998), 'EU Cohesion Policy and Competing Models of European Capitalism', *Journal of Common Market Studies*, 36, 457–77.

—— (forthcoming), *Images of Europe: Top Commission Officials and European Governance*, book manuscript.

Hooghe, L. and M. Keating (1994), 'The Politics of European Union Regional Policy', *Journal of European Public Policy*, 1, 367–93.

Hooghe, L. and G. Marks (1996), '"Europe with the Regions": Channels of Regional Representation in the European Union', *Publius: The Journal of Federalism*, 26, 73–91.

—— (1999), 'Making of a Polity: European Integration Since the 1980s', in H. Kitschelt, P. Lange, G. Marks and J. Stephens (eds), *Continuity and Change in Contemporary Capitalism*, Cambridge, Cambridge University Press.

Hosli, M. O. (1996), 'Coalitions and Power: Effects of Qualified Majority Voting in the Council of the European Union', *Journal of Common Market Studies*, 34, 255–73.

House of Commons (1995), Select Committee on European Legislation, *The 1996 Intergovernmental Conference: The Agenda. Democracy and Efficiency. The Role of National Parliaments*, Session 1994–95, HMSO.

Hovi, J. (1998), 'The Relevance of Unrealistic Models for Empirical Political Science', *Homo Oeconomicus*, 15, 45–59.

Hoyer, W. (1998), 'Nationale Entscheidungsstrukturen deutscher Europapolitik', in W.-D. Eberwein and K. Kaiser (eds), *Deutschlands neue Außenpolitik: Band 4 Institutionen und Ressourcen*, München, R. Oldenbourg Verlag, 75–86.

Hug, S. (1997), 'Integration Through Referendums', *Aussenwirtschaft*, 52, 287–310. Also forthcoming in Moser, P., G. Schneider and G. Kirchgässner (eds), *Decision Rules in the European Union: A Rational Choice Perspective*, London, Macmillan.

Hug, S. and P. Sciarini (2000), 'Referendums on Foreign Policy: Do Institutions Matter in Voter's Decision?', *Comparative Political Studies*.

Iida, K. (1993) 'When and How Do Domestic Constraints Matter? Two-Level Games with Uncertainty', *Journal of Conflict Resolution*, 37, 403–26.

Ikenberry, J. (1988), *Reasons of State: Oil Politics and the Capacities of the American Government*, Ithaca, Cornell University Press.

Immergut, E. (1992), *Health Politics: Interests and Institutions in Western Europe*, Cambridge, Cambridge University Press.

Janning, J. and P. Meyer (1998), *Deutsche Europapolitik: Vorschläge zur Effektivierung*, Gütersloh, Verlag Bertelsmann Stiftung.

Jepperson, R. (1991), 'Institutions, Institutional Effects, and Institutionalism', in W. Powell and P. DiMaggio (eds), *The New Institutionalism in Organizational Analysis*, Chicago, University of Chicago Press.

Jepperson, R., A. Wendt and P. Katzenstein (1996), 'Norms, Identity, and Culture in National Security', in P. Katzenstein (ed.), *The Culture of National Security: Norms and Identity in World Politics*, New York, Columbia University Press.

Joergensen, K. E. (ed.) (1997), *Reflective Approaches to European Governance*, London, Macmillan.

Joerges, C. and J. Neyer (1997a), 'From Intergovernmental Bargaining to Deliberative Political Processes: The Constitutionalisation of Comitology', *European Law Journal*, 3, 273–99.

—— (1997b), 'Transforming Strategic Interaction into Deliberative Problem-Solving: European Comitology in the Foodstuffs Sector', *Journal of European Public Policy*, 4, 609–25.

Johnson, J. (1993), 'Is Talk Really Cheap: Prompting Conversation between Critical Theory and Rational Choice', *American Political Science Review*, 87, 74–86.

Johnston, I. (1998), 'Socialization in International Relations' (unpublished manuscript).

Kaiser, D. (1996), 'Institutionelle Wandel im Europäischen Politikprozeß. Europäisches Parlament und Kommission – Ende einer natürlichen Allianz'. Diploma Thesis, Faculty of Public Administration, University of Konstanz.

Kastning, L. (1991), 'Informelles Regieren: Annäherung an Begrifflichkeit und Bedeutungsgehalt', in H.-H. Hartwich and G. Wewer (eds), *Formale und informale Komponenten des Regierens in den Bereichen Führung, Entscheidung, Personal und Organisation*, Opladen, Leske + Budrich.

Kato, J. (1996), 'Review Article: Institutions and Rationality in Politics – Three Varieties of Neo-Institutionalists', *British Journal of Political Science*, 26, 553–82.

Katzenstein, P. (1985), *Small States in World Markets: Industrial Policy in Europe*, Ithaca, NY, Cornell University Press.

—— 1996), 'Introduction', in P. Katzenstein (ed.), *The Culture of National Security: Norms and Identity in World Politics*, New York, Columbia University Press.

—— (1997), 'United Germany in an Integrating Europe', in P. Katzenstein (ed.), *Tamed Power: Germany in Europe*, Ithaca, NY, Cornell University Press.

Katzenstein, P., R. Keohane and S. Krasner (1998), 'International Organization and the Study of World Politics', *International Organization*, 52, 645–85.

Keck, M. and K. Sikkink (1998), *Activists Beyond Borders: Transnational Advocacy Networks in International Politics*, Ithaca, NY, Cornell University Press.

Keman, H. (1997), 'Approaches to the Study of Institutions', in B. Steunenberg and F. van Vught (eds), *Political Institutions and Public Policy*, Dordrecht, Kluwer, 1–27.

Keohane, R. and S. Hoffmann (1991), 'Institutional Change in Europe in the 1980s,' in R. Keohane and S. Hoffmann (eds), *The New European Community*, Boulder, CO, Westview Press.

Kerremans, B. (1996), 'Do Institutions Make a Difference? Non-Institutionalism, Neo-Institutionalism and the Logic of Common Decision-Making in the European Union', *Governance*, 9, 217–40.

Khalaf, R. (1997) 'Call to Strengthen Rules on Human Rights and Democracy', *Financial Times*, 11 February.

King, G., R. Keohane and S. Verba (1994), *Social Inquiry: Scientific Inference in Qualitative Research*, Princeton, Princeton University Press.

Kitschelt, H., P. Lange, G. Marks and J. Stephens (eds) (1999), *Continuity and Change in Contemporary Capitalism*, Cambridge, Cambridge University Press.

Knight, J. and I. Sened (1995), 'Introduction', in J. Knight and I. Sened (eds), *Explaining Social Institutions*, Ann Arbor, University of Michigan Press.

Knodt, M. (1998), 'Auswärtiges Handeln der deutschen Länder', in W.-D. Eberwein and K. Kaiser (eds), *Deutschlands neue Außenpolitik: Band 4 Institutionen und Ressourcen*, München, R. Oldenbourg Verlag, 153–66.

Koelble, T. A. (1995), 'The New Institutionalisms in Political Science and Sociology', *Comparative Politics*, 2, 231–43.

Koh, H. H. (1997), 'Review Essay: Why Do Nations Obey International Law?', *The Yale Law Journal*, 106, 2599–660.

Kohler-Koch, B. and M. Knodt (1997), 'Multi-Level Governance: The Joy of Theorizing and the Anguish of Empirical Research'. Paper presented at the European Consortium for Political Research 25th Joint Session, Universitaet Bern.

König, T. (1996), 'The Constitutional Development of European Integration', *Journal of Theoretical Politics*, 8, 553–9.

—— (1997), *Europa auf dem Weg zum Mehrheitssystem: Gründe und Konsequenzen nationaler und parlamentarischer Integration*, Opladen, Westdeutscher Verlag.

König, T. and H. Schulz (1997), 'The Efficiency of Legislative Decision Making in the European Union', Berkeley, Cal., Center for German and European Studies Working Paper 1.54, University of California.

König, T. and T. Bräuninger (1998a), *From an Ever-Growing Towards an Ever-Slower Union?*, Forschungsbericht 9806 des Europa-Instituts, Abt. Volkswirtschaftslehre. Saarbrücken, Universität des Saarlandes.

—— (1998b), 'The Inclusiveness of European Decision Rules', *Journal of Theoretical Politics*, 10, 125–42.

Krasner, S. (1984), 'Approaches to the State: Alternative Conceptions and Historical Dynamics', *Comparative Politics*, 16, 223–46.

—— (1988), 'Sovereignty: an Institutional Perspective', *Comparative Political Studies*, 21, 66–94.

Kratochwil, F. and J. G. Ruggie (1986), 'International Organization: A State of the Art on an Art of the State', *International Organization*, 40, 753–75.

Krehbiel, K. (1988), 'Spatial Models of Legislative Choice', *Legislative Studies Quarterly*, 13, 259–319.

Kreppel, A. and G. Tsebelis (1999), 'Coalition Formation in the European Parliament', *Comparative Political Studies*, 933–66.

Ladrech, R. (1994), 'Europeanization of Domestic Politics and Institutions: The Case of France', *Journal of Common Market Studies*, 32, 69–88.

Laffan, B. (1998), 'The European Union: A Distinctive Model of Internationalization', *Journal of European Public Policy*, 5, 235–53.

Laitin, D. (1998) *Identity in Formation: The Russian-Speaking Populations in the Near Abroad*, Ithaca, Cornell University Press.

Lane, J.-E. and R. Maeland (1995), 'Voting power under the EU Constitution', *Journal of Theoretical Politics*, 2, 223–30.

Lane, J.-E., R. Maeland and S. Berg (1995), 'The EU Parliament: Seats, States and Political Parties', *Journal of Theoretical Politics*, 7, 395–400.

Lane, J.-E., S. Berg and R. Maeland (1997), 'The Power Index Method and the EU', *Aussenwirtschaft*, 52. Also forthcoming in Moser, P., G. Schneider and G. Kirchgässner (eds), *Decision Rules in the European Union: A Rational Choice Perspective*, London, Macmillan.

Lane, J.-E. and M. Mattila (1998), 'Der Abstimmungsprozeß im Ministerrat', in T. König, E. Rieger and H. Schmitt (eds), *Europa der Bürger? Voraussetzungen, Alternativen, Konsequenzen*, Frankfurt, New York, Campus.

Lane, R. (1996) 'Positivism, Scientific Realism and Political Science: Recent Developments in the Philosophy of Science', *Journal of Theoretical Politics* 8, 361–82.

Lanzara, G. F. (1998), 'Self-Destructive Processes in Institution Building and Some Modest Countervailing Mechanisms', *European Journal of Political Research*, 33, 1–39.

Larsen, H. (1997), 'British Discourses on Europe: Sovereignty of Parliament, Instrumentality and the Non-Mythical Europe', in K. E. Joergensen (ed.), *Reflective Approaches to European Governance*, London, Macmillan.

Laursen, J. (1997), 'Nordic Ideas and Realities', in K. E. Joergensen (ed.), *Reflective Approaches to European Governance*, London, Macmillan.

Lee, M. (1990), 'The Ethos of the Cabinet Office: a Comment on the Testimony of Officials', *Public Administration*, 68, 235–42.

Leibfried, S. and P. Pierson (eds) (1995), *European Social Policy: Between Fragmentation and Integration*, Washington, DC, Brookings Institution.

Levi, M. (1997), *Consent, Dissent and Patriotism*, Cambridge, Cambridge University Press.

Levitt, B. and J. March (1996), 'Organizational Learning', in M. Cohen and L. Sproull (eds), *Organizational Learning*, London, Sage, 516–40.

Levy, J. (1994), 'Learning and Foreign Policy: Sweeping a Conceptual Minefield' (Review Article), *International Organization*, 48, 279–312.

Lindberg, L. and J. Campbell (1991), 'The State and the Organization of Economic Activity', in J. Campbell, R. Hollingsworth and L. Lindberg (eds), *Governance of the American Economy*, Cambridge, Cambridge University Press.

Lipson, C. (1991), 'Why are some International Agreements Informal?', *International Organization*, 45, 495–538.

Long, J. S. (1997), *Regression Models for Categorical and Limited Dependent Variables*, London, Sage.

Ludlow, P. (1994), 'The UK Presidency: A View from Brussels', *Journal of Common Market Studies*, 31, 246–60.

Ludlow, N. P. (1997), *Dealing with Britain: The Six and the First UK Application to the EEC*, Cambridge, Cambridge University Press.

Luhmann, N. (1962), 'Funktion und Kausalität', in N. Luhmann (ed.), *Soziologische Aufklärung*, Westdeutscher Verlag, Opladen.

Manow, P. (1996), 'Informalisierung und Parteipolitisierung – Zum Wandel exekutiver Entscheidungsprozesse in der Bundesrepublik', *Zeitschrift für Parlamentsfragen*, 27, 96–107.

March, J. and J. Olsen (1984), 'The New Institutionalism: Organizational Factors in Political Life', *American Political Science Review*, 78, 734–49.

—— (1989), *Rediscovering Institutions: The Organizational Basis of Politics*, New York, The Free Press.

—— (1996), Institutional Perspectives on Political Institutions, *Governance*, 9, 247–64.

—— (1998), 'The Institutional Dynamics of International Political Orders', *International Organization*, 52, 943–69.

Marks, G. (1993), 'Structural Policy and Multilevel Governance in the EC', in A. Cafruny and G. Rosenthal (eds) *The State of the European Community II: The Maastricht Debates and Beyond*, Boulder, CO, Lynne Rienner.

Marks, G., L. Hooghe and K. Blank (1996), 'European Integration from the 1980s: State-Centric v. Multi-Level Governance', *Journal of Common Market Studies*, 34, 341–78.

Marks, G. and C. Wilson (forthcoming), 'The Past in the Present: A Cleavage Theory of Party Positions on European Integration', *British Journal of Political Science*.

Marshall, G. (1989), 'Introduction', in G. Marshall (ed.), *Ministerial Responsibility*, Oxford, Oxford University Press.

Mattli, W. (1996), 'The Logic of Regional Integration: Europe and Beyond', unpublished manuscript, Columbia University.

Mattli, W. and A.-M. Slaughter (1995), 'Law and Politics in the European Union: A Reply to Garrett', *International Organization*, 49, 183–90.

—— (1998), 'Revisiting the European Court of Justice' (Review Essay), *International Organization*, 52, 177–209.

Mayntz, R. (1998), 'Informalisierung politischer Entscheidungsprozesse', in A. Görlitz and H.-P. Burth (eds), *Informelle Verfassung*, Baden-Baden, Nomos.

Mazey, S. and J. Richardson (1996), 'EU Policy-Making: A Garbage Can or an Anticipatory and Consensual Policy Style?', in Y. Mény, P. Muller and J.-L. Quermonne (eds), *Adjusting to Europe: The Impact of the European Union on National Institutions and Policies*, London, Routledge.

McCubbins, M. D. and T. Page (1987), 'A Theory of Congressional Delegation', in M. D. McCubbins and T. Sullivan (eds), *Congress: Structure and Policy*, Cambridge, Cambridge University Press.

McFadden, D. (1974), 'Conditional Logit Analysis of Qualitative Choice Behaviour', in P. Zarembka, *Frontiers in Econometrics*, New York, Academic Press.

McGowan, L. and S. Wilks (1995), 'The First Supranational Policy in the European Union: Competition Policy', *European Journal of Political Research*, 28, 141–69.

McKelvey, R. (1976), 'Intransitivities in Multidimensional Voting Models and Some Implications for Agenda Control', *Journal of Economic Theory*, 12, 472–82.

Milner, H. (1997), *Interests, Institutions, and Information: Domestic Politics and International Relations*, Princeton, Princeton University Press.

Mo, J. (1994) 'The Logic of Two-Level Games with Endogenous Domestic Coalitions', *Journal of Conflict Resolution*, 38, 402–22.

Mo, J. (1995) 'Domestic Institutions and International Bargaining: The Role of Agent Veto in Two-Level Games', *American Political Science Review* 89, 914–24.

Moravcsik, A. (1991), 'Negotiating the Single European Act: National Interests and Conventional Statecraft in the European Community', *International Organization*, 45, 19–56.

—— (1993) 'Preferences and Power in the European Community: A Liberal Intergovernmentalist Approach', *Journal of Common Market Studies*, 31, 473–524.

—— (1994), 'Why the European Community Strengthens the State: Domestic Politics and International Cooperation'. Working Paper #52, Center for European Studies, Harvard University.

—— (1997a), 'Taking Preferences Seriously: A Liberal Theory of International Politics', *International Organization*, 51, 513–53.

—— (1997b), 'Overcoming the "N=1 Challenge": The Case for Greater Rigor', *ECSA Journal*.

—— (1998) *The Choice for Europe: Social Purpose and State Power from Messina to Maastricht*, Ithaca, Cornell University Press.

—— (1999), 'A New Statecraft? Supranational Entrepreneurs and International Cooperation', *International Organization*, 53, 267–306.

Morrow, J. D. (1994), 'Modelling the Forms of International Cooperation: Distribution versus Information', *International Organization*, 48, 387–423.

Moser, P. (1996), 'The European Parliament as a Conditional Agenda Setter: What Are the Conditions? A Critique of Tsebelis (1994)', *American Political Science Review*, 90, 834–8.

—— (1997a), 'A Theory of the Conditional Influence of the European Parliament in the Cooperation Procedure', *Public Choice*, 91, 333–50.

—— (1997b), 'The Benefits of the Conciliation Procedure for the European Parliament', *Aussenwirtschaft*, 52, 57–62. Also forthcoming in P. Moser, G. Schneider, and G. Kirchgässner (eds), *Decision Rules in the European Union: A Rational Choice Perspective*, London, Macmillan.

—— (1999), 'The Impact of Legislative Institutions on Public Policy: A Survey', *European Journal of Political Economy*, 15, 1–33.

Moser, P., G. Schneider and G. Kirchgässner (eds) (forthcoming), *Decision Rules in the European Union: A Rational Choice Perspective*, London, Macmillan (also published as a special issue of *Aussenwirtschaft*, 52).

Mueller, D. C. (1996), *Constitutional Democracy*, New York, Oxford University Press.

—— (1997a), 'Federalism and the European Union: A Constitutional Perspective', *Public Choice*, 90, 255–80.

—— (1997b), 'Constitutional Public Choice', in D. C. Mueller (ed.), *Perspectives on Public Choice*, Cambridge, Cambridge University Press.

Nadelmann, E. (1990), 'Global Prohibition Regimes: The Evolution of Norms in International Society', *International Organization*, 44, 479–526.

Nicholls, A. (1994), *Freedom with Responsibility: The Social Market Economy in Germany 1918–1963*, Oxford, Clarendon Press.

Niskanen, William A. (1971), *Bureaucracy and Representative Government*, New York, Aldine-Atherton.

Nørgaard, A. S. (1996), 'Rediscovering Reasonable Rationality in Institutional Analysis', *European Journal of Political Research*, 29, 31–57.

North, D. (1981), *Structure and Change in Economic History*, New York, W. W. Norton & Co.

—— (1990), *Institutions, Institutional Change, and Economic Performance*, Cambridge, Cambridge University Press.

Nugent, N. (1994), *The Government and Politics of the European Community*, London, Macmillan.

—— (1996), 'Building Europe – A Need for More Leadership?', *Journal of Common Market Studies*, 34, 1–14.

Obradovic, D. (1997), 'Eligibility of Non-State Actors to Participate in European Union Policy Formation'. Paper presented at the Workshop on 'Non-State Actors and Authority in the Global System', University of Warwick.

Oehrgaard, J. (1997), '"Less than Supranational, More than Intergovernmental": European Political Cooperation and the Dynamics of Intergovernmental Integration', *Millennium*, 26, 1–29.

Olsen, J. (1995), 'European Challenges to the Nation State', Oslo, ARENA Working Paper 95/14.

—— (1996), 'Europeanization and Nation-State Dynamics', in S. Gustavsson and L. Lewin (eds), *The Future of the Nation State: Essays on Cultural Pluralism and Political Integration*, Stockholm, Nerenius and Santerus Publishers.

—— (1998), 'The New European Experiment in Political Organization'. Paper presented at the conference on 'Samples of the Future', SCANCOR, Stanford University.

Ordeshook, P. C. (1996), 'Engineering or Science: What is the Study of Politics?', in J. Friedman (ed.), *The Rational Choice Controversy: Economic Models of Politics Reconsidered*, New Haven, London, Yale University Press.

Ostrom, E. (1990), *Governing the Commons: The Evolution of Institutions for Collective Action*, New York, NY, Cambridge University Press.

—— (1991), 'Rational Choice Theory and Institutional Analysis: Toward Complementarity', *American Political Science Review*, 85, 237–43.

—— (1998), 'A Behavioral Approach to the Rational Choice Theory of Collective Action. Presidential Address American Political Science Association 1997', *American Political Science Review*, 92, 1–22.

Page, E. (1997), *People Who Run Europe*, Oxford, Oxford University Press.

Pahre, R. (1997), 'Endogenous Domestic Institutions in Two-Level Games and Parliamentary Oversight of the European Union', *Journal of Conflict Resolution*, 41.

Parker, G. (1998), 'Foreign Secretary Urges Curb on Brussels', *Financial Times*, 14 August.

Payne, D., R. Mokken and F. Stokman (1997), 'European Union Power and Regional Involvement: A Case Study of the Reform of the Structural Funds for Ireland', *Aussenwirtschaft*, 52. Also forthcoming in P. Moser, G. Schneider, and G. Kirchgässner (eds), *Decision Rules in the European Union: A Rational Choice Perspective*, London, Macmillan.

Pedler, R. and G. Schaefer (eds) (1996), *Shaping European Law and Policy: The Role of Committees and Comitology in the Political Process*, Maastricht, European Institute of Public Administration.

Peters, B. G. (1992), 'Bureaucratic Politics and the Institutions of the European Community', in A. Sbragia (ed.), *Euro-Politics: Institutions and Policy-Making in the New European Community*, Washington, Brookings Institution.

Pierson, P. (1993), 'When Effect Becomes Cause: Policy Feedback and Political Change', *World Politics*, 45, 595–628.

—— (1994), *Dismantling the Welfare State? Reagan, Thatcher and the Politics of Retrenchment*, NY, Cambridge University Press.

—— (1996), 'The Path to European Integration: A Historical Institutionalist Analysis', *Comparative Political Studies*, 29, 123–63.

—— (1998), 'The Path to European Integration: A Historical Institutionalist Analysis', in W. Sandholtz and A. Stone Sweet (eds), *European Integration and Supranational Governance*, Oxford, Oxford University Press.

—— (1999), 'Not Just What but When: Timing and Sequence in Political Processes', Harvard University, manuscript. Forthcoming in *Studies in American Political Development*.

Pollack, M. (1996), 'The New Institutionalism and EC Governance: The Promise and Limits of Institutional Analysis', *Governance*, 9, 429–58.

—— (1997), 'Delegation, Agency and Agenda Setting in the European Community', *International Organization*, 51, 99–134.

—— (1998), 'Constructivism, Social Psychology and Elite Attitude Change: Lessons from an Exhausted Research Program'. Paper presented at the 11th International Conference of Europeanists.

Putnam, R. (1973), *The Beliefs of Politicians*, New Haven, Yale University Press.

—— (1988) 'Diplomacy and Domestic Politics: The Logic of Two-Level Games', *International Organization*, 42, 427–60.

—— (1993), *Making Democracy Work: Civic Traditions in Modern Italy*, Princeton, NJ, Princeton University Press.

Ragin, C. C. (1987), *The Comparative Method*, University of California Press, Berkeley.

Rawls, J. A. (1971), *A Theory of Justice*, Cambridge, Belknap Press of Harvard University Press.

Ray, L. (1997), 'Politicizing Europe: Political Parties and the Changing Nature of Public Opinion about the European Union', Ph.D. thesis, University of North Carolina at Chapel Hill.

Rhodes, M., and B. Van Apeldoorn (1997), 'Capitalism versus Capitalism in Western Europe', in M. Rhodes, P. Heywood and V. Wright (eds), *Development in Western European Politics*, London, St. Martin's Press.

Richardson, J. (ed.) (1996), *Power and Policy Making in the European Union*, London, Routledge.

Riker, W. H. (1980), 'Implications from the Disequilibrium of Majority Rule for the Study of Institutions', *American Political Science Review*, 74, 432–47.

Ringquist, E. J. (1995), 'Political Control and Policy Impact in EPA's Office of Water Quality', *American Journal of Political Science*, 39, 336–63.

Risse, T. (1998), 'Let's Argue: Persuasion and Deliberation in International Relations'. Paper presented at the Third Pan-European Conference on International Relations, Vienna.

Risse, T. and K. Sikkink (1999), 'The Power of Principles: The Socialization of Human Rights Norms into Domestic Practices', in T. Risse, S. Ropp and K. Sikkink (eds), *The Power of Principles: International Human Rights Norms and Domestic Change*, Cambridge, Cambridge University Press.

Risse-Kappen, T. (ed.) (1995a), *Bringing Transnational Relations Back In: Non-State Actors, Domestic Structures and International Institutions*, Cambridge, Cambridge University Press.

—— (1995b), 'Democratic Peace – Warlike Democracies? A Social Constructivist Interpretation of the Liberal Argument', *European Journal of International Relations* 1, 491–517.

—— (1996), 'Exploring the Nature of the Beast: International Relations Theory and Comparative Policy Analysis Meet the European Union', *Journal of Common Market Studies*, 34, 53–80.

Rohrschneider, R. (1994), 'Report from the Laboratory: The Influence of Institutions on Political Elites' Democratic Values in Germany', *American Political Science Review*, 88, 927–41.

—— (1996), 'Cultural Transmission versus Perceptions of the Economy: The

Sources of Political Elites' Economic Values in the United Germany', *Comparative Political Studies*, 29, 78–104.

Rometsch, D. and W. Wessels (eds) (1996), *The European Union and Member States: Towards Institutional Fusion?*, Manchester, Manchester University Press.

Ross, G. (1995), *Jacques Delors and European Integration*, Oxford, Oxford University Press.

Ruggie, J. G. (1998a), 'What Makes the World Hang Together? Neo-Utilitarianism and the Social Constructivist Challenge', *International Organization*, 52, 855–85.

—— (1998b), *Constructing the World Polity: Essays on International Institutionalization*, New York, Routledge Press.

Sánchez-Cuenca, I. (2000), 'The Political Bases of Support for European Integration', *European Union Politics* 1.

Sandholtz, W. (1993a), 'Choosing Union: Monetary Politics and Maastricht', *International Organization*, 47, 1–39.

—— (1993b), 'Institutions and Collective Action: The New Telecommunications in Europe', *World Politics*, 45, 242–70.

—— (1996), 'Membership Matters: Limits of the Functional Approach to European Institutions', *Journal of Common Market Studies*, 34, 403–29.

Sandholtz, W. and J. Zysman (1989), '1992: Recasting the European Bargain', *World Politics*, 42, 95–128.

Sargent, T. (1993), *Bounded Rationality in Macroeconomics: The Arne Ryde Memorial Lectures*, Oxford, Clarendon Press.

Sbragia, A. (1993), 'The European Community: A Balancing Act', *Publius*, 23, 23–38.

Scharpf, F. W. (1985), 'Die Politikverflechtungsfalle – Europäische Integration und deutscher Föderalismus im Vergleich', *Politische Vierteljahresschrift*, 26, 323–56.

—— (1988), 'The Joint-Decision Trap: Lessons From German Federalism and European Integration', *Public Administration*, 66, 239–78.

—— (1996), 'Negative and Positive Integration in the Political Economy of European Welfare States', in G. Marks, F. Scharpf and W. Streeck (eds), *Governance in the European Union*, London, Sage.

—— (1997), *Games Real Actors Play: Actor-Centered Institutionalism in Policy Research*, Boulder, Westview.

Schelling, Thomas C. (1960), *The Strategy of Conflict*, Cambridge, MA, Harvard University Press.

Schmidt, S. K. (1996), 'Sterile Debates and Dubious Generalisations: European Integration Theory Tested by Telecommunications and Electricity', *Journal of Public Policy* 16 *(3)*, 233–71.

—— (1998), *Liberalisierung in Europa. Die Rolle der Europäischen Kommission*, Frankfurt a.M., Campus.

—— (2000), 'Only an Agenda Setter? The European Commission's Power over the Council of Ministers', *Journal of European Union Politics*.

Schmidt, V. (1995), 'The New World Order, Inc.', *Daedelus*, 124, 75–106.

Schneider, G. (1994a), 'Rational Choice und kommunikatives Handeln. Eine Replik auf Harald Müller', *Zeitschrift für Internationale Beziehungen*, 1, 357–66.

—— (1994b) 'Getting Closer at Different Speed: Strategic Interaction in Widening European Integration', in P. Allan and C. Schmidt (eds) *Game Theory and International Relations*, Cheltenham, Elgar.

—— (1995a), 'The Limits of Self-Reform: Institution Building in the European Community', *European Journal of International Relations*, 1, 59–86.

—— (1995b), 'Agenda-Setting in European Integration: The Conflict between Voters, Governments and Supranational Institutions', in F. Laursen (ed.), *The Political Economy of European Integration*, Maastricht, European Institute of Public Administration.

—— (1997), 'Choosing Chameleons: National Interests and the Logic of Coalition Building in the Commission of the European Union'. Paper presented at the 5th Biennial Meeting of the European Community Studies Association, Seattle.

—— (1998), 'Ideen, Interessen und Institutionen – Die Integrationsforschung im Zeichen der drei I', Inaugural address, Universität Konstanz.

Schneider, G. and L.-E. Cederman (1994), 'The Change of Tide in Political Cooperation: A Limited Information Model of European Integration', *International Organization*, 48, 633–62.

Schneider, G. and P. A. Weitsman (1995), 'Cooperation Among Equals: A Theory of Regional Integration', unpublished paper.

Schneider, G., P. A. Weitsman and T. Bernauer (1995), *Towards a New Europe: Stops and Starts in Regional Integration*, Westport, CT, Praeger.

Scully, R. M. (1997a), 'The European Parliament and the Co-Decision Procedure: A Reassessment', *Legislative Studies*, 3, 58–73.

—— (1997b), 'The European Parliament and Co-Decision: A Rejoinder to Tsebelis and Garrett', *Legislative Studies*, 3, 93–103.

Searing, D. S. (1991), 'Roles, Rules and Rationality in the New Institutionalism', *American Political Science Review*, 32, 47–68.

—— (1994), *Westminster's World: Understanding Political Roles*, Cambridge, Cambridge University Press.

Sears, D. O. and N. A. Valentino (1997), 'Politics Matters: Political Events as Catalysts for Preadult Socialization', *American Political Science Review*, 91, 45–65.

Simon, H. (1996), 'Bounded Rationality and Organizational Learning', in M. Cohen and L. Sproull (eds), *Organizational Learning*, London, Sage.

Singer, J. David (1968) (ed.), *Quantitative International Politics: Insights and Evidence*, New York, Free Press.

Skocpol, T. (1985), 'Bringing the State Back In: Strategies of Analysis in Current Research', in P. Evans, D. Rueschemeyer and T. Skocpol (eds), *Bringing the State Back In*, Cambridge, Cambridge University Press.

Skogstad, G. (1998), 'Ideas, Paradigms and Institutions: Agricultural Exceptionalism in the European Union and the United States', *Governance*, 11, 463–90.

Skowronek, S. (1982), *Building a New American State: The Expansion of National Administrative Capacities, 1877–1920*, New York, Cambridge University Press.

Soskice, D. (1999), 'Divergent Production Regimes: Coordinated and Uncoordinated Market Economies in the 1980s and 1990s', in H. Kitschelt, P.

Lange, G. Marks and J. Stephens (eds), *Continuity and Change in Contemporary Capitalism*, Cambridge, Cambridge University Press.

Soysal, Y. (1994), *Limits of Citizenship: Migrants and Postnational Membership in Europe*, Chicago, University of Chicago Press.

Stein, J. (1994), 'Political Learning by Doing: Gorbachev as Uncommitted Thinker and Motivated Learner', *International Organization*, 48, 155–83.

Steinmo, S., K. Thelen and F. Longstreth (eds) (1992), *Structuring Politics: Historical Institutionalism in Comparative Analysis*, NY, Cambridge University Press.

Steunenberg, B. (1994), 'Decision Making under Different Institutional Arrangements: Legislation by the European Community', *Journal of Institutional and Theoretical Economics*, 150, 642–69.

—— (1996), 'Agency Discretion, Regulatory Policy Making, and Different Institutional Arrangements', *Public Choice*, 86, 309–39.

—— (1997), 'Codecision and its Reform: A Comparative Analysis of Decision Making Rules in the European Union', in B. Steunenberg and F. A. van Vught (eds), *Political Institutions and Public Policy: Perspectives on European Decision Making*, Dordrecht, Kluwer.

—— (1998), 'Constitutional Change in the European Union: Parliament's Impact on the Reform of the Co-Decision Procedure', unpublished manuscript, University of Twente.

Steunenberg, B., C. Koboldt and D. Schmidtchen (1996), 'Comitology and the Balance of Power in the European Union: A Game Theoretic Approach', *International Review of Law and Economics*, 16, 329–44.

Steunenberg, B., C. Koboldt and D. Schmidtchen (1997), 'Beyond Comitology: European Policymaking with Parliamentary Involvement', *Aussenwirtschaft*, 52, 87–112. Also forthcoming in P. Moser, G. Schneider and G. Kirchgässner (eds), *Decision Rules in the European Union: A Rational Choice Perspective*, London, Macmillan.

Stone Sweet, A. and T. Brunell (1998), 'Constructing a Supranational Constitution: Dispute Resolution and Governance in the European Community', *American Political Science Review*, 92, 63–82.

Streeck, W. (1997), 'German Capitalism: Does it Exist? Can it Survive?', in C. Crouch and W. Streeck (eds), *Political Economy of Modern Capitalism*, London, Sage.

Taussig, A. (1970), 'European Integration and German Ministries', unpublished Ph.D. thesis, Harvard University.

Thelen, K. and S. Steinmo (1992), 'Historical Institutionalism in Comparative Politics', in S. Steinmo, K. Thelen and F. Longstreth (eds), *Structuring Politics: Historical Institutionalism in Comparative Analysis*, Cambridge, Cambridge University Press.

Tratt, J. (1966), *The Macmillan Government and Europe: A Study in the Process of Policy Development*, London, Macmillan.

Trumpf, J. (1988), 'Reflections from Three German Presidencies: High Marks for the German Coordination Model, Low Marks for the Presidency System', in W. Wessels and E. Regelsberger (eds), *The Federal Republic of Germany and the European Community: The Presidency and Beyond*, Bonn, Europa Union Verlag.

Tsebelis, G. (1990), *Nested Games: Rational Choice in Comparative Politics*, Berkeley, University of California Press.

—— (1994), 'The Power of the European Parliament as a Conditional Agenda Setter', *American Political Science Review*, 88, 128–42. (Unabridged version in G. Schneider, P. A. Weitsman and T. Bernauer (eds) (1995), *Towards a New Europe: Stops and Starts in Regional Integration*, Westport, CT, Praeger.)

—— (1996), 'More on the European Parliament as a Conditional Agenda Setter: Response to Moser', *American Political Science Review*, 90, 839–44.

—— (1997), 'Maastricht and the Democratic Deficit', *Aussenwirtschaft*, 52, 29–56. Also forthcoming in P. Moser, G. Schneider and G. Kirchgässner (eds), *Decision Rules in the European Union: A Rational Choice Perspective*, London, Macmillan.

Tsebelis, G. and G. Garrett (1997), 'Agenda Setting, Vetoes and the European Union's Co-decision Procedure', *The Journal of Legislative Studies*, 3, 74–92.

—— (2000), 'Legislative Politics in the European Union', *European Union Politics*, vol. 1, no. 1, February, 9–36.

Tsebelis, G. and A. Kreppel (1998), 'The History of Conditional Agenda-setting in European Institutions', *European Journal of Political Research*, 33, 41–71.

Tucker, E. (1997), 'European Union Asylum Seeker Policies Slammed', *Financial Times*, 4 December.

Underdal, A. (1998), 'Explaining Compliance and Defection: Three Models', *European Journal of International Relations*, 4, 5–30.

Vanberg, V. (1997), 'Subsidiarity, Responsive Government and Individual Liberty', in B. Steunenberg and F. A. van Vught (eds), *Political Institutions and Public Policy: Perspectives on European Decision Making*, Dordrecht, Kluwer.

Van Kersbergen, K. (1997), 'Between Collectivism and Individualism: The Politics of the Centre', in H. Keman (ed.), *The Politics of Problem-Solving in Postwar Democracies*, Basingstoke, Macmillan.

—— (1999), 'Contemporary Christian Democracy and the Demise of the Politics of Mediation', in H. Kitschelt, P. Lange, G. Marks and J. Stephens (eds), *Continuity and Change in Contemporary Capitalism*, Cambridge, Cambridge University Press.

Verba, S. (1965), 'Conclusion: Comparative Political Culture', in L. Pye and S. Verba (eds), *Political Culture and Political Development*, Princeton, Princeton University Press.

Wallace, H. (1985), 'The Presidency of the Council of Ministers of the European Communities: A Comparative Perspective', in C. O. Nuallain (ed.), *The Presidency of the European Council of Ministers*, London, Croom Helm.

—— (1992), 'Making Multilateral Negotiations Work', in W. Wallace (ed.), *The Dynamics of European Integration*, London, Pinter.

Wallace, H. and W. Wallace (1973), 'The Impact of Community Membership on the British Machinery of Government', *Journal of Common Market Studies*, 11, 243–62.

Webber, D. (ed.) (1999), *The Franco-German Relationship in the European Union*, London, Routledge.

Weber, S. (1994), 'Origins of the European Bank for Reconstruction and Development', *International Organization*, 48.

Weibull, J. W. (1995), *Evolutionary Game Theory*, Cambridge, MA, MIT Press.

Weingast, B. (1995), 'A Rational Choice Perspective on the Role of Ideas: Shared Belief Systems and State Sovereignty in International Cooperation', *Politics and Society*, 23, 449–64.

Weisberg, H. F. (1998), 'The Political Psychology of Party Identification'. Presented at the annual meeting of the American Political Science Association, Boston.

Wendt, A. (1992), 'Anarchy is What States Make of It: The Social Construction of Power Politics', *International Organization*, 46, 391–425.

—— (1994), 'Collective Identity Formation and the International State', *American Political Science Review*, 88, 384–96.

Wessels, W. (1991), 'The EC Council: The Community's Decisionmaking Centre', in R. Keohane and S. Hoffmann (eds), *The New European Community: Decisionmaking and Institutional Change*, Boulder, CO, Westview.

—— (1997) 'An Ever Closer Fusion? A Dynamic Macropolitical View on Integration Processes', *Journal of Common Market Studies*, 35, 267–99.

—— (1998), 'Comitology: Fusion in Action. Politico-Administrative Trends in the EU System', *Journal of European Public Policy*, 5, 209–34.

Westlake, M. (1995), *The Council of the European Union*, London, Catermill International Ltd.

Wewer, G. (1991), 'Spielregeln, Netzwerke, Entscheidungen – auf der Suche nach der anderen Seite des Regierens', in H.-H. Hartwich and G. Wewer (eds), *Regieren in der Bundesrepublik II. Formale und informale Komponenten des Regierens in den Bereichen Führung, Entscheidung, Personal und Organisation*, Opladen, Leske + Budrich.

Wiener, A. (1998), *'European' Citizenship Practice: Building Institutions of a non-State*, Boulder, CO, Westview Press.

Wilks, S. (1996), 'Regulatory Compliance and Capitalist Diversity in Europe', *Journal of European Public Policy*, 3, 536–59.

Wincott, D. (1995), 'Institutional Interaction and European Integration: Towards an Everyday Critique of Liberal Intergovernmentalism', *Journal of Common Market Studies*, 33, 597–609.

Wind, M. (1997), 'Rediscovering Institutions: A Reflectivist Critique of Rational Institutionalism', in K. E. Joergensen (ed.), *Reflective Approaches to European Governance*, London, Macmillan.

Wood, B. D. and R. Waterman (1993), 'The Dynamics of Political-Bureaucratic Adaptation', *American Journal of Political Science*, 37, 497–528.

Wright, V. (1996), 'The National Coordination of European Policy-making: Negotiating the Quagmire', in J. Richardson (ed.), *European Union: Power and Policy-Making*, London, Routledge.

Yee, A. S. (1997), 'Thick Rationality and the Missing "Brute Fact": The Limits of Rationalist Incorporations of Norms and Ideas', *Journal of Politics*, 59, 1001–39.

Zetterholm, S. (ed.) (1994), *National Cultures and European Integration: Exploratory Essays on Cultural Diversity and Common Policies*, Oxford, Berg.

Zimbardo, P. and M. Leippe (1991), *The Psychology of Attitude Change and Social Influence*, New York, McGraw Hill.

Zucker, L. (1991), 'The Role of Institutionalization in Cultural Persistence', in W.

Powell and P. DiMaggio (eds), *The New Institutionalism in Organizational Analysis*, Chicago, University of Chicago Press.

Zuern, M. (1997), 'Assessing State Preferences and Explaining Institutional Choice: The Case of Intra-German Trade', *International Studies Quarterly*, 41, 295–320.

Index